MOM, THE FLAG, AND APPLE PIE

MOM, THE FLAG, AND APPLE PIE

GREAT AMERICAN WRITERS ON GREAT AMERICAN THINGS

BY

MAX APPLE

ROBERT ALAN AURTHUR

RUSSELL BAKER

HAROLD BRODKEY

ART BUCHWALD

JULIA CHILD

HARRY CREWS

JOAN DIDION

NORA EPHRON

M. F. K. FISHER

WILLIAM PRICE FOX

MARSHALL FRADY

MARK GOODMAN

JOHN LEONARD

MERLE MILLER

WILLIAM C. MARTIN

GERALD NACHMAN

EDWIN NEWMAN

GRACE PALEY

GORDON PARKS

WALKER PERCY

JEAN STAFFORD

JOHN STEINBECK

ALEXANDER THEROUX

GORE VIDAL

JIM VILLAS

ANDY WARHOL

EUDORA WELTY

TOM WICKER

LARRY WOIWODE

TOM WOLFE

Compiled by the Editors of ESQUIRE

1976

DOUBLEDAY & COMPANY, INC., GARDEN CITY, NEW YORK

CONTENTS

Contents

MOM, THE FLAG, AND APPLE PIE

Great American Things

BY TOM WOLFE

What a spread! What a feast! What a weenie roast we have here!
Thirty great American writers writing about great American
things . . . very tasty! Don't delay! Get right to it! I won't hold
you up! I'm only here to put on record the things about America
that mean the most to American writers themselves. Not the
things that turn up in their books and articles—I mean the things
that writers actually *care* about, the things that set off the
deepest feelings they know. Don't expect *them* to mention such
matters. Not for a moment! They're like everybody else in that
respect—they'd sooner cut a main vein!

The perfect example is the well-known American writer. . . .
But perhaps it's best not to say exactly which well-known American writer—since we're about to surprise him in *an intimate act*.
He's in his apartment, a seven-room apartment on Riverside
Drive, on the West Side of Manhattan, in his study, seated at his
desk. As we approach from the rear, we notice a bald spot on the
crown of his head. It's about the size of a Ritz cracker, this bald
spot, freckled and toasty brown. Gloriously suntanned, in fact.
Around this bald spot swirls a corona of dark brown hair that becomes quite thick by the time it completes its mad Byronic rush
down the back over his turtleneck and out to the side in great
bushes over his ears. He knows the days of covered ears are
numbered, because this particular look has become somewhat
low rent. When he was coming back from his father's funeral,

half the salesmen lined up at O'Hare for the commuter flights, in their pajama-striped shirts and diamond-print double-knit suits, had groovy hair much like his. And to think that just six years ago such a hairdo seemed . . . so defiant!

Meeting his sideburns at mid-jowl is the neck of his turtleneck sweater, an authentic Navy turtleneck, and the sweater tucks into his Levi's, which are the authentic Original XX Levi's, the original straight stovepipes made for wearing over boots. He got them in a bona fide cowhand's store in La Porte, Texas, during his trip to Houston to be the keynote speaker in a lecture series on "The American Dream: Myth and Reality." (No small part of the latter was a fee of two thousand dollars plus expenses.) This outfit, the Navy turtleneck and the double-X Levi's, means work & discipline. *Discipline!* as he says to himself every day. When he puts on these clothes, it means that he intends to write, and do nothing else, for at least four hours. *Discipline,* Mr. Wonderful!

But on the desk in front of him—that's not a manuscript or even the beginnings of one . . . that's *last month's bank statement,* which just arrived in the mail. And those are his canceled checks in a pile on top of it. In that big ledger-style checkbook there (the old-fashioned kind, serious-looking, with no crazy Peter Max designs on the checks) are his check stubs. And those slips of paper in the promiscuous heap are all unpaid bills, and he's taking the nylon cover off his Texas Instruments desk calculator, and he is about to measure the flow, the tide, the mad sluice, the crazy current of the money that pours through his fingers every month and which is now running against him in the most catastrophic manner, like an undertow, a riptide, pulling him under—

—him and this apartment, which cost him $75,000 in 1972; $20,000 cash, which came out of the $25,000 he got as a paperback advance for his fourth book, *Under Uncle's Thumb,* and $536.36 a month in bank loan payments (on the $55,000 he borrowed) ever since, plus another $390 a month in so-called maintenance, which has steadily increased until it is now $460 a month . . . and although he already knows the answer, the round number, he begins punching the figures into the calculator . . . 536.36 plus . . . 460 . . . times 12 . . . and the calculator keys go *chuck chuck chuck chuck* and the curious little orange numbers, broken up like stencil figures, go trucking across the black path of the display panel at the top of the machine, giving a little orange shudder every time he hits the *plus* button, until there it is, stretching out seven digits long—11956.32—$12,000 a year! One thousand dollars a month—this is what he spends on his apartment alone!—and by May he will have to come up with another $6,000 so he can rent the house on Martha's Vineyard again *chuck chuck chuck chuck* and by September another $6,750—$3,750 to send his daughter Amy to Dalton and $3,000 to send his son Jonathan to Collegiate (on those marvelous frog-and-cricket evenings up on the Vineyard he and Bill and Julie and Scott and Henry and Herman and Leon and Shelly and the rest, all Media & Lit. people from New York, have discussed why they send their children to private schools, and they have pretty well decided that it is the educational turmoil in the New York public schools that is the problem—the kids just wouldn't be educated!—plus some considerations of their children's personal safety, as Leon once said in an exceptional burst of candor) and he punches that in . . . 6750 . . . *chuck chuck chuck chuck* . . . and hits the *plus* button . . . an orange shimmer . . . and beautiful! there's the figure—the three items, the apartment in town, the summer place and the children's schooling—$24,706.32!—almost $25,000 a year in fixed costs, just for a starter! for lodging and schooling! nothing else included! A grim nut!

It's appalling, and he's drowning, and this is only the beginning of it, just the basic grim nut—and yet in his secret heart he loves these little sessions with the calculator and the checks and the stubs and the bills and the marching orange numbers that stretch on and on . . . into such magnificently huge figures. It's like an electric diagram of his infinitely expanding life, a scoreboard showing the big league he's now in. Far from throwing him into a panic, as they well might, these tote sessions are one of the most satisfying habits he has. A regular vice! Like barbiturates! Calming the heart and slowing the respiration! Because it seems *practical*, going over expenses, his conscience sanctions it as a permissible way to avoid the only thing that can possibly keep him afloat: namely, more writing. . . . He's deep into his calculator trance now. . . . The orange has him enthralled. Think of it! He has now reached a stage in his life when not only a $1,000-a-month apartment but also a summer house on an island in the Atlantic is an absolute necessity—precisely that, absolute necessity. . . . It's appalling!—and yet it's the most inexplicable bliss!—nothing less.

As for the apartment, even at $1,000 a month it is not elegant. Elegance would cost at least twice that. No, his is an apartment of a sort known as West Side Married Intellectual. The rooms are big, the layout is good, but the moldings, cornices, covings and chair rails seem to be corroding. Actually, they are merely lumpy from too many coats of paint over the decades, and the parquet sections in the floor have dried out and are sprung loose from one another. It has been a long time since this apartment has had an owner who could both meet the down-payment nut *and* have the woodwork stripped and the flooring replaced. The building has a doorman but no elevator man, and on Sundays the door is manned by a janitor in gray khaki work clothes. But what's he supposed to do? He needs seven rooms. His son and daughter now require separate bedrooms. He and his wife require a third one (a third and fourth if the truth be known, but he has had to settle for three). He now needs, not just likes, this study he's in, a workroom that is his exclusively. He now *needs* the dining room, which is a real dining room, not a dogleg off the living room. Even if he is giving only a cocktail party, it is . . . *necessary* that they (one & all) note—however unconsciously—that he *does* have a dining room!

Right here on his desk are the canceled checks that have come in hung over from the cocktail party he gave six weeks ago. They're right in front of him now . . . $209.60 to the florists, Vince & Clutter, for flowers for the hallway, the living room, the dining room and the study, although part of that, $100, was for a bowl of tightly clustered silk poppies that will become a permanent part of the living-room decor . . . $138.18 to the liquor store (quite a bit was left over, however, meaning that the bar will be stocked for a while) . . . $257.50 to Mauve Gloves & Madmen, the caterers, even though he had chosen some of the cheaper hors d'oeuvres. He also tipped the two butlers $10 each, which made him feel a little foolish later when he learned that one of them was co-owner of Mauve Gloves & Madmen . . . $23.91 to the grocery store for he couldn't remember what . . . $173.95 to the Russian Tea Room for dinner afterward with Henry and Mavis (the guests of honor) and six other stragglers

. . . $12.84 for a serving bowl from Bloomingdale's . . . $20 extra
to the maid for staying on late . . . and he's chucking all these
figures into the calculator *chuck chuck chuck chuck* blink blink
blink blink *truck truck truck truck* the slanted orange numbers
go trucking and winking across the panel . . . 855.98 . . .
$855.98 for a cocktail party!—not even a dinner party!—ap-
palling!—and how slyly sweet. . . .

Should he throw in the library stairs as a party expense, too?
Perhaps, he thought, if he were honest, he would. The checks
were right here: $420 to Lum B. Lee Ltd. for the stairs them-
selves, and another $95 to the customs broker to get the thing
through customs and $45 to the trucker to deliver it, making a
total of $560! In any event, they're terrific . . . Mayfair heaven
. . . the classic English type, stairs to nowhere, going up in a spi-
ral around a central column, carved in the ancient bamboo style,
rising up almost seven feet, so he can reach books on his highest
shelf. . . . He had had it made extra high by a cabinetmaking
firm in Hong Kong, the aforementioned Lum B. Lee. . . . Now,
if the truth be known, the stairs are the result of a habit he has:
he goes around the apartment after giving a party and stands
where he saw particular guests standing, people who stuck in his
mind, and tries to see what they saw from that position; in other
words, how the apartment looked in their eyes. About a year ago
he had seen Lenny Johns of the *Times* standing in the doorway
of his study and looking in, so afterward, after Lenny and everyone else had gone, he took up the same position and looked in
. . . and what he saw did not please him. In fact, it looked sad.
Through Lenny Johns's eyes it must have looked like the basic
writer's workroom out of *Writer's Digest:* a plain Danish-style
desk (The Door Store) with dowel legs (dowel legs!), a
modernistic (modernistic!) metal and upholstery office swivel
chair, a low-slung (more Modernismus!) couch, a bank of undis-
tinguished-looking file cabinets, a bookcase covering one entire
wall but made of plain white-painted boards and using the wall
itself as its back. The solution, as he saw it—without going into
huge costs—was the library stairs—the stairs to nowhere!—an object indisputably useful and yet with an air of elegant folly!

It was after that same party that his wife had said to him:
"Who was that weepy-looking little man you were talking to so
much?"

"I don't know who you're talking about."

"The one with the three strands of hair pulled up from the side and draped over his scalp."

He knew she was talking about Johns. And he knew *she* knew Johns's name. She had met him before, on the Vineyard.

Meeting Lenny Johns socially was one of the many dividends of Martha's Vineyard. They have been going there for three summers now, renting a house on a hill in Chilmark . . . until it has become, well, a *necessity!* It's no longer possible to stay in New York over the summer. It's not fair to the children. They shouldn't have to grow up that way. As for himself, he's gotten to know Lenny and Bill and Scott and Julie and Bob and Dick and Jody and Gillian and Frank and Shelly and the rest in a way that wouldn't be possible in New York. But quite aside from all that . . . just that clear sparkling late-August solitude, when you can smell the pine and the sea . . . heading down the piney path from the house on the hill . . . walking two hundred yards across the marshes on the pedestrian dock, just one plank wide, so that you have to keep staring down at it . . . it's hypnotic . . . the board, the marsh grass, your own tread, the sound of the frogs and the crickets . . . and then getting into the rowboat and rowing across the inlet to . . . the *dune* . . . the great swelling dune, with the dune grass waving against the sky on top . . . and then over the lip of it—to the beach! the most pristine white beach in the world! and the open sea . . . all spread out before you—yours! Just that! the sand, the sea, the sky—and solitude! No gates, no lifeguard stands, no concessions, no sprawling multitudes of transistor radios and plaid plastic beach chairs . . .

It is chiefly for these summers on the Vineyard that he has bought a car, a BMW sedan—$7,200—but very lively! It costs him $76 a month to keep it in a garage in the city for nine months of the year, another $684 in all, so that the hard nut for Martha's Vineyard is really $6,684—but it's a necessity, and one sacrifices for necessities. After three years on the Vineyard he feels very possessive about the place, even though he's a renter, and he immediately joined in with the move to publish a protest against "that little Albanian with a pickup truck," as he was (wrongly) called, some character named Zarno or something who had assembled a block of fifty acres on the Vineyard and was going to develop it into 150 building lots—one third of an acre each! (Only dimly did he recall that the house he grew up in, in Chicago, had been on about one fifth of an acre and hadn't seemed terribly hemmed in.) Bill T—— wrote a terrific manifesto in which he talked about "these Snopes-like little men with their pickup trucks"—Snopes-like!—and all sorts of people signed it.

This campaign against the developers also brought the New York Media & Lit. people into contact for the first time with the Boston people. Until the Media & Lit. people began going there about ten years before, Martha's Vineyard had always been a Boston resort, "Boston" in the most proper social sense of the word. There wasn't much the Boston people could do about the New York people except not associate with them. When they said "New York people," they no doubt meant "Jews & Others," he figured. So when he was first invited to a Boston party, thanks to his interest in the anti-developers campaign, he went with some trepidation and with his resentment tucked into his waist-band like a .38. His mood darkened still more when he arrived in white ducks and an embroidered white cotton shirt, yoke-shoul-dered and open to the sternum—a little eccentric (actually a harmless sort of shirt known in Arizona as fruit western) but perfectly in the mood of standard New York People Seaside Funk—and found that the Boston men, to a man, had on jackets and ties. Not only that, they had on their own tribal colors. The jackets were mostly navy blazers, and the ties were mostly striped ties or ties with little jacquard emblems on them, but the pants had a go-to-hell air: checks and plaids of the loudest possi-ble sort, madras plaids, yellow-on-orange windowpane checks, crazy-quilt plaids, giant houndstooth checks, or else they were a solid airmail red or taxi yellow or some other implausible go-to-hell color. They finished that off with loafers and white crew socks or no socks at all. The pants were their note of Haitian abandon . . . weekends by the sea. At the same time the jackets and ties showed they had not forgotten for a moment where the power came from. He felt desolate. He slipped the loaded resent-ment out of his waistband and cocked it. And then the most amazing thing happened—

His hostess came up and made a fuss over him! Exactly! She had read *Under Uncle's Thumb!* So had quite a few of the men, infernal pants and all! Lawyers and investment counselors! They were all interested in him! Quite a stream—he hardly had to move from the one spot all evening! And as the sun went down over the ocean, and the alcohol rose, and all of their boiling teeth glistened—he could almost see something . . . *presque vu!* . . . a glimmer of the future . . . something he could barely make out . . . a vision in which America's best minds, her intellectuals, found a common ground, a natural unity, with the enlightened segments of her old aristocracy, her old money . . . the two groups bound together by . . . but by what? . . . he could *almost* see it, but not quite . . . it was *presque vu* . . . it was somehow a matter of taste . . . of sensibility . . . of grace, natural grace . . . just as he himself had a natural feel for the best British styles, which were after all the source of the Boston manners. . . . What were the library stairs, if they weren't that? What were the Lobb shoes?

For here, now, surfacing to the top of the pile, is the check for $248 to John Lobb & Sons Ltd. Boot Makers—that was the way he wrote it out, Boot Makers, two words, the way it was on their bosky florid London letterhead—$248!—for one pair of shoes!— from England!—handmade! And now, all at once, even as *chuck chuck chuck* he punches it into the calculator, he is swept by a wave of sentiment, of sadness, sweet misery—guilt! Two hundred and forty-eight dollars for a pair of handmade shoes from England . . . He thinks of his father. He wore his first pair of Lobb shoes to his father's funeral. Black cap toes they were, the most formal daytime shoes made, and it was pouring that day in Chicago and his incomparable new shoes from England were caked with mud when he got back to his father's house. He took the shoes off, but then he froze—he couldn't bring himself to remove the mud. His father had come to the United States from Russia as a young man in 1922. He had to go to work at once, and in no time, it seemed, came the Depression, and he struggled through it as a tailor, although in the forties he acquired a dry-cleaning establishment and, later, a second one, plus a diaper-service business and a hotel-linen service. But this brilliant man—oh, how many times had his mother assured him of that!—had had to spend all those years as a tailor. This cultivated man!—more assurances—oh, how many yards of Goethe and Dante had he heard him quote in an accent that gripped the English language like a full nelson! And now his son, the son of this brilliant, cultivated but uneducated and thwarted man—

now his son, his son with his education and his literary career, his son who had never had to work with his hands more than half an hour at a stretch in his life—his son had turned up at his funeral in a pair of handmade shoes from England! . . . Well, he let the mud dry on them. He didn't touch them for six months. He didn't even put the shoe trees (another $47) in. Perhaps the goddamned boots would curl up and die.

The number . . . 248 . . . is sitting right up there in slanted orange digits on the face of the calculator. That seems to end the reverie. He doesn't want to continue it just now. He doesn't want to see the 6684 for Martha's Vineyard up there again for a while. He doesn't want to see the seven digits of his debts (counting the ones after the decimal point) glowing in their full, magnificent, intoxicating length. It's time to get serious! *Discipline!* Only one thing will pull him out of all this: work . . . writing . . . and there's no way to put it off any longer. *Discipline,* Mr. Wonderful! This is the most difficult day of all, the day when it falls to his lot to put a piece of paper in the typewriter and start on page one of a new book, with that horrible arthritic siege—writing a book!—stretching out ahead of him (a tubercular blue glow, as his mind comprehends it) . . . although it lifts his spirits a bit to know that both *The Atlantic* and *Playboy* have expressed an interest in running chapters as he goes along, and *Penthouse* would pay even more, although he doesn't want it to appear in a one-hand magazine, a household aid, as literary penicillin to help quell the spirochetes oozing from all the virulent vulvas. . . . Nevertheless! help is on the way! Hell! —there's not a magazine in America that wouldn't publish something from this book!

So he feeds a sheet of paper into his typewriter, and in the center, one third of the way down from the top, he takes care of the easy part first—the working title, in capital letters:

RECESSION AND REPRESSION:
POLICE STATE AMERICA
AND THE SPIRIT OF '76

Mom

BY GRACE PALEY

The mother is at the open window. She calls the child home. She's a fat lady. She leans forward, supporting herself on her elbows. Her breasts are shoved up under her chin. Her arms are broad and heavy.

I am not the child. She isn't my mother. Still, in my head where remembering is organized for significance (not usefulness), she leans far out. She looks up and down the block. The technical name of this first seeing is "imprint." It often results in lifelong love. I play in the street, she stands in the window. I wanted her to call me home to the dark mysterious apartment behind her back, where the father was already eating and the others sat at the kitchen table and waited for the child.

She was destined, with her meaty bossiness, her sighs, her suffering, to be dumped into the villain room of social meaning and psychological causation. When this happened to her she had just touched the first rung of the great American immigrant ladder. Her husband was ahead of her, her intentional bulk kept him from slipping. Their children were a couple of rungs above them. She believed she would follow them up into the English language, education and respect.

Unfortunately, science and literature had turned against her. What use was my accumulating affection when the brains of the opposition included her son the doctor and her son the novelist? Because of them, she never even had a chance at the crown of

apple pie awarded her American-born sisters and accepted by
them when they agreed to give up their powerful pioneer dispo-
sitions.

What is wrong with the world? the growing person might
have asked. The year was 1932 or perhaps 1942. Despite the
worldwide fame of those years, the chief investigator into human
pain is looking into his own book of awful prognoses. He looks
up. Your mother, probably, he says.

As for me, I was not paying attention. I missed the mocking
campaign.

The mother sits on a box, an orange crate. She talks to her
friend who also sits on an orange crate. They are wearing
housedresses, flowered prints, large, roomy, unbelted, sleeveless.
Each woman has a sweater on her lap, for coolness could arrive
on an after-supper breeze and remain on the street for the summer night.

The first mother says: Ellie, after thirty you notice it? the
years fly fast.

Oh, it's true, says the second mother.

I am so shocked by this sentence that I fall back against the
tenement, breathing hard. I think, Oh! Years! The next sentence
I remember is said about twenty minutes later.

Ellie, I'll tell you something, if you don't want to have so many
children, don't sleep in a nightgown, sleep in pajamas, you're
better off.

Sometimes even that doesn't help, says the second mother.

This is certainly an important sentence, I know. It is serious,
but they laugh.

Summer night in the east Bronx. The men are inside playing
pinochle. The men are sleeping, are talking shop. They have
gone to see if Trotsky is still sitting on a bench in Crotona Park.
The street is full of mothers who have run out of the stuffy house
to look for air, and they are talking about my life.

At three o'clock in the autumn afternoon, the American-born
mother opens the door. She says there is no subject that cannot
be discussed with her because she was born in this up-to-date
place, the U.S.A. We have just learned several words we believe
are the true adult names of the hidden parts of our bodies, the

parts that are unnameable. (Like God's name says a brother just
home from Hebrew school. He is smacked.) The American-born
mother says those are the worst words of all, never to use them
or think of them, but to always feel free to talk to her about anything else.

The Russian-born mother has said on several occasions that
there are no such words in Russian.

At three forty-five the Polish-born mother stands at the kitchen
table, cutting fine noodles out of dough. Her face is as white as
milk, her skin is so fine you would think a Polish count had married an English schoolmistress to make a lady-in-waiting for
Guinevere. You would think that later in life, of course.

One day an aunt tells us the facts which are as unspeakable as
the names of the body's least uncovered places. The grandfather
of the Polish mother was a fair-haired hooligan. He waited for
Easter. Through raging sexual acts on the body of a girl, his grief
at the death of God might be modulated—transformed into joy
at His Resurrection.

When you're home alone lock the door double, said the milky
Polish mother, the granddaughter of the fair hooligan.

On Saturday morning, at home, all the aunt-mothers are argu-
ing politics. One is a Zionist, one is a Communist, one is a
Democrat. They are very intelligent and listen to lectures at
Cooper Union every week. One is a charter member of the
I.L.G.W.U. She said she would leave me her red sash. She forgot
however. My friend and I listen, but decide to go to the movies.
The sight of us at the door diverts their argument. Are you going
out? Did you go to the bathroom first? they cry. We mean did
you go for everything? My friend and I say yes, but quietly. The
married aunt with one child says, The truth, be truthful. Did you
go? Another aunt enters the room. She has been talking to my
own mother, the woman in whose belly I gathered flesh and
force and became me. She says, There's real trouble in the world,
leave the children alone. She has just come to the United States
and has not yet been driven mad by all the requirements for
total health and absolute sanitation.

That night, my grandmother tells a story. She speaks the common language of grandmothers—that is, not a word of English.
She says, He came to me from the north. I said to him No, I
want to be a teacher. He said, Of course, you should. I said,

What about children. He said, No, not necessarily children. Not so many, no more than two. Why should there be? I liked him. I said, All right.

There were six. My grandmother said: You understand this story. It means make something of yourself.

That's right, says an aunt, the one who was mocked for not having married, whose beauty, as far as the family was concerned, was useless, because no husband ever used it.

And another thing, she said, I just reminded myself to tell you. Darling, she said, I know you want to go to the May Day parade with your friends, but you know what? Don't carry the flag. I want you to go. I didn't say don't go. But don't carry the flag. The one who carries the flag is sometimes killed. The police go crazy when they see that flag.

I *had* dreamed of going forth with a flag—the American flag on July 4, the red flag of the workers on May Day. How did the aunt know this? Because I know you inside out, she said, since you were born. Aren't you *my* child, too?

The sister-mother is the one who is always encouraging. You can do this, you can get an A, you can dance, you can eat squash without vomiting, you can write a poem. But a couple of years later when love and sex struck up their lively friendship, the sister was on the worried mother's side, which was the sad side, because my mother would soon be dying.

One evening I hear the people in the dining room say that my mother is going to die. I remain in the coat closet, listening. She is not going to die soon, I learn. But it will happen. One of the men at the table says that I must be told. I must not be spoiled. Others disagree. They say I have to go to school and do my homework. I have to play. Besides it will be several years.

I am not told. Thereafter I devote myself to not having received that knowledge. I see that my mother gazes sadly at me, not reproachfully, but with an anxious look, as I wander among the other mothers, leaning on their knees, writing letters, making long phone calls. She doesn't agree with their politics, what will become of mine? Together with the aunts and grandmother she worked to make my father strong enough and educated enough so he could finally earn enough to take care of us all. She was successful. Despite this labor, time has passed. Her life is a known closed form. I understand this. Does she? This is the last secret of all. Then for several years, we are afraid of each other. I fear her death. She is afraid for my life.

Of which fifty years have passed, much to my surprise. Using up the days and nights in a lively manner, I have come to the present, daughter of mothers and mother to a couple of grown-up people. They have left home. What have I forgotten to tell? I have told them to be kind. Why? Because my mother was. I have told them when they drop a nickel (or even a shirt) to leave it for the gleaners. It says so in the Bible and I like the idea. Have I told them to always fight for mass transportation and not depend on the auto? Well, they know that. Like any decent kids of Socialist extraction, they can spot the oppressor smiling among the oppressed. Take joy in the struggle against that person, that class, that fact. It's very good for the circulation; I'm sure I said that. Be brave, be truthful, but do they know friendship first, competition second, as the Chinese say? I did say better have a trade, you must know something to be sure of when times are hard, you don't know what the Depression was like, you've had it easy. I've told them everything that was said *to* me or *near* me. As for the rest, there is ordinary place and terrible time—aunts, grandparents, neighbors, all my pals from the job, the playground and the P.T.A. It is on the occasion of their one hundred thousandth bicentennial that I have recalled all those other mothers and their histories.

The Flag

BY RUSSELL BAKER

At various times when young, I was prepared to crack skulls, kill and die for Old Glory. I never wholly agreed with the LOVE IT OR LEAVE IT bumper stickers, which held that everybody who didn't love the flag ought to be thrown out of the country, but I wouldn't have minded seeing them beaten up. In fact, I saw a man come very close to being beaten up at a baseball park one day because he didn't stand when they raised the flag in the opening ceremonies, and I joined the mob screaming for him to get to his feet like an American if he didn't want lumps all over his noodle. He stood up, all right. I was then thirteen, and a Boy Scout, and I knew you never let the flag touch the ground, nor threw it out with trash when it got dirty (you burned it), nor put up with disrespect for it at the baseball park.

At eighteen, I longed to die for it. When World War Two ended in 1945 before I could reach the combat zone, I moped for months about being deprived of the chance to go down in flames under the guns of a Mitsubishi Zero. There was never much doubt that I would go down in flames if given the opportunity, for my competence as a pilot was such that I could barely remember to lower the plane's landing gear before trying to set it down on a runway.

I had even visualized my death. It was splendid. Dead, I would be standing perhaps four thousand feet up in the sky. (Everybody knew that heroes floated in those days.) Erect and dashing, surrounded by beautiful cumulus clouds, I would look just as good as ever, except for being slightly transparent. And I would smile, devil-may-care, at the camera—oh, there would be cameras there and the American flag would unfurl behind me across five hundred miles of glorious American sky, and back behind the cumulus clouds the Marine Band would be playing *The Stars and Stripes Forever*, but not too fast.

Then I would look down at June Allyson and the kids, who had a gold star in the window and brave smiles shining through their tears, and I would give them a salute and one of those brave, wistful Errol Flynn grins, then turn and mount to paradise, becoming more transparent with each step so the audience could get a great view of the flag waving over the heavenly pastures.

Okay, so it owes a lot to Louis B. Mayer in his rococo period. I couldn't help that. At eighteen, a man's imagination is too busy with sex to have much energy left for fancy embellishments of patriotic ecstasy. In the words of a popular song of the period, there was a star-spangled banner waving somewhere in The Great Beyond, and only Uncle Sam's brave heroes got to go there. I was ready to make the trip.

All this was a long time ago, and, asinine though it now may seem, I confess it here to illustrate the singularly masculine pleasures to be enjoyed in devoted service to the stars and stripes. Not long ago I felt a twinge of the old fire when I saw an unkempt lout on a ferryboat with a flag sewed in the crotch of his jeans. Something in me wanted to throw him overboard, but I didn't, since he was a big muscular devil and the flag had already suffered so many worse indignities anyhow, having been pinned in politicians' lapels, pasted on cars to promote gasoline sales, and used to sanctify the professional sports industry as the soul of patriotism even while the team owners were instructing their athletes in how to dodge the draft.

For a moment, though, I felt some of the old masculine excitement kicked up by the flag in the adrenal glands. It's a man's flag, all right. No doubt about that. Oh, it may be a scoundrel's flag, too, and a drummer's flag, and a fraud's flag, and a thief's flag. But first and foremost, it is a man's flag.

Except for decorating purposes—it looks marvelous on old New England houses—I cannot see much in it to appeal to women. Its pleasures, in fact, seem so exclusively masculine and its sanctity so unassailable by feminist iconoclasts that it may prove to be America's only enduring, uncrushable male sex symbol.

Observe that in my patriotic death fantasy, the starring role is not June Allyson's, but mine. As defender of the flag, I am not only the hero but also have a wonderful time en route to enshrinement. I am able to leave a humdrum job, put June and the kids with all their humdrum problems behind me, travel the world with a great bunch of guys, do exciting things with powerful flying machines and, fetchingly uniformed, strut exotic saloons on my nights off.

In the end, I walk off with all the glory and the big scene.

And what does June get? Poor June. She gets to sit home with the kids the rest of her life dusting my photograph and trying to pay the bills, with occasional days off to visit the grave.

No wonder the male pulse pounds with pleasure when the stars and stripes come fluttering down the avenue with the band smashing out those great noises. Where was Mrs. Teddy Roosevelt when Teddy was carrying it up San Juan Hill? What was Mrs. Lincoln doing when Abe was holding it aloft for the Union? What was Martha up to while George Washington was carrying it across the Delaware? Nothing, you may be sure, that was one tenth as absorbing as what their husbands were doing.

Consider some of the typical masculine activities associated with Old Glory: dressing up in medals. Whipping cowards, slackers and traitors within an inch of their miserable lives. Conquering Mount Suribachi. Walking on the moon. Rescuing the wagon train. Being surrounded by the whole German Army and being asked to surrender and saying, "You can tell Schicklgruber my answer is 'Nuts!'" In brief, having a wonderful time. With the boys.

Yes, surely the American flag is the ultimate male sex symbol. Men flaunt it, wave it, punch noses for it, strut with it, fight for it, kill for it, die for it.

And women—? Well, when do you see a woman with the flag? Most commonly when she is wearing black and has just received it, neatly folded, from coffin of husband or son. Later, she may wear it to march in the Veterans Day parade, widows' division.

Male pleasures and woman's sorrow—it sounds like the old

definition of sex. Yet these are the immemorial connotations of
the flag, and women, having shed the whalebone girdle and
stamped out the stag bar, nevertheless accept it, ostensibly at
least, with the same emotional devotion that men accord it.

There are good reasons, of course, why they may be reluctant
to pursue logic to its final step and say, "To hell with the flag,
too." In the first place, it would almost certainly do them no
good. Men hold all the political trumps in this matter. When little girls first toddle off to school, does anyone tell them the facts
of life when they stand to salute the flag? Does anyone say, "You
are now saluting the proud standard of the greatest men's club
on earth"? You bet your chewing gum nobody tells them that. If
anyone did, there would be a joint session of Congress presided
over by the President of the United States to investigate the entire school system of the United States of America.

What little girls have drilled into them is that the flag stands
for one nation indivisible, with liberty and justice for all. A few
years ago, the men of the Congress, responding to pressure from
the American Legion (all men) and parsons (mostly all men),
all of whom sensed perhaps that women were not as gullible as
they used to be, revised the Pledge of Allegiance with words in-
timating that it would be ungodly not to respect the flag. The
"one nation indivisible" became "one nation *under God,* indivisible," and another loophole for skeptics was sealed off. The
women's movement may be brave, but it will not go far taking
on national indivisibility, liberty, justice and God, all in one
fight. If they tried it, a lot of us men would feel perfectly
justified in raising lumps on their lovely noodles.

Philosophically speaking, the masculinity of the American flag
is entirely appropriate. America, after all, is not a motherland—
many places still are—but a fatherland, which is to say a vast na-
tion-state of disparate people scattered over great distances, but
held together by a belligerent, loyalty-to-the-death devotion to
some highly abstract political ideas. Since these ideas are too
complex to be easily grasped, statesmen have given us the flag
and told us it sums up all these noble ideas that make us a country.

Fatherland being an aggressive kind of state, the ideas it em-
bodies must be defended, protected and propagated, often in

blood. Since the flag is understood to represent these ideas, in a kind of tricolor shorthand, we emote, fight, bleed and rejoice in the name of the flag.

Before fatherland there was something that might be called motherland. It still exists here and there. In the fifties, when Washington was looking for undiscovered Asiatic terrain to save from un-American ideologies, somebody stumbled into an area called Laos, a place so remote from American consciousness that few had ever heard its name pronounced. (For the longest time, Lyndon Johnson, then Democratic leader of the Senate, referred to it as "Low Ass.") Federal inspectors sent to Laos returned with astounding information. Most of the people living there were utterly unaware that they were living in a country. Almost none of them knew the country they were living in was called Laos. All they knew was that they lived where they had been born and where their ancestors were buried.

What Washington had discovered, of course, was an old-fashioned motherland, a society where people's loyalties ran to the place of their birth. It was a Pentagon nightmare. Here were these people, perfectly happy with their home turf and their ancestors' graves, and they had to be put into shape to die for their country, and they didn't even know they had a country to die for. They didn't even have a flag to die for. And yet, they were content!

The point is that a country is only an idea and a fairly modern one at that. Life would still be going on if nobody had ever thought of it, and it would probably be a good deal more restful. No flags. Not much in the way of armies. No sharing of exciting group emotions with millions of other people ready to do or die for national honor. And so forth. Very restful, and possibly very primitive, and almost surely very nasty on occasion, although possibly not as nasty as occasions often become when countries disagree.

I hear my colleagues in masculinity protesting. "What? No country? No flag? But there would be nothing noble to defend, to fight for, to die for, in the meantime having a hell of a good time doing all those fun male things in the name of!"

Women may protest, too. I imagine some feminists may object to the suggestion that fatherland's need for prideful, warlike and aggressive citizens to keep the flag flying leaves women pretty much out of things. Those who hold that sexual roles are a simple matter of social conditioning may contend that the flag can offer the same rollicking pleasures to both sexes once baby girls are trained as thoroughly as baby boys in being prideful, warlike and aggressive.

I think there may be something in this, having seen those harridans who gather outside freshly desegregated schools to wave the American flag and terrify children. The question is whether women really want to start conditioning girl babies for this hitherto largely masculine sort of behavior, or spend their energies trying to decondition it out of the American man.

In any case, I have no quarrel with these women. Living in fatherland, they have tough problems, and if they want to join the boys in the flag sports, it's okay with me. The only thing is, if they are going to get a chance, too, to go up to paradise with the Marine Band playing *The Stars and Stripes Forever* back behind the cumulus clouds, I don't want to be stuck with the role of sitting home dusting their photographs the rest of my life after the big scene is ended.

Apple Pie

BY M. F. K. FISHER

It is as meaningless to say that something is "as American as apple pie" as it is to assert proudly that a Swedish or Irish grandfather who emigrated to Minnesota was "a first American." Both the pie and the parent sprang from other cultures, and neither got here before the Indian.

Be that as it is, and nonetheless, most of us today would fight staunchly to defend the rights and honors of what we choose to consider our own dish . . . or at least one of our own *great* dishes. The fact that it came here from England, with the Pilgrims up North and the Cavaliers down South, long before we were a nation, and that it was probably brought in recognizable form to England by William the Conqueror in 1066 or so, cannot mar the fine polish of how we feel about apple pie as a part of our comparatively youthful heritage.

There are as many opinions about perfection in this national dish as there are about hangover cures. A man-on-the-street survey, no matter who conducts it nor how nor where, will turn up firm contradictions based on knowledge or prejudice or plain wishful thinking. A lot of people have never really had the chance to eat a decent apple pie, but after a minute's sensual reflection will know positively what they would expect if they did. They can taste it on their mind's tongue: thin flaky pastry and hunks of sweet apples bathed in a syrup; rich but sturdy dough filled with finely sliced tart apples seasoned with cinnamon; an upper and lower crust in a traditional pie pan; an upper crust only, in a deep dish; a bottom crust with crosses of dough over the filling. . . .

It is all a dream, unless one has a quaint old-country grandma or an equally rare bakery. We order apple pie doggedly in everything from expensive steak houses to the corner drugstore, and gallantly disguise it with vanilla ice cream "a la mode," or eat packaged ersatz "Cheddar" alongside, or even tolerate it (in what can only be a form of chauvinism) with cheese baked under the top crust, or raisins added, or some other such heinous desecration of what apple pie can be.

It can be very very good, like the little girl with the curl in the middle of her forehead. Since the possibilities for its being equally horrid have been hinted at, and no mention at all has been made of bad bakery products and tasteless but somewhat less dangerous frozen goods, I'll try a more positive look at what *can* happen to this adopted beauty of a dish.

Like anything fit to be put on the table, it cannot be whipped out in a few minutes from bad supplies and a bored heart. A really good apple pie takes perhaps an hour and a half to get from the peelings to the table. This does not count buying the apples and seeing that the other supplies are on hand . . . and even having a kitchen and an oven! If the pie smells as good as it should, people will want to eat it immediately, but it should wait for a while and be served gently warm. It is almost as easy to make two or six as one, and some of the batch can be frozen or stored. In simpler days, extra pies were put outside the kitchen window, safe from four-legged friends of course, or down in the icy cellar. A two-crust pie risks becoming soggy if not eaten soon, and pioneer cooks found that, for keeping, it was wise to bake one or two deep-dish pies with only a top crust.

So, given the ingredients and the essentials—like pan, stove, oven—one goes calmly about the game, which can become as skilled as eye surgery or Wimbledon, of concocting an apple pie to fit the sensual expectations and requirements of its eaters. It should leave them happy but expectant of the next time and with excellent digestion.

A woman who is eminent in this branch of gastronomical therapy tells me:

Peel, core, and slice about six tart apples into a bowl. Sugar

them, add a little cinnamon and a jigger of good brandy or bourbon, and stir them well. While they sit, make a light rich dough,
and roll it out (never back and forth but *out*). Have the oven at
450°. Line the pan(s), heap in the apples, dot generously with
butter. Cover with top crust, seal edges, and cut a slash in the
top. Bake fast for ten minutes, and then reduce heat to 350° for
about thirty to forty minutes or until the apples feel tender when
speared through the peekhole.

She adds a few casual asides to this basically plain procedure:
if the apples are too mild, stir a little lemon juice into them; add
a couple of tablespoonsful of cornstarch if you think the pie will
be too soupy . . . and if it runs over, throw salt onto the juice in
the oven; don't mention the brandy if Aunt Jenny, who is president of the W.C.T.U., asks why the pie is so tasty, since she
wouldn't admit that all the alcohol has long since evapo-
rated. . . .

There is a surprising scarcity of such fundamental recipes in
our old kitchen manuals, because in early America any cook
worth his or her salt knew perforce how to produce a pie by puberty, so that there was no need to write the rules. Many of the
existing directions are, of course, impractical by now, but even a
modern amateur can take a good look at a standard guide like
Mrs. Rombauer or Fanny Farmer and roll out a decent crust.
And there are real apples almost always in the markets. There is
sugar, cinnamon, even lemon juice in an emergency. Margarine
is procurable if butter is not.

To sound realistic rather than wishful for a minute, a "homemade" pie that might bring some joy to a person used to drugstore offerings can be fabricated with a bought crust and a can
of "pie apples," if rather heavily seasoned and gussied. It tastes
fairly good, perhaps because it is actually made in the home
(which is where the oven is). But comparisons are said to be
odious. . . .

Possibly our national appetite for apple pie could be called a
syndrome, or even a mystique, and perhaps we can blame a lot
of it on a very nice quiet religious eccentric named John Chap-
man. He was a New Englander (1774–1845) who spent the last
forty years of his life wandering around what is now Ohio-In-
diana-Illinois, planting apple seeds, yes, "Planting the trees that
would march/ In his name to the great Pacific,/ Like Birnam

Wood to Dunsinane,/ Johnny Appleseed swept on." That is what Carl Sandburg sang about Johnny, and another poet wrote, "Let all unselfish spirits heed/The story of Johnny Appleseed," and my own grandfather is said to have rested under Johnny's bending orchard boughs on his way to survey the Iowa territory for Mr. Lincoln. That was in about 1864. He said that the trees were half wild but fruitful and that people still talked affectionately of the crazy gentle man as if he were still there.

Apple trees have grown in temperate zones for as long as we can tell (how about the Garden of Eden?), and they are a tough rich beautiful tree, a boon to us all in spite of Eve's slip of the tongue. They are intricately woven into our legends and myths and religious fantasies, from Aphrodite to William Tell. There are said to be about 7,600 varieties of them, almost all edible in one form or another. They will live a long time even in high places but not on deserts.

Apples keep well in cool cellars and can be partially or wholly cooked and used in preserves and sauces, or dried, as pioneer Americans found. (A fine pie can be made of dried apple slices let swell to their right size in warm water overnight. Then the pie can be baked in time for breakfast, while the men are at their first chores. Pie for breakfast is as American as . . .) An apple a day is said to keep the doctor away, and certainly it should, if the eater has a good stomach and strong teeth and can breathe good air and a few other things that otherwise might bring the pill boys hurrying in. The best apples now available, unless there is a venerable orchard nearby, are marketed as Rome Beauties, mostly for cooking; Northern Spies, McIntoshes, Jonathans for eating; Gravensteins for both. This is a northern California estimate, and I know there are countless other choices in our country and that I would blush to make this one anywhere but here.

A pie is always a baked dish with a crust on top for me. It can have a top and bottom crust, especially if filled with fruit. But if it has only a bottom crust it is a tart. This simplifies life. In England, where our pies came from, they can be either tarts or pies, depending on what is in them; that is, fruit can be topless or bottomless, but meat is always with a top and is called a pie and not a tart. (A pasty, usually with meat and vegetables in it, is what we call a turnover.) In France a *tarte* is a tart, topless and unashamed, except for a slight lacing of strips of pastry and a hint of a blush from the sweet glaze over it.

(It is interesting or even significant that Mrs. Irma Rombauer, whose *Joy of Cooking* is as staunchly American as Mrs. Isabella Beeton's *Book of Household Management* is British, states flatly of her French apple pie—really an open-face *tarte* on *galette* crust—that it is "the prince"! Her Gallic recipe is as *echt* as *Apfelkuchen,* although I feel patriotically that her rule for plain Midwestern apple pie is equally noble.)

I try to stay positive about several American institutions, including apple pie, but it is hard not to make firm and even derisive statements about what is fobbed off on us just because we seem to have a compulsive craving for the dish. How dare the local U-Help Drugs display, much less sell, what I see boldly cut onto plates on glass shelves behind the fair-tressed serving maid? What good will a scoop of vanilla ice cream lend it? But I may *need* some quick energy from sugar or glucose, the taste of ex-fruit, the sustenance of dead fat and emasculated flour. . . . The crust is inedible, like slippery cardboard on the bottom and sugared newsprint on top. The apples are canned vintage, embalmed for posterity in a rare chemical syrup. As for the scoop of. . . . Back to the wall, I can dig between the two crusts and eat some shiny lumps and think of other days.

Perhaps it is true that national surveys show that American males now prefer chocolate pie to apple, and although I can understand, I refuse to believe it. Myself, I have never eaten chocolate pie in a good restaurant or coffee shop, much less in my own home, but once I was served a chocolate meringue pie in a New York apartment that had been "decorated" in browns and blacks to match the pet dachshund, and it was an experience in nothingness, except perhaps calorically. The flavor was so delicately un-chocolate as to vanish within the frothy high-piled filling, and the crust was equally discreet and neither light nor heavy, flaky nor rich nor . . . *crusty*. The little dog had much more character, and a forthright approximation of our national dish, even from a stylish caterer, would have matched him better.

Vanilla ice cream is the best camouflage of outrage at the local U-Helps, but if an honorable, decent, healthy, respectable apple pie is at hand, I would send it down my happy gullet either unassisted or with one of two special things: a piece of good Cheddar cheese, English or American. (It can be called rat-trap, where I came from.) The other is plain thick cream, poured from a pitcher and preferably into a soup plate over the piece of pie.

Once I stayed for a time in southern Illinois and lived from one Sunday-noon invitation to the next, less aware of the elegant old house, a station of the Underground on the Mason-Dixon line in the Civil War, than of the fact that not only one pie would be served for dessert but *two*. They were mince and apple, and both were just hot enough to melt the ice cream served from a chilled bowl. The ice cream was made with maple sugar, to pile on top of the slices of pie, each on a separate plate. This was a dizzying reward to a half-starved college student. It was as near as I ever came to New England, where shaved maple sugar and plain cream are eaten now as in the seventeenth century with apple dumplings, pies, pandowdies, anything with a good crust.

Myself, given such a crusty pie made with tart apples and the right sugar-cinnamon-butter, that is all I need for a whole meal, a private sensual satisfying supper. I agree with Robert Louis Stevenson's seemingly infantile prattling in *A Child's Garden of Verses:* "The friendly cow all red and white,/ I love with all my heart./ She gives me cream with all her might,/ To eat with apple tart."

In other words, apple pie as we make it now, whether at a U-Help or in an Idaho cabin or a New York kitchenette-studio, is unique to America. It assumes ethnic tinges depending on where we live and who bore us there, but the shape is formally *ours:* a two-crust round baked shallow dish or pan, containing sliced apples, spices, sugar and butter (with perhaps lemon juice or brandy).

I'll eat it anytime I can find a good one. Or, I'll stay home and bake one, which is probably what we all should do.

Guns

BY LARRY WOIWODE

Once in the middle of a Wisconsin winter I shot a deer, my only one, while my wife and daughter watched. It had been hit by a delivery truck along a country road a few miles from where we lived and one of its rear legs was torn off at the hock; a shattered shin and hoof lay steaming in the red-beaded snow. The driver of the truck and I stood and watched as it tried to leap a fence, kicked a while at the top wire it was entangled in, flailing the area with fresh ropes of blood, and then went hobbling across a pasture toward a wooded hill. Placid cows followed it with a curious awe. "Do you have a rifle with you?" the driver asked. "No, not with me. At home." He looked once more at the deer, then got in his truck and drove off.

I went back to our Jeep where my wife and daughter were waiting, pale and withdrawn, and told them what I was about to do, and suggested that they'd better stay at home. No, they wanted to be with me, they said; they wanted to watch. My daughter was three and a half at the time. I got my rifle, a .22, a foolishly puny weapon to use on a deer but the only one I had, and we came back and saw that the deer was lying in some low brush near the base of the hill; no need to trail its blatant spoor. When I got about a hundred yards off, marveling at how it could have made it so far in its condition through snow that came over my boot tops, the deer tried to push itself up with its front legs, then collapsed. I aimed at the center of its skull, thinking, *This will be the quickest,* and heard the bullet ricochet off and go singing through the woods.

The deer was on its feet, shaking its head as though stung, and I fired again at the same spot, quickly, and apparently missed. It was now moving at its fastest hobble up the hill, broadside to me, and I took my time to sight a heart shot. Before the report even registered in my mind, the deer went down in an explosion of snow and lay struggling there, spouting blood from its stump and a chest wound. I was shaking by now. Deer are color-blind as far as science can say, and as I went toward its quieting body to deliver the coup de grace, I realized I was being seen in black and white, and then the deer's eye seemed to home in on me, and I was struck with the understanding that I was its vision of approaching death. And then I seemed to enter its realm through its eye and saw the countryside and myself in shades of white and gray. *But I see the deer in color,* I thought.

A few yards away, I aimed at its head once more, and there was the crack of a shot, the next-to-last round left in the magazine. The deer's head came up, and I could see its eye clearly now, dark, placid, filled with an appeal, it seemed, and then felt the surge of black and white surround and subsume me again. The second shot, or one of them, had pierced its neck; a gray-blue tongue hung out over its jaw; urine was trickling from below its tail; a doe. I held the rifle barrel inches from its forehead, conscious of my wife's and daughter's eyes on me from behind, and as I fired off the final and fatal shot, felt myself drawn by them back into my multicolored, many-faceted world again.

I don't remember my first gun, the heritage is so ingrained in me, but know I've used a variety of them to kill birds, reptiles, mammals, amphibians, plant life, insects (bees and butterflies with a shotgun), fish that came too close to shore—never a human being, I'm quick to interject, although the accumulated carnage I've put away with bullets since boyhood is probably enough to add up to a couple of cows, not counting the deer; and have fired, at other targets living and fairly inert, an old ten gauge with double hammers that left a welt on my shoulder that lasted a week, a Mauser, a twelve-gauge sawed-off shotgun, an M-16, at least a dozen variations on the .22—pump, bolt action, lever action, target pistols, special scopes and sights and stocks

—a .410 over-and-under, a zip gun that blew up and scattered shrapnel that's still imbedded in my arm, an Italian carbine, a Luger, and, among others, a fancily engraved, single-trigger, double-barreled twenty gauge at snowballs thrown from behind my shoulder out over a bluff; and on that same bluff on the first day of this year, after some wine and prodding, I found myself at the jittering rim of stutters from a paratrooper's lightweight machine gun with a collapsible, geometrically reinforced metal stock, watched the spout of its trajectory of tangible tracers go off across the night toward the already-set sun, and realized that this was perhaps the hundredth weapon I'd had performing in my hands.

I was raised in North Dakota, near the edge of the West, during the turbulence and then the aftermath of the Second World War, which our country ended in such an unequivocal way there was a sense of vindication about our long-standing fetish for guns, not to say pride in it, too. "Bang! Bang! You're dead," returns to me from that time without the least speck of friction or reflection. When we weren't playing War, or Cowboys and Indians, or Cops and Robbers, we were reading War Comics (from which you could order for less than a dollar little cardboard chests of plastic weaponry and soldiers to stage your own debacles), or Westerns, or listening to *The Lone Ranger* and *Richard Diamond, Private Detective,* and other radio shows—all of which openly glorified guns, and the more powerful the better.

My fantasies, when I was frustrated, angry, or depressed, were rife with firearms of the most lethal sort, flying shot, endless rounds of shattering ammunition; the enemy bodies blown away and left in bloody tableaux. And any gun was an engineered instrument—much more far-ranging and accurate than bows and arrows or slingshots—that detached you from your destructiveness or crime or sometimes even from being a source of death.

I've only owned three firearms in my life as an adult. Two I brought back to the shops within a week after I'd bought them, realizing I was trying to reach out in some archaic way, and the limits to my maturity and imagination that that implied, plus the bother to my daughter of their powing sounds; and the third, the .22, after trembling over it a few years and using it to shoot holes in the floor to enact a between-the-legs suicide, I gave away. To my younger brother. Who was initiated into the buck-fever fra-

ternity in the forests of northern Wisconsin when he was an adolescent by a seasoned local who said to him, "If you see anything
moving out there tomorrow, boy, *shoot* it. You can check out
later what it is. Nobody gives a shit up here." And on a hunting
trip years later, an acquaintance from the village my brother
lived in then, a lawyer, was shot in the head with a deer rifle, but
somehow survived. And even went back to practicing law. It was
thought to be an accident at first, what with all the bullets
embroidering the air that day, and then rumor had it that another member of the party hunting on adjoining land, an old
friend of the lawyer's, had found out a week before the season
that the lawyer had been having his wife for a while. The two
men were polite enough to one another in the village after that,
my brother said, but not such good friends, of course. Just balanced, justice-balanced males.

For months and seasons after I'd shot the crippled doe, every
time we passed the field in our Jeep, my daughter would say,
"Here's where Daddy shooted the deer." In exactly that manner,
using the tone and detachment of a storyteller or tourist guide.
And I'd glance into the rearview mirror and see her in her car
seat, studying the hill with troubled and sympathetic eyes. One
day I stopped. "Does it bother you so much that I shot it?" I
asked. There was no answer, and then I saw that she was nod-
ding her head, her gaze still fixed on the hill.

"Well, if I wouldn't have, it could have suffered a long time.
You saw how badly hurt it was. It couldn't have lived that way. I
didn't like doing it, either, but it was best for the deer. When I
told the game warden about it, he even thanked me and said,
'Leave it for the foxes and crows.' They have to eat, too, you
know, and maybe the deer made the winter easier for them."
And I thought, Oh, what a self-justifying fool and ass and pig
you are. Why didn't you leave her at home? Why didn't you go
to the farmer whose land the deer was on, which would have
been as quick or quicker than going back for the .22—a man
who would have had a deer rifle, or at least a shotgun with rifled
slugs, and would have put the deer away with dispatch in one
shot and might have even salvaged the hide and venison? And
who could say it wouldn't have lived, the way some animals do
after tearing or chewing off a limb caught in a trap? Who was to
presume it wouldn't have preferred to die a slow death in the

brush, looking out over the pasture, as the crimson stain widening in the snow drew away and dimmed its colorless world until all went black? Why not admit that I was a common back-country American and, like most men of my mold, had used an arsenal of firearms to kill and was as excited about putting away a deer as moved by compassion for its suffering? Then again, given my daughter's understanding and the person I am, perhaps she sensed this, and more.

I once choked a chicken to death. It was my only barefaced, not to say barehanded, confrontation with death and the killer in me and happened on my grandparents' farm. I couldn't have been more than nine or ten and no firearms were included or necessary. I was on my knees and the chicken fluttered its outstretched wings with the last of the outraged protest. I gripped, beyond release, above its swollen crop, its beak gaping, translucent eyelids sliding up and down. An old molting specimen. A hen, most likely; a worse loss, because of eggs, than a capon or cock. My grandfather, who was widely traveled and world-wise, in his eighties then, and had just started using a cane from earlier times, came tapping at that moment around the corner of the chicken coop and saw what I was doing and started gagging at the hideousness of it, did a quick assisted spin away and never again, hours later nor for the rest of his life, for that matter, ever mentioned the homicidal incident to me. Keeping his silence, he seemed to understand; and yet whenever I'm invaded by the incident, the point of it seems to be his turning away from me.

My wife once said she felt I wanted to kill her. A common enough feeling among long-married couples, I'm sure, and not restricted to either sex (I know, for instance, that there were times when she wanted to kill me), but perhaps with firsthand experience infusing the feeling, it became too much to endure. I now live in New York City, where the clock keeps moving toward my suitcase, alone, and she and my daughter in the Midwest. The city has changed in the seven years since the three of us lived here together. There are more frivolous and not-so-frivolous wares—silk kerchiefs, necklaces and rings, roach clips, rolling papers, socks, a display of Florida coral across a convertible top, books of every kind—being sold in the streets than anybody can remember seeing in recent years. People openly saying that soon it will be like the thirties once were, with us *all* in the streets selling our apples, or whatever, or engaged in a tacit and friendly sort of gangsterism to survive. Outside my window, a spindly deciduous species has a sign strung on supporting posts on either side of it, in careful handlettering, that reads, THIS TREE GIVES OXYGEN. GIVE IT LOVE. More dogs in the streets and parks than they'd remembered, and more canine offal sending up its open-ended odor; at least half the population giving up cigarette smoking, at last, for good, they say, and many actually are. The mazed feeling of most everywhere now of being in the midst of a slowly forging and forgiving reciprocity. An air of bravura about most everybody in maintaining one's best face, with a few changes of costumish clothing to reflect it, perhaps, no matter what might yet evolve. A unisex barbershop or boutique on nearly every other block, it seems.

Sometimes I think this is where I really belong. Then a man is gunned down in a neighborhood bar I used to drop into and the next day a mob leader assassinated, supposedly by members of his own mob. *Perhaps this is where I'm most at home,* I equivocate again and have an image of myself in a Stetson traveling down a crosstown street at a fast-paced and pigeon-toed shamble toward the setting sun (setting this far east, but not over my wife and daughter yet), my eyes cast down and shoulders forward, hands deep in my empty Levi's pockets, a suspect closet-faggot-cowboy occasionally whistled at by queens.

I won't (and can't) refute my heritage, but I doubt that I'll use a firearm again, or, if I do, only in the direst sort of emergency. Which I say to protect my flanks. The bloody, gun-filled fantasies seldom return now, and when they do they're reversed: I'm the one being shot, or shot at, or think I am.

Coca-Cola

BY JEAN STAFFORD

At one time there was a widely held belief among edgy mothers that Coca-Cola derived its name from cocaine, which was one of its principal ingredients (in the vernacular of the South and the West, it was referred to as "dope"), and that it was habit-forming. The pause that refreshes could lead quicker than you might think to the Big Sleep. My own mother had it on good authority ("Never mind who told me") that an aspirin tablet pulverized and added to a glass of Coca-Cola produced the same effect as a Mickey Finn: under the influence of this witch's brew, many unwitting girls had been despoiled ("stripped" was the way my mother put it) by concupiscent mountebanks posing as Fuller Brush men. I could not puzzle out the stratagem of these seductions. Did the impostor, on learning that the lady of the house was not at home, offer her dumb daughter a cooling drink, which, it just so happened, he had in his sample case, and, while she was gone to get glasses, remove the caps with a can opener he had at the ready and as quick as a wink insinuate the aspirin into one of the bottles? It seemed a risky ploy—what if the lady of the house or a real Fuller Brush man showed up before the dark deed was done? On the several occasions I tried to pin my mother down to facts and figures, she sent me to the store on a trumped-up errand or reminded me that Christmas was drawing nigh and I had not finished the potholder I was blanket-stitching for my grandmother.

Whenever I was taken to a soda fountain, I supinely ordered cherry phosphate or Hires root beer—the latter passed muster despite the flagrantly taboo word "beer" in its name. And then, in my eleventh year, when it was springtime in the Rockies, a brother and sister newly arrived in Colorado from the East (I think they came from Des Moines) invited me to go up to the foothills for a picnic one Saturday. They were swells. I had read about picnic hampers, but I had never seen one and I was impressed by theirs. It was wicker, lined with sunflower-printed calico, and Fabrikoid loops held in place a nest of folding drinking cups, salt and pepper shakers, a jar of dill pickles and a thermos. The sandwiches, with the crusts trimmed, were cut in four triangles and neatly wrapped in waxed paper and in red pencil were labeled "Minced Ham," "Tuna & Lettuce," "Sardines w. Gentleman's Relish." There were, as well, three hard-boiled eggs made fuchsia by being submersed in beet juice, and three Charleston Chews.

The thermos, which was large, held Coca-Cola, and on learning this, I was awed by the sophistication of my companions and, even more, by the hedonism of their parents: my friends' father bought syrup and he carbonated it with a seltzer bottle right at home, a procedure having much in common with operating a still in the cellar. Alarmed and titillated, in my mind's eye I saw my mother's furrowed brow and her quaking underlip, but her face was immediately obliterated by that of a grinning Fuller Brush man with a black goatee and horns growing sprucely out of his panama.

Naturally I didn't let on how grass-green I was, and if Lloyd and Lucy saw how I had to hold my folding cup with both hands, they courteously paid no heed as we drank our aperitif. Never before had I tasted anything so delicious, and no subsequent Coca-Cola has quite measured up to that first one drunk in a shady dingle where the magpies screamed "nevermore" and the doleful wind in the lodgepole pines intoned the *dies irae*. The effervescence was boldly astringent and as clean as a knife; the flavor suggested the corrupt spices of Araby and a hint, perhaps, of brimstone.

I was not much for eating, but I managed most of my share of the sandwiches and two dill pickles and, passing up the eccentrically colored eggs, ate the whole of my Charleston Chew.

There was still a good deal of Coca-Cola left after we'd finished our meal and now Lloyd, the older of my hosts, passed around a sat-on half pack of cubebs, which their father, a tubercular, smoked incessantly. The sneaky brand name was Cold Golds, and while there might not have been a cough in a carload—as the authentic Old Golds claimed for themselves—for him and his jaded children, my first puff, which reached no farther than the tip of my tongue, set me off into paroxysms. The cure, it appeared, for this kind of croup, was more Coca-Cola. It was as plain as a pikestaff that I had never smoked before, but those decadent dudes from Iowa were patient with me and, persevering under their tutelage and with the help of the pop, I worked my way through to the bitter end of my first coffin nail.

Sin giddied me. There we were, lolling about on the pine needles, attracting wood ticks, like three old tars drinking cocaine highballs and smoking opium in a Shanghai den. But all of a sudden, something went wrong in paradise; a telltale sourness gathered where my tonsils once had been. I got up and with as much insouciance as I could summon, but without daring to speak, hightailed it to a cave where I threw up. I blamed the Sardines w. Gentleman's Relish, which I had not liked at all, or possibly the cubeb—truth to tell I had found it vile. Purged and clearheaded but much enfeebled, I went back to Lloyd and Lucy with the unlikely story that I had just remembered that my brother had asked me to check one of his skunk traps. Lloyd refilled my folding cup.

Let me tell you I eyed it with misgivings. I knew he wasn't an unlicensed Fuller Brush man, but there *was* the possibility that the Coca-Cola rather than the flossied-up sardines or the quasi-medicinal cigarette had undone me. Nevertheless, I sipped it, then took a proper swallow, then gulped down the rest and asked for more. I learned then that Coca-Cola is, for me, the specific for almost every variety of dyspepsia; later I found it to be, as well, soothing to a sore throat, a surefire cure for a hangover (save for the katzenjammer gravis that time and reformation of character alone can ease) and the greatest of all thirst quenchers. South of the Mason-Dixon line, it is prescribed from the cradle to the final rocking chair for thrush, gout, undulant fever, prickly heat and insanity. My own physician, a fastidious and astute diagnostician associated with one of the prominent teaching hospitals of New York City, recommends it more often than he does vitamins. This may have to do, in part, with the fact that he is himself a heavy user. He has had some rather unpleasant dustups with his colleagues and their nurses with whom he shares offices when, without asking leave, they have helped themselves to his supply of Coke in the communal refrigerator. Recently, he has found a way to postpone losing his temper if his need is compelling and the cupboard is bare: the chief technician in the X-ray room has a fully stocked private fridge that she keeps locked. She had given Dr. R—— a key; that may sound like intramural hanky-panky, but such rumors are without foundation. The arrangement is strictly businesslike and thanks to Mrs. J——'s predilection and her no-nonsense housewifery Dr. R——, never deprived of Coke, practices sounder medicine than he would do if his mind were on his thirst and not on my gallbladder.

Once I saw Coca-Cola put dramatically to four purposes simultaneously: on an August evening in 1959, in Alexandria, Louisiana, when the temperature was a little over 101° and the humidity was just short of precipitation, I was one of a throng listening to the late Governor Earl K. Long on the stump for re-election. He held a bottle of Coca-Cola, which now he held aloft to emphasize the goodness of his intentions or, more cordially, to toast his constituents (I thought of the Statue of Liberty, whom James Agee once described as "the toastmistress of Bedloe's Island"), now swigged to cool his throat, and now applied to his handkerchief to mop his sweating brow. The fourth office the drink performed was not evident to the naked eye, but it was generally agreed among friends and foes alike that there was a good dollop of Southern Comfort in the bottle to keep his oratory zinging along like an American bald eagle that had caught the scent of a liberal carpetbagger from New York City.

I don't remember ever seeing Lloyd and Lucy again, but they had changed my life. Sometimes, unless the offering was one hundred percent guaranteed to terrorize me within an ace of death, I would skip the Saturday movie and use half the price of admission on a Coke in a drugstore, but one in a neighborhood far from my own lest my mother stop by for a bottle of Hinds honey and almond hand lotion. Occasionally I had a squirt of cherry or lemon or lime added, but I preferred the

drink straight, preferred, as the company now accurately adver-
tises it, "The Real Thing." But then I learned a way to have my
cake and drink it, too; there was a fraternity at the University of
Colorado in Boulder where I lived whose members were so rich
and lazy that they didn't bother to return the empties for refund,
so under the cover of dark, a couple of times a week, I
scavenged the trash cans in back of their house; I frequented the
town dump, as well, and in this way, easily supported my habit
and in addition could afford to let zombies, big old apes, and
Lon Chaney make my blood run cold on Saturday afternoon and
cause me to walk and scream in my sleep on Saturday night. The
fact that I had the longest list of contagious diseases on record at
the board of health and single-handedly started a prominent
scarlet fever epidemic could, I suppose, be attributed to my
unfastidious commerce. But, as I look on it, you've got to take
the bitter with the sweet.

Besides the apocryphal (so far as I know) persuasion that
Coca-Cola and aspirin produced a downer, so it was believed
among the university students that ammonia added to Coca-Cola
transformed it into an upper, and during finals week, when everybody was boning up on push moraines for examinations in ge-
ology and Cardinal Newman for those in Victorian prose, the
soda jerks all over town were making this appalling mixture
hand over fist till closing time. I tried it only once and it had the
same effect on me as Sardines w. Gentleman's Relish.

I do not hold with the adulteration of Coca-Cola. In the early
forties when I lived in Baton Rouge, I did knock back a good
many cuba libres which were fashionable just then. I used to
pour Coca-Cola into ice-cube trays, dainty up each cell with a
mint leaf and have the mixture and the cooler ready for the rum.
But I did not partake of a beverage thought up and daily drunk
by a Bostonian with whom I was closely (and legally) associated at the time; he called it Postbellum Shandygaff and it
consisted of one bottle of beer, one bottle of ale and two trays of
my Coca-Cola ice cubes. The vessel from which he swilled it was
a glass vase intended for gladioli, larkspur, African daisies and
other long-stemmed flowers.

There are those, I am told, who baste hams with Coca-Cola,
but I do not personally know anyone who makes a practice of
this. Mr. John Shinn of Sylacauga, Alabama, who is now resident

in the town on Long Island where I live, read me a recipe for "congealed Coca-Cola salad" that he had found in an old Deep South cookery book. What you do is this: you open up a can of crushed pineapple and drain it but retain the juice, and then a can of pitted Bing cherries and treat that in the same way. Then you bring the combined juices to the boiling point and add a package of black cherry gelatin and one of strawberry gelatin. Cool. Add one cup of chopped nutmeats and one cup of *cottage cheese* (italics mine), two "regular" bottles of Coca-Cola. Combine all ingredients. Chill until firm: yield, ten to twelve servings. It is to be hoped that no bridge-club hostess ever gilded this lily with a topping of whipped cream to which shredded coconut had been added. Do you suppose that self-improving ladies in New England, forgathered to discuss the 100 Best Books, were served "Moxie surprise"?

Within the past twelvemonth, I have had it demonstrated to me that Coca-Cola, sprayed from an atomizer, can immediately and permanently defrost a windshield in near-zero weather.

When Miss Ann Honeycutt (originally of Bossier Parish, Louisiana) and Mr. Joseph Mitchell (from Black Ankle County, North Carolina) lunch together in a seafood restaurant, they drink Coke, finding it far superior to white wine as an accompaniment to poached striped bass, grilled shad and fried blowfish.

One morning a few years ago, Mr. Craig Claiborne (born in Sunflower, Mississippi) was in Kyoto walking off an exquisite breakfast that had included salty fish, rice, strange and ambrosial pickles. He was on the last lap of a round-the-world eating tour and was dizzied by the incommensurable varieties of dishes he had ingested (and had not always *digested*) in the famous cities and the unsung hamlets of the seven continents. It was a hot day as he strolled slowly through the streets on his way to a celebrated market; and abruptly he was stopped in his tracks by the spectacle of a Coca-Cola vending machine. He dropped the necessary coin of the realm into the slot and as he drank the soothing syrup of his childhood, the roads to Xanadu and Mandalay, the pleasure domes of Tunis, the pubs of Melbourne and the dining rooms of Balinese plantations vanished. He had not, he told me, ever been so refreshed by such a pause and tears of homesickness bedimmed his vision. I may have made this up (and I can't check because he is eating his way through the

Basque country), but I think he said he booked passage to San Francisco at once, skipping Samoa.

Dick and Carrie Nye Cavett own and sporadically occupy a big old house with bats in the belfry on a butte overlooking the Atlantic Ocean not many miles away from me. Now and again when Miss Carrie Nye (a native of Greenwood, Mississippi, and a Delta queen if you ever saw one) is feeling puny after feeding, lodging, tap-dancing with and picking up after a large number of long-term sleep-over guests, she gets into an outsize and stentorian Land-Rover and comes to my house for treatment. She could take it at home, but the mister can, on occasion, be finicking and while his voice would not be raised, his gorge would be and, thoughtful wife that she is, she spares him what *is* a pretty unusual spectacle. I have ready on a tray a jar of pickled onions, a basin of crystallized ginger and one of Planters dry-roasted pecans; with this collation, she drinks plentifully of Coca-Cola and bourbon. After considerable experimentation, she has come to the conclusion that just any bourbon won't do. The Jack Daniel's people will be relieved to know that their illustrious sippin' whiskey won't do *at all*. She has settled on Early Times. When she arrives she is limp and slow-moving, her hair is lackluster and she has trouble focusing her eyes. If she speaks at all, it is in a whisper bordering on a whimper. Sometimes her sneakers are on the wrong feet. But by the time she has ingested her health food and her restorative elixir, her hair takes on the sheen of rain-washed, sun-dried quaking-aspen leaves, her eyes —both those in the front of her head and those in the back—are all-seeing and the timbre returns to her voice. Vanquished altogether are her stomachache and her liver attack and she is as lithe and strong as a cheetah. She shoots out my driveway in her truck as if she were going into the 175th lap of the Indianapolis 500.

It is no longer true that the sun never sets on the British Empire. But it doesn't set on the Coca-Cola Company and hasn't for a long time. Now you can drink it in more than one hundred thirty countries. During World War II, Coke became a global household word. Mr. John Rebhan, the most unorthodox landscape architect on eastern Long Island—he looks on flowers only as accessories to shrubs and trees—fought in the Pacific in World War II and told me once that immediately after their debarkation from the troopship on Guam, the men were taken on a tour of a brand-new bottling plant to be reassured that, along with Old Glory and Bob Hope, Coca-Cola would be with them at the front.

In the course of an engaging and illuminating telephone conversation with Mr. William Pruett, vice-president of public relations at the Mother Plant in Atlanta, I learned that very early on in the North African campaign, General Eisenhower ordered the installation of ten plants so that the men could keep their whistles wet and their powder dry. (Mr. Pruett, by the way, has an uncle in Sylacauga, Alabama, and John Shinn, Esq., reports that Dr. Pruett and *his* Uncle Jay Shinn often have breakfast together. At four A.M., their usual rising hours, they plan the menu over the telephone and meet at six. Recently, Shinn Esq.'s mother got the news from her cook who had got it from Dr. Pruett's cook that the pièce de résistance at their last meal had been fried pigs' feet.)

When the screw tops for soft drinks came in some years ago, I was dismayed that Coca-Cola followed in the lead of its Johnny-come-lately imitators. Putting it in all-aluminum cans had been bad enough, putting it in family-size quarts and picnic-size half gallons had been shameful, replacing its original elegant green glass (the color was known as Georgia green) with a clear non-returnable bottle had been an unbecoming concession to the tawdry times. But the screw top was the limit. I could never get it off; I used the hot-water method, I used pliers, I punctured the top with an ice pick.

So I took up the all-aluminum cans, angry and repelled. One day I removed the plastic webbing that binds together an eight-pack. I found that one can contained nothing but air. It was not dented or perforated or in any other way mutilated; it was simply empty and always had been and always would be. Since it weighed no more than a postage stamp, I sent it, together with a strong letter, to the public relations department of the New York branch. A few days later, from the window of my study upstairs, I saw a speckless crimson station wagon, bearing in white the legend "Coca-Cola" written in its fine, aristocratic script, come into my drive and I went down to receive two young men, clean-shaven, wearing white duck trousers and navy blazers with "Coca-Cola" rather than "Eton" or "Hyannisport Yacht Club" on the left breast pocket. I was sorry they did not wear boaters. They brought the heartfelt apologies of Management and we chatted pleasantly in my parlor for half an hour. They, and Management, were aesthetically in complete agreement with me and wished that we could turn back the clock to the days of the six-and-a-half-ounce green glass bottle, the contents of which, with crushed ice, precisely filled the graceful soda-fountain glass with the company hallmark. But stiff competition had made it necessary for them to knuckle under and toady to a generation that had been bamboozled by their plagiarists. The courtly emissaries had driven a tidy distance from up island to pay this call on me, and I was touched. Before they took their leave, they said they had a token to make amends for my can of air and from the back of that chaste red station wagon they brought me two wooden cases of green, glass, six-and-a-half-ounce bottles of The Real Thing. When they had gone, I stood a moment on the back porch and recited the Pledge of Allegiance with my right hand on my heart.

It is once more possible to get bottles with caps that are removed in the normal way. And I am told that green glass returnable bottles are still available; I suspect, however, that most of these are kept in Dixie, just as the best scotch never leaves Scotland and the best California wines have to be drunk in California. But the taste is different; it is sweeter; I think there is less caffeine in it. Something is gone—possibly cocaine. In certain quarters of the Deep South it still retains its grand old razzmatazz, but I don't get down that way much any more, so I worry along with what I can get in New York State. All the same, while it has lost a good deal of its gumption, it is without peer and it has no challengers for the National Drink title. (I have heard of Parisian hostesses who place a bottle of it among the liqueurs if American guests are present.)

Now an eight-pack costs as much as a six-pack of beer or a bottle of passable French wine. A couple of years ago in mid-February, as I was picking up my week's supply, I found a paper heart hung round the neck of one bottle and on it was the tender but down-to-earth enjoinder, BUY SOMEONE YOU LOVE A COKE. That valentine said more about brotherhood and more about the economy than politicians running for office and *Forbes* magazine put together could say in a month of Sundays.

The Evangelist

BY WILLIAM C. MARTIN

I AM UN-REAL. I AM incredible. I AM unbelievable to those who think only on the limited conscious level of mind.

I AM incredible because I am making the impossible possible. I am teaching people how to make the impossible possible by using their own indwelling God-given Mind Power.

I AM God appearing as ME. I AM the Master Mind thinking as Me. I AM the Almighty acting as Me. This is the truth even of you, and of every man. I AM the Divine Sweetheart of the Universe, loving and being loved forever.

—Dr. Frederick J. Eikerenkoetter II,
better known as "Reverend Ike"

"It is very important to note," cautions Reverend Ike, "that when I speak in this way, I am referring to the Divine Presence and not to the human personality at all. Otherwise, it makes me sound like an egomaniac." Well, yes, one could get that impression. And the gold-plated church and the Rolls-Royce and the Mercedes limousines and the clothes that would make a pimp blush do little to counteract such an impression. But it might, it just might be wrong. The evidence is mounting that Dr. Eikerenkoetter is concerned not only with bettering his own lot

—an aim he freely admits—but also with assisting his million-plus, mostly black followers to better theirs and to gain a positive and healthy self-image in the bargain. Not only is he rapidly rising into the ranks of the half dozen or so most successful American evangelists of this century, he is also gaining sufficient recognition as an important practitioner of "self-image psychology" to merit a recent invitation to share his thoughts with the Department of Psychiatry at the Harvard Medical School.

Reverend Ike has come a long way, honey. I started following his career in the mid-sixties, when he ran the Miracle Temple in Boston's South End. At the time, I regarded him as little more than a stylish storefront rip-off artist. An aide concedes this might have been true about the Reverend in 1965, but that Ike has changed. Whatever his motives then or now, it is unquestionably true that the gospel Reverend Ike preaches today is a long way from what he was preaching in 1965, and that whether or not he is still ripping off black folk, he is doing a great deal more.

Since Jonathan Edwards and George Whitefield stoked the Great Awakening in New England, popular evangelists in America have utilized a limited range of techniques: dark warnings of approaching doom and calls to repentance (Billy Graham), sometimes mixed with detailed interpretation of biblical prophecy (the Armstrongs of Ambassador College); hypernationalism (Carl McIntire and Billy James Hargis); faith healing (the early Oral Roberts, the late A. A. Allen, and the current Kathryn Kuhlman); and charismatic enthusiasm (several exponents of the Jesus Movement). In rather sharp contrast, Reverend Ike has no use for doom-saying, is essentially apolitical, directs his aides to remove those members of the audience overcome with glossolalia or the holy barks, and has even dropped faith healing from his repertoire. "I was good at it, too," he recalls with amusement. "I'd knock people down and pray over them and grease them with oil and give them prayer cloths. I used to break up canes and yank people out of wheelchairs. I'd either heal them or kill them."

In place of these time-tested techniques, Reverend Ike has substituted a blatantly this-worldly blend of ideas that have appeared earlier under the banners of New Thought, Christian Science, Positive Thinking, and home psychotherapy, all served up with liberal helpings of street slogans ("Stick around. Don't be a clown. Pick up on what I'm putting down"), ingeniously applied scripture, and extravagant testimonials from satisfied users. The end product, which Dr. Eikerenkoetter calls the Science of Living, makes Thomas Harris and Norman Vincent Peale sound like depressive paranoids with a bad case of the poor mouth. It also constitutes, like the Black Muslim teachings of Elijah Muhammad, a major religious alternative to the fundamental Christianity traditionally associated with American blacks.

Little in Frederick Eikerenkoetter's background foreshadowed his present role as philosopher, psychologist, and pastor to the masses. At age fourteen, he followed his father into the ministry when he became Assistant Pastor of the Bible Way Church in Ridgeland, South Carolina. After graduating from high school in 1952, he attended several fundamentalist Bible colleges, spent two years in the Air Force chaplain service, then returned to South Carolina to found the United Church of Jesus Christ for All People Inc. In 1964 he moved his ministry north and established the Miracle Temple in Boston. In 1966, he transferred his operation to New York City. During these years, Reverend Ike's nickel bag of theology contained essentially the same opiates as those of other storefront street-dealers: temporary painkillers and the promise of the Ultimate High. After a year or two in the ghetto, however, Ike decided his parishioners were suffering from an overdose. The White Horse of Hope had gone lame. "I looked around and discovered people were already in hell. They no longer needed to be told they were going to hell. They needed a way out. At that point I began to develop answers to the present issues of life. I am no longer interested in what is to come later. I am interested in *now*. That's all there is."

Perhaps because he realized his growing band of followers was not equipped to kick fundamentalism cold turkey or perhaps for the more selfish reason that a nationwide evangelistic campaign and a flourishing radio ministry were bringing cascades of money from fundamentalist disciples, Reverend Ike continued to sound like a typical "healer and blesser," lacing his broadcasts and publications with stories of marvelous cures and instant riches wrought by his prayers and the little prayer cloths he sent to those who worked the Blessing Plan, the central mechanism of which was and still is a regular donation to Reverend Ike. Despite the obvious risk in quitting a winner, however, Ike was beginning to chafe. In a 1969 interview between services during a Houston appearance, he confided he was about ready to make his break with fundamentalism. "I am fed up with it. I've had it with all these ideas and this tradition and I can't preach it any more. I have been culling out these negative ideas one by one, and when I get a few more things clear in my mind, I am going to begin to unteach some of those who have been mistaught. My presentation is going to change. Right now I sound just like another Holy Roller, but when I get my philosophy together, I will change my method of presentation."

By 1972, Reverend Ike not only had his philosophy together, but he had abandoned all pretense of being a fundamentalist. In fact, although the umbrella organization for his activities is called the United Christian Evangelistic Association, Ike acknowledges that his message can be called "Christian" or even "religious" only by stretching the terms beyond their conventional meanings. Now, on the road or at home in New York, Reverend Ike explicitly proclaims that:

"The Science of Living is not church doctrine, religious dogma, or theology. It is the teaching of how a person may live a positive, dynamic, healthy, happy, successful, prosperous life through the consciousness of the Presence of God—Infinite Good —already within everyone. . . .

"The Science of Living teaches you how to become a dynamic person. You UNLEARN sickness and know health. You UNLEARN poverty and know prosperity. You learn how to break every limitation and solve every problem YOURSELF. Sickness, age, fear, worry, tension, every human torment drops away, and a NEW YOU begins to live more abundantly."

The basic philosophical tenet of the Science of Living is that Mind is the only effective causative agent. Because this is the case, the whole duty of man is to comprehend the workings of his own mind, to apprehend its relation to other minds and to the Divine Mind present in every man, and to apply Mind Power to the affairs of everyday life.

From this starting point, Reverend Ike moves quickly to

demythologize the pillars of orthodox Christian faith. God is not "someone else, somewhere else, sometime else," but the Divine Mind "within you HERE and NOW." Jesus is "the Master Mind working in you" and Christ and Lord are but synonyms for the Cosmic Law of Mind, a law that operates with the immutability of the law of gravity. "The Cosmic Law of Mind," Reverend Ike explains, "is the universal principle which inevitably brings to pass the materialization of every subjective realization. Just like the law of gravity, it is in action everywhere. If you throw a heavy object into the air, you know it is coming down and you get out of the way. In the Science of Living, we learn to think only those thoughts that we want to see and hear in our lives, because those thoughts are going to come to pass, whether we are conscious of them or not. The scripture puts it beautifully in *Proverbs 23:7* ('As a man thinketh, so is he') and in *Galatians 6:7* ('Whatsoever a man soweth [in his subconscious mind] that shall he also reap'). When you work consciously, confidently, and correctly with the Lord—the Cosmic Law of Mind— He will give you the desires of your heart. That is why the scripture says, 'Keep your heart with all diligence, for out of it are the issues of life.'"

In similar fashion, the devil is dismissed as nothing more than ignorance, being "born again" gives way to being "magnetized into the universal subconscious," and salvation is conceived as victory over the only sin worth talking about, negative thinking. Reverend Ike also tosses Heaven onto the heap of discarded theological baggage. "We are not interested in Pie in the Sky bye and bye. We want our pie now, with ice cream on it, and a cherry on top."

The pie of which Reverend Ike speaks is a money pie. Nothing about his ministry stands out more boldly than his unabashed love of money. Undoubtedly, it is also a major factor in his popularity. According to Ike, it is not the *love*, but the *lack* of money that is the root of all evil. A special "Green Power" edition of his *Action!* magazine pictures two fist-sized rolls of twenty-dollar bills and asks, "What's wrong with money, success, and prosperity?" Inside this and other publications, one finds more rolls and stacks of bills and even a vase filled with flowers made of folded money. Several 1972 issues featured a piece called *The Money*

Rake! and offered tips on how to rake money in with the right attitude:

DON'T BE A HYPOCRITE ABOUT MONEY

Admit openly and inwardly that you like money. Say "I like money. I need money. I want money. I love money in its RIGHT PLACE. Money is not sinful. Money is GOOD. . . ."

BE CAREFUL WHAT YOU THINK OR SAY ABOUT MONEY

As long as you think and say things such as "Money is hard to get" and "I can't get hold of any money," that is just the way it will be.

STOP COMPLAINING ABOUT HIGH PRICES

Say, instead, "I give thanks for money to pay whatever price for whatever I need."

STOP LOOKING FOR "SOMETHING FOR NOTHING"

A person with a hope to get something for nothing is open to be cheated and swindled by others who have the same thing in mind but are "slicker" than he is.

Reverend Ike readily acknowledges that the basic principles of Mind Science are not unique to him, although he claims to have arrived at them independently before discovering similar notions in the writings of professional optimists from Mary Baker Eddy's mentor, Phineas Quimby, to Dr. Peale and Maxwell Maltz. In any case, it is relatively unusual fare to be dishing out to folk reared on fundamentalism, as most of his followers have been. How does he accomplish the task of communicating what must be regarded as heresy to his rapidly expanding flock? Impressively, that's how.

"You will note"—he smiles—"that I quote the Bible a great deal. As you know, fundamentalist people accept the authority of the scriptures. They are programed to believe anything a scripture is quoted in front of. So I take the scriptures and I reinterpret them in the light of the Science of Living, and that helps a lot of them make the transition more easily." In addition to scripture, Reverend Ike also draws on other images from the familiar tradition, as when a lesson from a Science of Living study guide asserts that the words of the spiritual, "Deep River, my home is over Jordan," express "a deep-seated realization on the part of man as to his proper place in Divine Mind. . . . Once this is established in our thought pattern, through our crossing over Jordan in consciousness to its positive side, we shall find that we have reached the Promised Land [Divine Consciousness]."

But Ike is not simply trying to see how far the old wineskins will stretch. With the same caution—admirable or otherwise—that led him to hold back from declaring his true convictions until several years after he had formed them, he has limited the amount of pure, uncut Mind Science dispensed to his mass audience until first testing the tolerance level of the folks in the home church in New York. He tells them, "You understand, of course, that when I am speaking to the Babylonians, I have to communicate in a language they understand, but when I talk to you, I can speak in another tongue." In the last two years, the message at home and abroad has become progressively uniform, to the point that anyone who believes Reverend Ike is just another pulpit-pounding soul saver simply hasn't been paying attention. Today, using calculated profanity, sharp perception of soft spots in what he repeatedly calls "the old religion," and a heavy dose of what Phineas Quimby used to call Animal Magnetism, Ike often launches into what amounts to a frontal assault on beliefs his hearers have held since childhood: "Coming up in Sunday School and in organized Protestant religion, we always thought of the Lord as some old gray-haired man sitting up in the sky in a great big chair. And with one hand he was writing all the bad deeds that were being done and in the other hand he had a great big stick with which he was going to beat the hell out of the bad people. And we used to pray to this Lord and say, 'Please, Lord, do this and do that.' I'm sorry to have to tell you this, Saints, but that is a false idea. There is nobody up in the sky who is going to do a damn thing for you. And yet religious people pray and fast and punish themselves, trying to impress some God-in-the-sky, and the preachers take the Bible and beat them down with it, and you will go back to this kind of preaching, like a damn fool, week after week, trying to get some man-in-the-sky to run your life for you. It breaks my heart to tell you good religious people this, but the only one who runs your life is you. And if you don't take conscious control of your life and operate your own mind, your life will just be a total mess! The Lord is not going to do a damn thing. You are the only one who can tell you what you can or can't have. When you pray, you are talking to yourself. So stop this kneeling down for your prayers, or somebody will catch you humped over and you'll get kicked in the behind. If you are going to pray, just stand right up, put your hand on your hip, let your backbone slip, and say, real sassy-like, 'Can't nooooooobody tell *me* what *I* can't have.'"

Excursions such as this move Reverend Ike's audiences to titter with scandalized laughter and to look around nervously as if half expecting a bolt of lightning to come crashing through the roof, but there is clearly an exhilaration present as they shake their hips not only in obedience to Ike's direction but also in bold defiance of their religious past. He is onto something, and he knows it. "Frankly, I've been rather surprised," he admits, "at how fundamentalists and even semiliterate people from the backwoods have come to this and have accepted it. So many have said to me, 'You know, Reverend Ike, I have felt this for a long time, but I never had the occasion to hear anybody say it. When you told me God is in Me, this sort of confirmed what I have been feeling.'"

Along with scripture, familiar symbols, and out-front Positive Thinking, Reverend Ike also gets his points across by means of a technique long favored by mass evangelists—unremitting bombardment. Listeners to his daily broadcasts hear of case after case of those who have profited from Reverend Ike's teaching and receive constant encouragement to "get out of the ghetto and into the get-mo'." The bimonthly *Action!* magazine, sent free to anyone who requests it, is also jammed with testimonials, sermons, expositions on Mind Science, and instructions on how to hear and see even more. A letter a month, preferably with a contribution, brings a special Success Idea, which is yet another formulation of the basic theme: "How to use Mind Power to get more Green Power." If requested, each Success Idea comes with a prayer cloth, a tiny scarlet remnant of Reverend Ike's days as a healer and blesser.

In each publication and broadcast, Reverend Ike urges his followers to write him regularly. Undoubtedly, he hopes and expects most will enclose money, but he makes a great deal of the letter-writing process itself, claiming that even though he does not read every letter personally, he knows what they say by means of "subconscious correlation" and "vibratory affinity" and that the very process of writing to him will start things happening. In support of this, he produces letter after letter from correspondents who tell of the good fortune that befell them within minutes after they dropped their letters into the mailbox. When I asked him how he accounted for these occurrences, he pondered the question a moment, then allowed it was a demonstration of something called *graphotherapeutics*. "To write," he explained, "you must focus your attention rather definitely and positively. Once the mind is directed in a certain way and certain ideas are clarified in the mind, other ideas which help to bring about the realization of the first idea begin to happen." Is it possible that people might confuse graphotherapeutics with magic? "Yes, there is that possibility. I have found that belief works, whether a person understands the mental mechanics of it or not." But, to be fair, Reverend Ike is not really trying to have it both ways. A subsequent edition of *Action!* addressed this issue squarely: "Some call it A MIRACLE! Others call it MAGIC! But I have stripped away all of the religious and superstitious NONSENSE, and I have revealed *IT* to be MIND POWER!"

Reverend Ike's approach has firmly established him as the poor man's Peale and he has, as they say, done well by doing good. His daily radio program is heard on approximately 270 stations and he confidently predicts that the weekly *Joy of Living* telecast will be seen nationwide within a few months. His personal appearances regularly draw crowds of five to ten thousand, and a memorable service at Madison Square Garden in 1972 drew over twenty thousand. A mailing list generated primarily by letters containing contributions is rapidly climbing toward two million and raising huge sums of money in the process. Figures on the total income from the Blessing Plan and other revenue-gathering activities are unavailable, but Reverend Ike concedes that "the church is very rich." Much of the money, of course, goes to pay for broadcasts, printing, postage, professional staff, and the standard operational expenses for such an organization. But Reverend Ike comes in for his share. His personal salary is said to be a relatively modest $40,000, but this is augmented by an almost unlimited expense account that enables him to purchase jewelry and clothes that, by his own reckoning, cost $1,000 a week, and to enjoy the use of Association-owned homes and luxurious automobiles.

The crown jewel of Reverend Ike's organization is the United Palace and Science of Living Institute, a former Loew's theatre that occupies a city block on Broadway and 175th and serves as a mother of a church. Besides providing formal instruction in the Science of Living and granting honorary doctorates to its President and Founder (Ike holds the D.Sc.L. and Ph.D. ScL. degrees), the Institute offers courses in secretarial training, money management, yoga, speech, drama, and fine arts. A bookstall in the space where the candy counter used to be displays *I'm OK, You're OK, Jonathan Livingston Seagull, Working with the Law, Open Your Mind to Prosperity, Try Giving Yourself Away,* and *Move Ahead with Positive Thinking.* The church also provides academic and family counseling, college scholarships, drug-abuse and prison programs, and sponsors free plays and concerts.

A staff of associates operates the church in Reverend Ike's absence, but he conducts classes and services on an average of two weekends a month. Sunday meetings are scheduled in the afternoon, to avoid conflicts with churches of the old religion. The official starting time is usually three o'clock, but the action begins at least an hour earlier, as scattered clumps of ten or fifteen people gather to hear church leaders discuss the Science of Living. About two-thirty, Reverend Ike appears onstage without fanfare, and announces that he wants to exchange smiles and hugs with the assembly. "You know, you are not blessed unless you put on a smile, even if your wig cost a hundred dollars." As a spotlight follows him up and down the aisles, he pauses every few rows, flashes his teeth, and wraps his arms around himself in an enormous autoerotic bear hug. The folks in each section mirror the gesture and say with him, "MMMMMMMMMMM, there is healing and blessing even in a smile."

As soon as Reverend Ike has made the circuit, a mammoth stage bearing a fifty-voice chorus rises into view. The chorus is good, but Ike notes he would like to see some improvement before an upcoming telecast. "We have some good singers who haven't joined the choir yet, and some of you who have joined it need to volunteer for the usher board. I'm going to be damn blunt with you. Television is expensive. If you have a voice like a sour lemon, get the hell out of my choir. Anything that doesn't look, act, sound, and smell like the Christ, the Son of the Living God, won't go on my TV show, because I'm mean and clean and everybody on the screen is going to have to look like they are kin to me."

When the chorus has finished, it drops out of sight and the gold curtain opens to reveal an opulent set curtained and carpeted in deep red and featuring a Louis XV desk flanked by two throne-like wing chairs covered in red velvet, each sporting an embossed golden crown that lies just above Reverend Ike's head when he sits down. The chairs strike an outsider as a bit immoderate until the Reverend explains the symbolism: "The crowns represent the Divine Royalty of the individual. I put two out there for a purpose—so that people will not get the idea that this is a chair where only Reverend Ike sits. We do not believe in the exclusive divinity of any man. Anybody can sit in those chairs. When I call people to testify, regardless of who they are, they sit in those chairs."

The testimony of Edward Milton, Jr., is typical of those who sit on the Throne of Man: "Reverend Ike, I was working on two or three jobs making money but I couldn't seem to see where it was going. I was shacking up with a woman and was all hung up. So, after I heard you on the radio, I decided to write you. That was in July. I started working with the Blessing Plan and using your Success Ideas. By November I was blessed with a brand-new Buick Electra 225! And January twenty-first I married a nice young lady. And by August 1972, I was blessed with an eighteen-thousand-dollar home. We have it furnished beautifully." Reverend Ike is delighted: "You couldn't keep any money. You couldn't accumulate anything. Doing nothing but shacking and backtracking, huh? You women had better say 'Amen.' I tell all the ladies in my congregation, 'Don't fool around with those men who don't have anything, never did have anything, and don't look like they're going to get anything.' These little girls come up to me and say, 'Reverend Ike, I want to get married!' I say, 'Your boyfriend have any money?' They say, 'No, but we have love.' I say, 'You try paying the rent with that! See how many groceries that will buy.'"

The sermon for the day is typical: "Are You on Your Side?"

Under each of the main headings—(1) "Be Your Own Cheer-leader and Others Will Join in the Cheering," (2) "Be the President of Your Own Fan Club," and (3) "Play the Game of Life in Your Favor"—Reverend Ike tells stories of the Wright brothers, whose daddy was a bishop and told them it was blasphemy to think that man could fly, but who looked up in the sky and saw birds fly and said in their hearts, "If birds fly over the rainbow, why then O why can't I?" and of Thomas Edison whose school-master said he could not learn but who had a light in his heart and lit up the world.

To punctuate the proclamation, Reverend Ike pauses every three or four minutes to ask the congregation to shake at least three hands and say, "Come on. You can make it. I see you making it big," or to repeat an affirmation such as, "I'm a FUN person . . . God in me is full of fun . . . The blues do not interest me . . . I light up the atmosphere with my happiness . . . I fizz like a bottle of French champagne . . . I move from glory to glory. . . . So it is. It cannot be otherwise. . . . Thank you God-in-Me, Thank you Lord, Thank you Cosmic Law of Mind."

To close the service Reverend Ike leads his parishioners in a Visualization Prayer Treatment. The mental mechanics of the V.P.T. are evidently similar to those of graphotherapy. By concentrating on the good they desire, those undergoing the Treatment automatically set up subconscious vibrations that will "enable their imaginations to build a bridge of incident over which they can pass to the condition they have consistently imagined." Like a magnificent tawny lion, Reverend Ike lounges in one of the crown chairs and directs his flock to "lean back, stretch your legs, close your two outer eyes, open the inner eye of faith, and follow me into the Theatre of the Mind." Then, at his direction, they repeat his every phrase, giving each the same sensual caress he does: "As I look on the stage of my imagination, I see who I am in God and who God is in me. My divine self is healthy, strong, and bubbling over with the joy of the Lord. Prosperous ideas constantly unfold in my mind, leading and guiding me into ways of success. It feels so good to have money. I am going to pick out a car. MMMMMMMMMM, doesn't this leather smell wonderful! Now I am going to rub my hand around the steering wheel and feel the notches on the underside of the wheel. Oh, this is wonderful. Now I see myself on a Caribbean cruise. I can smell the flowers around me, I can taste the tangy tropical drinks. I can hear my friends telling me how good I look when I come back from my vacation. And all that I see, I can have because the Lord, the Law of Mind gives it to me. Thank you Father."

Back from St. Thomas-in-the-Mind, Reverend Ike brings the service to a close with a matter-of-fact announcement: "Now, I want you to give me some money. Give whatever you want to, but remember one thing. If there is a sin in this church, it is making noise during the offering. Please do not give change. Change makes me nervous in the service." The crowd laughs at the line they have heard before and Reverend Ike says, "Bless your hearts. I'm just teasing you because I love you. And you know that." As uniformed and white-gloved sisters collect the offering in plastic buckets—"The Scripture says, 'My cup runneth over,' so we use buckets"—Reverend Ike commends them for their generosity. "We have never had a financial problem in this church and we never shall. I am not personally a millionaire, but I have made this church a multimillionaire. Besides being a minister, I am a pretty sharp businessman. You have to admit, a fool couldn't do all this. Look around you and see how I am spending your money. That is liquid gold we are putting on the walls and the ceiling, and if you look carefully you will find a few drops of it on the rug. The complete renovation will take another year and about another one and a half million. But it's worth it. Anything I am connected with, I glorify."

When the service ended a few minutes later, Reverend Ike repaired to a private suite in the Palace to shower and change clothes. As he sipped a thick revivifying blend of milk, raw egg, and banana, I asked him to respond to the criticism of black militants who claim he is draining the ghetto of money that should go for shoes, milk, and rent, and spending it instead on cars, clothes, and gold-leaf paint. One senses he has answered the question before. "If I could say that tomorrow morning I am going to lead five thousand people up to city hall to demand more welfare, they would say, 'Oh, gee, Reverend Ike is great.' But the black ministers and the black militants and the white liberals who teach people to demand handouts are doing minorities a disfavor, by breaking down their sense of self-sufficiency. We say to the poor, 'Look, the white people are not responsible to deliver you. As long as you have to depend on the President, or the Governor, or the Mayor, you're not free. You're a slave. You can't eat until they feed you. You can't eat until you line up and get those damn stamps. Don't look for handouts. Welfare has its place, but don't make it a resting place.'"

Reverend Ike does not shrink from the anti-sociological implications of his brand of classic individualism—"You could take all the people from the ghetto and move them downtown into Fifth Avenue mansions and ten minutes later they will have brought the ghetto with them. That's because the environment you live in is the environment that lives in you." But on other occasions, his pronouncements sound like moderately respectable social psychology: "I take issue with the do-gooders in the federal government and some of the so-called liberals who are good at giving people negative labels for themselves. In Washington, D.C., they have certain rubber stamps. One says, 'Poor People,' and they select a group of people and categorize them as Poor People. If people don't fit in that category they have another stamp that says, 'Culturally Deprived,' and another that says, 'Underprivileged.' This is negative self-image psychology. That is just another psych job. Don't you let this world put any labels on you. This is what the Bible means when it says, 'Be not conformed to this world.' Don't you take anything from this world. Any kind of sob story you've got, I can match it. Don't tell me, 'Reverend Ike, I'm black. Nobody likes me.' I'm medium black myself!!! I came from a broken home. I walked four miles to school every day and four miles back. You don't need any more sympathy and welfare; you need a kick where your brains are. I could still be down in South Carolina sitting on a log in the woods talking about 'poor black me.' Instead, when I was a little barefoot boy working in an auto mechanic shop, the head mechanic would look at me and say, 'Boy, do you think you will ever amount to anything?' I would straighten up, hold my shoulders back, tilt my chin and answer, 'Yes, sir!'"

Like most super-individualists, Reverend Ike fails to recognize that others may not be quite so well equipped for the Game of Life as he, and that social, political, and economic structures do, in fact, make a difference. Still, it is no doubt true that a positive self-image gives a person a leg up on the ladder of success, whatever the odds. And Reverend Ike's people are nothing if not positive. I talked to as many as I could before and after services and found them unequivocally excited about possession of a new sense of self-confidence and reporting improvement in all areas of their lives—school, jobs, marriages, and bank accounts. They understand what Reverend Ike is saying, recognize it is a radical departure from "the old church down South," and are pleased with the difference. Clearly, they agree with the Reverend's motto: "You can't lose with the stuff I use."

An Epilogical Testimony

After my last visit with Reverend Ike, I spent the night on Long Island with old friends who assured me we would have no difficulty making an eight-twenty flight from La Guardia the next morning. The time they allowed for the trip would have been comfortable in the middle of the night, but at seven-fifteen A.M. we discovered that others had also made plans to drive into the city via the Long Island Expressway. After forty minutes and four accident bottlenecks, the map showed we had averaged an inch every ten minutes and still had six inches to go. Obviously, it was time for a Visualization Prayer Treatment. I heard myself telling the stewardess that no, I did not want a cocktail at eight-thirty in the morning. I struggled vainly with the button that was supposed to make my seat recline. I put on the stereo earphones and discovered the right channel was dead and all I could get was a left ear full of percussion. I tried to breathe through the cigar smoke exhaled by a seatmate who insisted no one was going to tell him he had to sit in the back of the plane to smoke. I heard the captain say we were experiencing a loss of cabin pressure and realized it had been so long since I had paid attention to the stewardesses' instructions about the oxygen equipment that I had forgotten what to do and would undoubtedly explode or implode momentarily. But, in the Theatre of my Mind, I was on that plane!

Wonderfully, the traffic began to move more swiftly. Then, in cruel rebuke to the Scientific Life, the car threw a fan belt and we pulled into a service station. In a moment, in the twinkling of an eye, I dashed into the street. Two blocks away, a yellow cab was stopped in front of a school. I flagged him to my position and asked if he could make it to La Guardia in ten minutes. "No. Get in." Inside, he told me, "Mister, you don't know how lucky you are to find a cab out here. I just happened to be bringing my daughter to school." He knew a shortcut, but cautioned against optimism. "When we get back on the freeway, we'll really hit the heavy traffic. I don't think we can make it." Moments later, we pulled onto a virtually empty freeway. "Mister, I can't explain it. I come by here at this time every morning, and this is the first time I have seen the traffic this light in ten years. It's a miracle." At eight-seventeen we stopped at the Eastern terminal. A porter asked, "Where you going?" I told him Houston, and he said "Gate thirty-five. Run!"

A few minutes later, as we taxied down the runway, I pondered the events of the morning. Most of my skepticism returned when I noted that the seat reclined properly and no one was blowing smoke in my face. Still, just to be safe, I paid careful attention to the oxygen routine. And I thought, "I AM incredible, because I have made the impossible possible. I AM on this plane. So it is. It cannot be otherwise. Thank you, Cosmic Law of Mind."

The Shopping Center

BY JOAN DIDION

They float on the landscape like pyramids to the boom years, all those Plazas and Malls and Esplanades. All those Squares and Fairs. All those Towns and Dales, all those Villages, all those Forests and Parks and Lands. Stonestown. Hillsdale. Valley Fair, Mayfair. Northgate, Southgate, Eastgate, Westgate. Gulfgate. They are toy garden cities in which no one lives but everyone consumes, profound equalizers, the perfect fusion of the profit motive and the egalitarian ideal, and to hear their names is to recall words and phrases no longer quite current. Baby Boom. Consumer Explosion. Leisure Revolution. Do-It-Yourself Revolution, Backyard Revolution. Suburbia. "The *Shopping Center*," the Urban Land Institute could exult in 1957, "is today's extraordinary retail business evolvement . . . the automobile accounts for suburbia, and suburbia accounts for the shopping center."

It was a peculiar and visionary time, those years after World War II to which all the Malls and Towns and Dales stand as climate-controlled monuments. Even the word "automobile," as in "the automobile accounts for suburbia and suburbia accounts for the shopping center," no longer carries the particular freight it did then: as a child in the late forties in California I recall reading and believing that the "freedom of movement" afforded by the automobile was "America's fifth freedom." The trend was up. The solution was in sight. The frontier had been reinvented, and its shape was the subdivision, that new free land on which all settlers could recast their lives' tabula rasa. For one perishable moment there the American idea seemed about to achieve itself via F.H.A. housing and the acquisition of major appliances, and a certain enigmatic glamour attached to the architects of this new-found land. They made something of nothing. They gambled and sometimes lost. They staked the past to seize the future. I have difficulty now imagining a childhood in which a man named Jere Strizek, the developer of Town and Country Village outside Sacramento (143,000 square feet gross floor area, 68 stores, 1,000 parking spaces, the Urban Land Institute's "prototype for centers using heavy timber and tile construction for informality"), could materialize as a role model, but I had such a childhood, just after World War II, in Sacramento. I never met nor even saw Jere Strizek, but at the age of twelve I imagined him a kind of frontiersman, a romantic and revolutionary spirit, and in the indigenous grain he was.

I suppose James B. Douglas and David D. Bohannon were, too.

I first heard of James B. Douglas and David D. Bohannon not when I was twelve but a dozen years later, when I was living in New York, working for *Vogue,* and taking, by correspondence, a University of California Extension course in shopping-center theory. This did not seem to me eccentric at the time. I remember sitting on the cool floor in Irving Penn's studio and reading, in *The Community Builders Handbook,* advice from James B. Douglas on shopping-center financing. I recall staying late in my pale blue office on the twentieth floor of the Graybar Building to memorize David D. Bohannon's parking ratios. My "real" life was to sit in this office and describe life as it was lived in Djakarta and Caneel Bay and in the great châteaux of the Loire Valley, but my dream life was to put together a Class A regional shopping center with three full-line department stores as major tenants.

That I was perhaps the only person I knew in New York, let alone on the Condé Nast floors of the Graybar Building, to have memorized the distinctions among "A," "B," and "C" shopping centers did not occur to me (the defining distinction, as long as I have your attention, is that an "A" or regional center has as its major tenant a full-line department store that carries major appliances, a "B" or community center has as its major tenant a junior department store that does not carry major appliances, and a "C" or neighborhood center has as its major tenant only a supermarket): my interest in shopping centers was in no way casual. I did want to build them. I wanted to build them because I had fallen into the habit of writing fiction, and I had it in my head that a couple of good centers might support this habit less taxingly than a pale blue office at *Vogue*. I had even devised an original scheme by which I planned to gain enough capital and credibility to enter the shopping-center game: I would lease warehouses in, say, Queens, and offer Manhattan delicatessens the opportunity to sell competitively by buying cooperatively, from my trucks. I see a few wrinkles in this scheme now (the words "concrete overcoat" come to mind), but I did not then. In fact I planned to run it out of the pale blue office.

James B. Douglas and David D. Bohannon. In 1950 James B. Douglas had opened Northgate, in Seattle, the first regional center to combine a pedestrian mall with an underground truck tunnel. In 1954 David D. Bohannon had opened Hillsdale, a forty-acre regional center on the peninsula south of San Francisco. That is the only solid bio I have on James B. Douglas and David D. Bohannon to this day, but many of their opinions are engraved on my memory. David D. Bohannon believed in preserving the integrity of the shopping center by not cutting up the site with any dedicated roads. David D. Bohannon believed that architectural setbacks in a center looked "pretty on paper" but caused "customer resistance." James B. Douglas advised that a small-loan office could prosper in a center only if it were placed away from foot traffic, since people who want small loans do not want to be observed getting them. I do not now recall whether it was James B. Douglas or David D. Bohannon or someone else altogether who passed along this hint on how to paint the lines around the parking spaces (actually this is called "striping the lot," and the spaces are "stalls"): make each space a foot wider than it need be—ten feet, say, instead of nine—when the center first opens and business is slow. By this single stroke the developer achieves a couple of important objectives, the appearance of a popular center and the illusion of easy parking, and no one will really notice when business picks up and the spaces shrink.

Nor do I recall who first solved what was once a crucial center dilemma: the placement of the major tenant vis-à-vis the parking lot. The dilemma was that the major tenant—the draw, the raison d'être for the financing, the Sears, the Macy's, the May Company—wanted its customer to walk directly from car to store. The smaller tenants, on the other hand, wanted that same customer to *pass their stores* on the way from the car to, say, Macy's. The solution to this conflict of interests was actually very simple: *two major tenants*, one at each end of a mall. This is called "anchoring the mall," and represents seminal work in shopping-center theory. One thing you will note about shopping-center theory is that you could have thought of it yourself, and a course in it will go a long way toward dispelling the notion that business proceeds from mysteries too recondite for you and me.

A few aspects of shopping-center theory do in fact remain impenetrable to me. I have no idea why the Community Builders' Council ranks *Restaurant* as deserving a Number One or "Hot Spot" location but exiles *Chinese Restaurant* to a Number Three, out there with *Power and Light Office* and *Christian Science Reading Room*. Nor do I know why the council approves of enlivening a mall with "small animals" but specifically, vehemently, and with no further explanation, excludes "monkeys." If I had a center I would have monkeys, and Chinese restaurants, and Mylar kites and bands of small girls playing tambourine.

A few years ago at a party I met a woman from Detroit who told me that the Joyce Carol Oates novel with which she identified most closely was *Wonderland.*
I asked her why.
"Because," she said, "my husband has a branch there."
I did not understand.
"In Wonderland the center," the woman said patiently. "My husband has a branch in Wonderland."
I have never visited Wonderland but imagine it to have bands of small girls playing tambourine.

A few facts about shopping centers.
The "biggest" center in the United States is generally agreed

to be Woodfield, outside Chicago, a "super" regional or "leviathan" two-million-square-foot center with four major tenants.

The "first" shopping center in the United States is generally agreed to be Country Club Plaza in Kansas City, built in the twenties. There were some other early centers, notably Edward H. Bouton's 1907 Roland Park in Baltimore, Hugh Prather's 1931 Highland Park Shopping Village in Dallas, and Hugh Potter's 1937 River Oaks in Houston, but the developer of Country Club Plaza, the late J. C. Nichols, is referred to with ritual frequency in the literature of shopping centers, usually as "pioneering J. C. Nichols," "trail-blazing J. C. Nichols," or "J. C. Nichols, father of the center as we know it."

Those are some facts I know about shopping centers because I still want to be Jere Strizek or James B. Douglas or David D. Bohannon. Here are some facts I know about shopping centers because I never will be Jere Strizek or James B. Douglas or David D. Bohannon: a good center in which to spend the day if you wake sad and fearful in Honolulu, Hawaii, is Ala Moana, major tenants Liberty House and Sears. A good center in which to spend the day if you wake sad and fearful in Oxnard, California, is The Esplanade, major tenants the May Company and Sears. A good center in which to spend the day if you wake sad and fearful in Biloxi, Mississippi, is Edgewater Plaza, major tenant Godchaux's. Ala Moana in Honolulu is larger than The Esplanade in Oxnard, and The Esplanade in Oxnard is larger than Edgewater Plaza in Biloxi. Ala Moana has carp pools. The Esplanade and Edgewater Plaza do not.

These marginal distinctions to one side, Ala Moana, The Esplanade, and Edgewater Plaza are the same place, which is precisely their role not only as equalizers but in the sedation of anxiety. In each of them one moves for a while in an aqueous suspension not only of light but of judgment, not only of judgment but of "personality." One meets no acquaintances at The Esplanade. One gets no telephone calls at Edgewater Plaza. "It's a hard place to run into for a pair of stockings," a friend complained to me recently of Ala Moana, and I knew that she was not yet ready to surrender her ego to the idea of the center. The last time I went to Ala Moana it was to buy the New York *Times*. Because the New York *Times* was not in, I sat on the mall for a while and ate caramel corn. In the end I bought not the

New York *Times* at all but two straw hats at Liberty House, four bottles of nail enamel at Woolworth's, and a toaster, on sale at Sears. In the literature of shopping centers these would be described as impulse purchases, but the impulse here was obscure. I do not wear hats, nor do I like caramel corn. I do not use nail enamel. Yet flying back across the Pacific I regretted only the toaster.

The State of the Union

BY GORE VIDAL

"How can you say such awful things about America when *you live in Italy?*" Whenever I go on television, I hear that plangent cry. From vivacious Barbara Walters of the *Today* show (where I was granted six minutes to comment on last November's elections) to all the other vivacious interviewers across this great land of ours, the question of my residency is an urgent matter that must be mentioned as soon as possible so that no one will take seriously a single word that that awful person has to say about what everybody knows is not only the greatest country in the history of the world but a country where vivacious Barbara Walters et al. can make a very pretty penny peddling things that people don't need. "So if you no liva here," as sly fun-loving Earl Butz might say, "you no maka da wisecracks."

Usually I ignore the vivacious challenge: the single statement on television simply does not register; only constant repetition penetrates . . . witness the commercials. Yet on occasion, when tired, I will rise to the bait. Point out that I pay full American tax—fifty percent of my income contributes to the support of the Pentagon's General Brown, statesman/soldier and keen student of the Protocols of the Elders of Zion. Remind one and all that I do spend a good part of my time in the land of the free, ranging up and down the countryside for months at a time discussing the state of the union with conservative audiences (no use talking to the converted), and in the process I manage to see more of the country than your average television vivacity ever does. In fact, I know more about the relative merits of the far-flung Holiday Inns than anyone who is not a traveling salesman or a presidential candidate.

Last fall I set out across the country, delivering pretty much the same commentary on the state of the union that I have been giving for several years, with various topical additions, subtractions. In one four-week period I gave fifteen lectures, starting with the Political Union at Yale and then on to various colleges and town forums in New York, New Jersey, West Virginia, Nebraska, Missouri, Michigan, Washington, Oregon, California. . . .

October 29. Bronxville, New York. A woman's group. Ten-thirty in the morning in a movie house where Warhol's *Frankenstein* was playing. Suitable, I decide. In the men's room is a life-size dummy of a corpse that usually decorates the lobby. Creative management.

Fairly large audience—five, six hundred. Very conservative—abortion equals euthanasia. Watergate? What about Chappaquiddick? Our dialectic would not cause Plato to green with Attic envy.

I stack the cards of my text on the lectern. Full light on me. Audience in darkness. Almost as restful as the creative stillness of a television studio. I feel an intimacy with the camera that I don't with live audiences. Had I played it differently I might have been the electronic Norman Thomas, or George Brent.

I warn the audience: "I shall have to refer to notes." Actually, I read. Could never memorize anything. No matter how many times I give the same speech, the words seem new to me . . . like Eisenhower in 1952: "If elected in November," the Great Golfer read dutifully from a text plainly new to him, "I will go to . . . *Korea?*" The voice and choler rose on the word "Korea." No one had told him about the pledge. But go to Korea he did, resentfully.

I reassure the audience that from time to time I will look up from my notes, "in order to give an air of spontaneity." Get them laughing early. And often. Later the mood will be quite grim out there as I say things not often said in this great land of ours where the price of freedom is eternal discretion.

For some minutes, I improvise. Throw out lines. Make them

laugh. I've discovered that getting a laugh is more a trick of timing than of true wit (true wit seldom provokes laughter; rather
the reverse). I tell them that although I mean to solve most of
the problems facing the United States in twenty-seven minutes—
the time it takes to read my prepared text (question time then
lasts half an hour, longer if one is at a college and speaking in
the evening), I will not touch on the number one problem facing
the country—the failing economy (this is disingenuous: politics
is the art of collecting and spending money and everything I say
is political). "I leave to my friend Ken Galbraith the solving of
the depression." If they appear to know who Galbraith is, I
remark how curious it is that his fame is based on two books,
The Liberal Hour, published just as the right-wing Nixon criminals hijacked the presidency, and *The Affluent Society,* published
shortly before we went broke. Rueful laughter.

I begin the text. Generally the light is full in one's eyes while
the lectern is so low that the faraway words blur on my cards. I
crouch; squint. My heart sinks as flashbulbs go off and cameras
click: my second chin is not particularly noticeable when viewed
straight on but from below it has recently come to resemble
Hubert Humphrey's bullfrog swag. Do I dare to wear a scarf? Or
use metal clamps to tuck the loose skin up behind the ears like a
certain actress who appeared in a television play of mine years
ago? No. Let the flesh fall to earth in full public view. Soldier on.
Start to read.

"According to the polls, our second principal concern today is
the breakdown of law and order. Now, to the right wing, law
and order is often just a code phrase meaning 'get the niggers.'
To the left wing it often means political oppression. When we
have one of our ridiculous elections—ridiculous because they are
about nothing at all except personalities—politicians declare a
war on crime which is immediately forgotten after the election."

I have never liked this beginning and so I usually paraphrase.
Shift lines about. Remark that in the recent presidential election
(November 7, 1972) sixty-two percent of the people chose not to
vote. "They aren't apathetic, just disgusted. There is no choice."

Sometimes, if I'm not careful, I drift prematurely into my analysis of the American political system: there is only one party in
the United States, the Property party (thank you, Dr. Lundberg,
for the phrase) and it has two wings: Republican and Democrat.

Republicans are a bit stupider, more rigid, more doctrinaire in their laissez-faire capitalism than the Democrats, who are cuter, prettier, a bit more corrupt—until recently (nervous laugh on that)—and more willing than the Republicans to make small adjustments when the poor, the black, the anti-imperialists get out of hand. But, essentially, there is no difference between the parties. Those who gave Nixon money in '68 also gave money to Humphrey.

Can one expect any change from either wing of the Property party? No. Look at McGovern. In the primaries he talked about tax reform and economic equality . . . or something close to it. For a while it looked as if he was nobly preparing to occupy a long box at Arlington. But then he was nominated for President and he stopped talking about anything important. Was he insincere in the primaries? I have no idea. I suspect he was just plain dumb, not realizing that if you speak of economic justice or substantial change you won't get the forty million dollars a Democratic candidate for President needs in order to pay for exposure on television where nothing of any real importance may be said. Remember Quemoy? and her lover Matsu?

Once I get into this aria, I throw out of kilter the next section. Usually I do the Property party later on. Or in the questions and answers. Or not at all. One forgets. Thinks one has told Kansas City earlier in the evening what, in fact, one had said that morning in Omaha.

Back to law and order.

"An example: roughly eighty percent of police work in the United States has to do with the regulation of our private morals. By that I mean, controlling what we drink, eat, smoke, put into our veins—not to mention trying to regulate with whom and how we have sex, with whom and how we gamble. As a result, our police are among the most corrupt in the Western world."

Nervous intake of breath on this among women's groups. Some laughter at the colleges. Glacial silence at Atlantic City. Later I was told, "We've got a lot of a very funny sort of element around here . . . you know, from Philadelphia, originally. Uh . . . like Italian." I still don't know quite what was meant.

"Not only are police on the take from gamblers, drug pushers, pimps, but they find pretty thrilling their mandate to arrest prostitutes or anyone whose sexual activities have been proscribed by

a series of state legal codes that are the scandal of what we like
to call a free society. These codes are very old of course. The
law against sodomy goes back fourteen hundred years to the Emperor Justinian, who felt that there should be such a law because, as everyone knew, sodomy was a principal cause of
earthquake."

"Sodomy" gets them. For elderly, good-hearted audiences I
paraphrase; the word is not used. College groups get a fuller discussion of Justinian and his peculiar law, complete with quota-
tions from Procopius. California audiences living on or near the
San Andreas fault laugh the loudest—and the most nervously.
No wonder.

"Cynically one might allow the police their kinky pleasures in
busting boys and girls who attract them, not to mention their
large incomes from the Mafia and other criminal types, *if* the
police showed the slightest interest in the protection of persons
and property, which is why we have hired them. Unhappily for
us, the American police have little interest in crime. If anything,
they respect the criminal rather more than they do the hapless
citizen who has just been mugged or ripped off.

"Therefore, let us remove from the statute books all laws that
have to do with *private* morals—what are called victimless
crimes. If a man or woman wants to be a prostitute that is his or
her affair. It is no business of the state what we do with our
bodies sexually. Obviously laws will remain on the books for the
prevention of rape and the abuse of children, while the virtue of
our animal friends will continue to be protected by the S.P.C.A."

Relieved laughter at this point. He can't be serious . . . or is he?

"Let us end the vice squad. What a phrase! It is vice to go to
bed with someone you are not married to or someone of your
own sex or to get money for having sex with someone who does
not appeal to you—incidentally, the basis of half the marriages
of my generation."

Astonished laughter at this point from middle-aged women
. . . and by no means women liberationists. I speak only to, as
far as I am able, conservative middle-class audiences off the
beaten track—Parkersburg, West Virginia; Medford, Oregon;
Longview, Washington. If the women respond well, I improvise;
make a small play: "Marvin may not be handsome but he'll be a
good provider . . . and so Marion walks down the aisle a martyr

to money." Encouraging that "nice" women are able to acknowledge their predicament openly. I got no such response five years ago.

"Let us make gambling legal. Those who want to lose their money gambling should have every right to do so. The principal objectors to legalized gambling are the Mafia and the police. *They* will lose money. Admittedly a few fundamentalist Christians will be distressed by their neighbors' gambling, but that is a small price to pay for the increased revenue to the cities, states and federal government, not to mention a police force which would no longer be corrupted by organized crime.

"All drugs should be legalized and sold at cost to anyone with a doctor's prescription."

Intake of breath at this point. Is *he* a drug addict? Probably. Also, varying degrees of interest in the subject, depending on what part of the country you are in. Not much interest in Longview because there is no visible problem. But the college towns are alert to the matter as are those beleaguered subs close to the major urbs.

"For a quarter of a century we have been brainwashed by the Bureau of Narcotics, a cancer in the body politic that employs many thousands of agents and receives vast appropriations each year in order to play cops and robbers. And sometimes the cops we pay for turn out to be themselves robbers or worse. Yet for all the legal and illegal activities of the Bureau the use of drugs is still widespread. But then if drugs were entirely abolished thousands of agents would lose their jobs, and that would be unthinkable."

Around in here I take to discussing the findings of one doctor who had recently been on television warning of the perils of pot. Apparently too much pot smoking will enlarge the breasts of young males (Myra Breckinridge would have had a lot to say on this subject but I may not) while reducing their fertility. I say, "Isn't this *wonderful?*" using a Nixon intonation; and recommend that we get all the males in the country immediately on pot. The women laugh happily; a sort of pill for the male has always been their dream. Equality at last.

I play around with the idea of southern senators doing television commercials, pushing the local product: "Get your high with Carolina Gold." I imitate Strom Thurmond, puffing happily.

"How would legalization work? Well, if heroin was sold at cost in a drugstore it would come to about fifty cents a fix—to anyone with a doctor's prescription. Is this a good thing? I hear the immediate response: Oh, God, every child in America will be hooked. But will they? Why do the ones who get hooked get hooked? They are encouraged to take drugs by the pushers who haunt the playgrounds of the cities. But if the drugs they now push can be bought openly for very little money then the pushers will cease to push.

"Legalization will also remove the Mafia and other big-time drug dispensers from the scene, just as the repeal of Prohibition eliminated the bootleggers of whiskey forty years ago."

I feel I'm going on too long. My personal interest in drugs is slight. I've tried opium, hashish, cocaine, LSD, and pot, and liked none of them except cocaine, which leaves you (or at least me) with no craving for more. Like oysters. If in season, fine. Otherwise, forget them. Pot and opium were more difficult for me because I've never smoked cigarettes and so had to learn to inhale. Opium made me ill; pot made me drowsy.

"The period of Prohibition—called the noble experiment—brought on the greatest breakdown of law and order the United States has known until today. I think there is a lesson here. Do not regulate the private morals of people. Do not tell them what they can take or not take. Because if you do, they will become angry and antisocial and they will get what they want from criminals who are able to work in perfect freedom because they have paid off the police.

"Obviously drug addiction is a bad thing. But in the interest of good law and good order, the police must be removed from the temptation that the current system offers them and the Bureau of Narcotics should be abolished.

"What to do about drug addicts? I give you two statistics. England with a population of over fifty-five million has eighteen hundred heroin addicts. The United States with over two hundred million has nearly five hundred thousand addicts. What are the English doing right that we are doing wrong? *They* have turned the problem over to the doctors. An addict is required to register with a physician who gives him at controlled intervals a prescription so that he can buy his drug. The addict is content. Best of all, society is safe. The Mafia is out of the game. The police are unbribed, and the addict will not mug an old lady in order to get the money for his next fix."

Eleanor Roosevelt maintained that you should never introduce more than one "new" thought per speech. I'm obviously not following her excellent advice. She also said that if you explain things simply and in proper sequence people will not only understand what you are talking about but, very often, they will begin to realize the irrationality of some of their most cherished prejudices.

One of the reasons I took the trouble to spell out at such length the necessity of legalizing drugs was to appeal not to the passions of my audience, to that deeply American delight in the punishing of others so perfectly exploited by Nixon-Agnew-Reagan, but to appeal to their common sense and self-interest. If you *give* an addict his drugs, he won't rob you. The police won't be bribed. Children won't be hooked by pushers. Big crime will wither away. Some, I like to think, grasp the logic of all this.

"I worry a good deal about the police because traditionally they are the supporters of fascist movements and America is as prone to fascism as any other country. Individually, no one can blame the policeman. He is the way he is because Americans have never understood the Bill of Rights. Since sex, drugs, alcohol, gambling are all proscribed by various religions, the states have made laws against them. Yet, believe it or not, the United States was created entirely separate from any religion. The right to pursue happiness—as long as it does not impinge upon others—is the foundation of our state. As a modest proposal, this solution to the problem of law and order is unique: *it won't cost a penny*. Just cancel those barbarous statutes from our Puritan past and the police will be obliged to protect us—the job they no longer do.

"Meanwhile, we are afflicted with *secret* police of a sort which I do not think a democratic republic ought to support. In theory, the F.B.I. is necessary. For the investigation of crime. But in all the years that the F.B.I. has been in existence the major criminals—the Mafia, Cosa Nostra—have operated freely and happily. Except for the busting of an occasional bank robber or car thief, the F.B.I. has not shown much interest in big crime. Its time has been devoted to spying on Americans whose political beliefs did not please the late J. Edgar Hoover, a man who hated Commies, blacks and women in more or less that order."

This generally shocked and never got a laugh. Needless to say, my last lecture was given before the F.B.I.'s scrutiny of "dissidence" became public; not to mention the C.I.A.'s subsequent admission that at least ten thousand Americans are regularly spied upon by that mysterious agency whose charter is to subvert wicked foreigners not lively homebodies.

"The F.B.I. has always been a collaborating tool of reactionary politicians. The Bureau has also had a nasty talent for amusing Presidents with lurid dossiers on the sex lives of their enemies.

"I propose that the F.B.I. confine its activities to *organized* crime and stop pretending that those who are against undeclared wars like Vietnam or General Motors or pollution want to overthrow the government and its Constitution with foreign aid. Actually, in my lifetime, the only group of any importance that has come near to overthrowing the Constitution was the Nixon Administration."

A number of cheers on this. When I am really wound up I do a number of Nixon turns. I have the First Criminal's voice down . . . well, pat. I do a fair Eisenhower, and an excellent F.D.R. Am working on Nelson Rockefeller right now. No point to learning Ford.

"So much, as General Eisenhower used to say, for the domestic front. Now some modest proposals for the future of the American empire. At the moment things are not going very well militarily. Or economically. Or politically.

"At the turn of the century we made our bid for a world empire. We provoked a war with Spain. We won it and ended up owning the Spanish territories of Cuba and the Philippines. The people of the Philippines did not want us to govern them. So we killed three million Filipinos, the largest single act of genocide until Hitler."

Much interest in this statistic. Taken from Galloway and Johnson's book, *West Point: America's Power Fraternity*. Recently I got a letter from a Filipino scholar who has been working on the subject. She says that no one will ever know the exact number killed because no records were kept. But whole towns were wiped out, every man, woman and child slaughtered. The American Army does admit that perhaps a quarter million were killed during the "mopping up." The spirit of My Lai is old with us.

"The first and second world wars destroyed the old European empires, and created ours. In 1945 we were the world's greatest power, not only economically but militarily—we alone had the atom bomb. For five years we were at peace. Unfortunately those industries that had become rich during the war *combined* with the military—which had become powerful—and together they concluded that it was in the best interest of the United States to maintain a vast military establishment.

"Officially this was to protect us from the evil Commies. Actually it was to continue pumping federal money into companies like Boeing and Lockheed and keep the Pentagon full of generals and admirals while filling the pork barrels of congressmen who annually gave the Pentagon whatever it asked for, *with* the proviso that key military installations and contracts be allocated to the home districts of senior congressmen." Tough sentence to say. Never did get it right.

"Nobody in particular was to blame. It just happened. To justify our having become a garrison state, gallant Harry Truman set about deliberately alarming the American people. The Soviet was dangerous. We must have new and expensive weapon systems. To defend the free world. The cold war began. The irony is that the Soviet was not dangerous to us *at that time*. Millions of their people had been killed in the war. Their industries had been shattered. Most important, they did not have atomic weapons and we did.

"So, at the peak of our greatness, we began our decline."

Absolute silence at this point.

"Instead of using the wealth of the nation to improve the lot of our citizens, we have been wasting over a third of the federal budget on armaments and on the prosecution of secret and/or undeclared wars. We have drafted men into the Army in peacetime, something the founders of this country would have been appalled at. We have been, in effect, for thirty-three years a garrison state whose main purpose has been the making of armaments and the prosecution of illegal wars—openly as in Vietnam and Cambodia, secretly as in Greece and Chile. Wherever there is a choice between a military dictatorship—like Pakistan—and a free government—like India—we support the dictator. And then wonder why we are everywhere denounced as hypocrites.

"This is not good for character. This is not good for business. We are running out of raw materials. Our currency is worth less and less. Our cities fall apart. Our armed forces have been, literally, demoralized by what we have done to them in using them for unjust ends.

"In a third of a century the only people who have benefited from the constant raid on our treasury and the sacrifice of our young men have been the companies that are engaged in making instruments of war—with the connivance of those congressmen who award the contracts and those generals who, upon early retirement, go to work for those same companies.

"What to do? A modest and obvious proposal: cut the defense budget. It is currently about a quarter of the national budget—eighty-five billion eight hundred million dollars. Unhappily both Ford and Rockefeller are loyal servants of the Pentagon. *They* will never cut back. They will only increase a military budget that is now projected for the end of the decade to cost us one hundred fourteen billion dollars a year. This is thievery. This is lunacy.

"Conservative estimates say that we can cut the budget by ten percent and still make the world free for I.T.T. to operate in. I propose we aim to cut it by two thirds in stages over the next few years. I propose also a reduction of conventional forces. We need maintain no more than an army, navy, air force of perhaps two hundred thousand highly trained technicians whose task would be to see that anyone who tried to attack us would be destroyed.

"A larger army only means that we are bound to use it sooner or later. To attack others. We have learned that from experience. Generals like small wars because there is a lot of money being spent and, of course, they get promoted. I might be more tolerant of their not unnatural bias *if* they could actually *win* a war, but that seems beyond their capacity. They prefer a lot of activity; preferably in an undeveloped country blasting gooks from the air.

"I would also propose phasing out the service academies. And I was born in the cadet hospital at West Point where my father was an instructor."

To relieve the tension that has started to build, I wander off the track. Describe how I was delivered by one Major Snyder. Later Ike's doctor. "It's only gas, Mamie," he is supposed to have said to Mrs. Eisenhower when the President was having his first heart attack.

"The academies have created an un-American military elite that has the greatest contempt for the institutions of this country, for democratic institutions anywhere. Over the years West Point graduates have caused grave concern. On two occasions in the last century the academy was nearly abolished by Congress. I do not think, despite the virtues of an Omar Bradley, say, that the system which has helped lock us into a garrison state ought to continue."

Often, at this point, I recall an evening at my family's house shortly after the second war began. A group of West Point generals took some pleasure in denouncing that Jew Franklin D. Rosenfeld who had got us into the war on the wrong side. We ought to be fighting the Commies not Hitler. But then F.D.R. was not only a kike, he was sick in the head—and not from polio but from syphilis. Anyway, everything could be straightened out —with just one infantry brigade they would surround the White House, the Capitol, remove the Jew. . . .

My lecture tour ended just as General Brown made his memorable comments on international Jewry and its fifth column inside the United States. I've since heard from several people who said they'd not believed my story until General Brown so exuberantly confirmed what I'd been saying.

"The motto of the academy is 'Duty, Honor, Country.' Which is the wrong order of loyalties. Worse, the West Point elite has created all around the world miniature West Points. Ethiopia, Thailand, Latin America are studded with academies whose function is to produce an elite not to fight wars—there are no wars in those parts of the world—but to *limit* democracy.

"West Point also trains many of these past and future oligarchs —like the present dictator of Nicaragua, Somoza. Retired West Pointers also do profitable business in those nations that are dominated by West Point-style elites.

"Finally, the best result of ceasing to be a garrison state would be economic. Until the energy crisis, the two great successes in the world today were Japan and Germany and they have small military establishments. The lesson is plain: no country needs more military power than it takes to deter another nation from attacking it.

"Now none of these proposals is of much use if we do not reduce our population. The U.S. is now achieving a replacement rate of population. This is a startling and encouraging reduction of population but there are still too many of us and we ought to try by the next century to reduce our numbers by half. The problem is not lack of room. In area we have a big enough country, though we are gradually covering the best farmland with cement and poisoning the lakes and rivers.

"The problem is our way of living. With six percent of the world's population we use forty percent of the world's raw resources. This unnatural consumption is now ending. We are faced with shortages of every kind and we will have to change the way we live whether we want to or not.

"Obviously fewer Americans means less consumption and more for everybody. How do we stop people from breeding? First, by not constantly brainwashing the average girl into thinking that motherhood must be her supreme experience. Very few women are capable of being good mothers; and very few men of being good fathers. Parenthood is a gift, as most parents find out too late and most children find out right away. So a change in attitude will help; and that seems to be happening.

"More radically, I would say that no one ought to have a child *without* permission from the community. A sort of passport must be issued to the new citizen. How these passports will be allotted I leave to the wisdom of the democracy. Perhaps each girl at birth might be given the right to have one child with the understanding that if she decided to skip the hard work of motherhood she could pass that permission on to a woman who wanted two or three or four children.

"For those who gasp and say that this is interfering with man's most sacred right to add as many replicas of himself as he likes to the world, let me point out that society does not let you have more than one husband or wife, a restriction which I have heard no conservative complain of, even though any Moslem would find it chilling, and Mrs. Richard Burton would find it square."

Mrs. Burton is thrown in, cheaply, to reduce the tension that is mounting. Most members of the audience believe that the right to have as many children as they want is absolute; and to limit population by law seems a terrible imposition. Yet most of them take for granted that the government has the right to control most aspects of our private lives (remember the legendary prisoner of Alcatraz who served time for going down on his wife?).

During the question-and-answer period someone invariably says that I have contradicted myself. On the one hand, I would allow free drugs, prostitution, gambling, and all sorts of wickedness while, on the other, I would restrict the right to have children—well, isn't that interfering with people's private lives?

The answer is obvious: adding a new citizen to a country is a public not a private act, and affects the whole community in a way that smoking pot or betting on horses does not. After all, the new citizen will be around a long time after his parents have departed. Doesn't it then make sense that if there is insufficient space, food, energy, the new citizen ought not to be born?

"In an age of chronic and worsening shortages, I would propose that all natural resources—oil, coal, minerals, water—be turned over to the people, to the government."

Two years ago when I made this proposal, the response was angry. The dread word "communism" was sounded. Not to mention "free enterprise," "American way." Now hardly anyone is much distressed. Even die-hard conservatives have fallen out of love with the oil industry.

"But since none of us trusts our government to do anything right—much less honest—national resources should be a separate branch of the government, coequal with the other three but interconnected so that Congress can keep a sharp eye on its funding and the courts on its fairness. The President, any President, on principle, should be kept out of anything that has to do with the economy.

"Much of today's mess is due to Johnson's attempt to conquer Asia without raising taxes, and to Nixon's opportunistic mucking about with the economy at election time. These Presidential ninnies should stick to throwing out baseballs, and leave the important matters to serious people."

The hatred Americans have for their own government is pathological, if understandable. At one level it is simply thwarted greed: since our religion is making a buck, giving a part of that buck to any government is an act against nature.

At this point, without fail, a hot-eyed conservative will get to his feet and say that it is ridiculous to nationalize anything since it is not possible for a government agency to operate efficiently or honestly.

I then ask: isn't this a democratic society? and aren't those who do the government's work not an abstract enemy to be referred to as "them" but simply ourselves? Are you trying to say that we are, deep down, a nation of crooked fuck-ups? (Naturally, I euphemize.)

The point still does not penetrate. So I shift ground. Agree that the United States was founded by the brightest people in the country—and we haven't seen them since. Nice laugh. Tension relaxes a bit.

I agree that most people who go into government are second-raters. The bright ones go into the professions or into moneymaking. This flatters the audience. I suggest that we ought to "change our priorities." Businesslike phrase. Perhaps our schools should train a proper civil service. Train people who prefer payment in honor rather than in money. England, France, Scandinavia attract bright people into government despite low salaries.

This deeply disturbs the audience. First, you must never say that another country handles anything better than we do. Second, although the word "honor" makes no picture at all in the American head, "money" comes on a flashing vivid green for go.

Someone then says that socialist Sweden is a failure because everybody commits suicide, the logic being that a society without poverty will be so boring that death is the only way out. When I tell them that fewer Swedes commit suicide than Americans, they shake their heads. *They know.*

The next questioner says that England's National Health Service is a flop. This is not true but he would have no way of knowing since the newspapers he reads reflect the A.M.A.'s dark view of socialized medicine. Incidentally, England is always used as an example of what awful things will happen to you when you go socialist.

I point out that England's troubles are largely due to the energy crisis and an ancient unsolved class war. I mention England's successful nationalization of steel some years ago. I might as well be speaking Greek. The audience has no way of knowing any of these things. Year after year, the same simple false bits of information are fed them by their rulers and they absorb them, like television commercials.

I do find curious and disturbing the constant hatred of government which is of course a hatred of themselves. Do these "average" Americans know something that I don't? Is the world really Manichaean? Perhaps deep down inside they really believe that we are all crooked fuck-ups, and murderous ones, too (thank you, Lieutenant Calley, President Johnson). After all, the current national sport is shoplifting. For once, I am probably too optimistic about my country.

"Now those who object to nationalizing our resources in the name of free enterprise must be reminded that the free enterprise system ended in the United States a good many years ago. Big oil, big steel, big agriculture avoid the open marketplace. Big corporations fix prices among themselves and thus drive out of business the small entrepreneur. Also, in their conglomerate form, the huge corporations have begun to challenge the very legitimacy of the state.

"For those of you who are in love with Standard Oil and General Motors and think that these companies are really serving you, my sympathy. I would propose, however, that the basic raw resources, the true wealth of the country, be in our hands, not in theirs. We would certainly not manage our affairs any worse than they have.

"As for the quality of our life, well, it isn't much good for most people because most people haven't got much money. Four point four percent own most of the United States. To be part of the four point four you must have a net worth of at least sixty thousand dollars."

This projected figure is from the I.R.S., and I find it hard to believe. Surely individual net worth is higher. In any case, recent figures show that most of the country's ownership is actually in the hands of one percent with, presumably, a much higher net capital.

"This gilded class owns twenty-seven percent of the country's real estate. Sixty percent of all corporate stock, and so on. They keep the ninety-five point six percent from rebelling by the

American brand of bread and circuses: whose principal weapon is the television commercial. From babyhood to grave the tube tells you of all the fine things you ought to own because other people (who are nicer looking and have better credit ratings than you) own them.

"The genius of our ruling class is that it has kept a majority of the people from ever questioning the inequity of a system where most people drudge along, paying heavy taxes for which they get *nothing* in return while I.T.T.'s taxes in 1970 went down, despite increased earnings."

For any Huey Long in embryo, I have a good tip: suggest that we stop paying taxes until the government gives us something in return for the money we give it.

"We get freedom!" vivacious Barbara Walters positively yelled into my ear during our six minutes on the *Today* show. To which the answer is you don't have freedom in America if you don't have money and most people don't have very much, particularly when what they do make goes to a government that gives nothing back. I suppose vivacious Barbara meant that they are free to watch television's God-awful programing which they pay for when they buy those shoddy things the networks advertise.

"I would propose that no one be allowed to inherit more than, let us say, a half million dollars, while corporate taxes obviously must be higher.

"We should also get something back for the money we give the government. We should have a national health service, something every civilized country in the world has. Also, improved public transport. Also, schools which do more than teach conformity. Also, a cleaning of the air, of the water, of the earth before we all die of the poisons let loose by a society based on greed.

"Television advertising should be seriously restricted if not eliminated. Although the TV commercial is the only true art form our society has yet contrived, the purpose of all this beauty is sinister—to make us want to buy junk we don't need by telling us lies about what is being sold.

"Obviously, the bright kids know that what is being sold on the screen is a lot of junk but that is corruption, too, because then everyone who appears on the screen is also thought to be selling junk and this is not always true, even at election time.

"Fascism is probably just a word for most of you. But the reality is very much present in this country. And the fact of it dominates most of the world today. Each year there is less and less freedom for more and more people. Put simply, fascism is the control of the state by a single man or by an oligarchy, supported by the military and the police. This is why I keep emphasizing the dangers of corrupt police forces, of uncontrolled *secret* police, like the F.B.I. and the C.I.A. and the Bureau of Narcotics and the Secret Service and Army counterintelligence and the Treasury men—what a lot of sneaky types we have, spying on us all!

"From studying the polls, I would guess that about a third of the American people at any given moment would welcome a fascist state. This is because we have never been able to get across in our schools what the country was all about. I suspect that the reason for this failure is the discrepancy between what we were meant to be and what we are—a predatory empire—is so plain to children that they regard a study of our Constitution as just another form of television commercial and just as phony. This is sad. Let us hope it is not tragic. The means exist to set things right."

Now for the hopeful note, struck tinnily, I fear. But the last "solution" I offer is a pretty good one.

"In the end, we may owe Richard Nixon a debt of gratitude. Through his awesome ineptitude we have seen revealed the total corruption of our system. From the Rockefellers and the Kennedys who buy elections—and people—to the Agnews and Nixons who take the money from those who buy, we are perfectly corrupt. What to do?

"How do we keep both the corrupting Kennedys and Rockefellers as well as the corrupted Nixons and the Agnews *out* of politics?

"I propose that no candidate for any office be allowed to buy space on television or in any newspaper or other medium. This will stop cold the present system where Presidents and congressmen are bought by corporations and gangsters. To become President you will not need thirty, forty, fifty million dollars to smear your opponents and present yourself falsely on TV commercials.

"Instead television (and the rest of the media) would be required by law to provide prime time (and space) for the various candidates.

"I would also propose a four-week election period as opposed to the current four-year one. Four weeks is more than enough time to present the issues. To show us the candidates in interviews, debates, *un*controlled encounters in which we can actually see who the candidate really is, answering tough questions, his record up there for all to examine. This ought to get a better class into politics."

There is about as much chance of getting such a change in our system approved by Congress as there is of replacing the faces on Mount Rushmore with those of Nixon and company. After all, the members of the present Congress got there through the old corrupt route and, despite the probity of individual members, each congressman is very much part of a system which now makes it impossible for anyone to be elected President who is not beholden to those interests that are willing to give him the millions of dollars he needes to be a candidate.

Congress' latest turn to the screw is glorious: when paying income tax, each of us can now give a dollar to the Presidential Election Campaign Fund. This means that the two major parties can pick up thirty million dollars apiece from the taypayers while continuing to receive, under the counter, another thirty or so million from the milk, oil, insurance, etc. interests.

"Since Watergate, no one can say that we don't know where we are or who we are or what sort of people we have chosen to govern us. Now it remains to be seen if we have the power, the will to restore to the people a country which—to tell the truth—has never belonged to the ninety-five point six percent but certainly ought to, as we begin our third—and, let us not hope, terminal—century."

I ended the series with a noon lecture at a college in Los Angeles . . . not U.C.L.A. They told me this so often that now I've forgotten what the school was actually called. No matter. They have doubtless forgotten what I've said. In a sense, I've forgotten, too. The act of speaking formally (or informally, for that matter) is rather like the process of writing: at the moment it is all-absorbing and one is absolutely concentrated. Then the great eraser in one's brain mercifully sweeps away what was said, written.

But impressions of audiences do remain with me. The young appear to have difficulty expressing themselves with words. Teachers tell me that today's students cannot read or write with any ease (having read the prose of a good many American academies, I fear that the teachers themselves have no firm purchase on our beautiful language).

Is television responsible? Perhaps. Certainly if a child does not get interested in reading between six and thirteen he will never be able to read or write (or speak) well and, alas, the prepubescent years are the years of tube addiction for most American children.

Naturally that small fraction of one percent which will maintain the written culture continues, as always, but they must now proceed without the friendly presence of the common reader who has become the common viewer, getting his pleasure and instruction from television and movies. A new kind of civilization is developing. I have no way of understanding it.

As I make these notes, I am troubled by the way that I responded to the audiences' general hatred of the government. Yes, *we* are the government—but only in name. I realize that I was being sophistical when I countered their cliché that our government is dishonest and incompetent with that other cliché: you are the government.

Unconsciously, I seem to have been avoiding the message that I got from one end of the country to the other: we hate this system that we are trapped in but we don't know who has trapped us or how. We don't know what our cage really looks like because we were born in it and have nothing to compare it to, but if anyone has the key to the lock then where the hell is he?

Most Americans lack the words, the concepts that might help them figure out what has happened; and it is hardly their fault. Simple falsities have been drummed into their heads from birth (Sweden=socialism=suicide) so that they will not rebel, not demand what is being withheld them . . . and that is not Nixon's elegant "a piece of the action" but justice. Social justice.

The myth of upward social mobility dies hard; but it dies. Working-class parents produce children who will be working class while professional people produce more professionals.

Merit has little to do with one's eventual place in the hierarchy.
We are now locked into a class system nearly as rigid as the one
that the Emperor Diocletian impressed upon the Roman empire.

Yes, I should have said, our rulers *are* perfectly corrupt but
they are not incompetent: in fact, they are extremely good at ex-
ercising power over those citizens whom they have so nicely
dubbed "consumers." But the consumers are not as dopey as they
used to be and when they have to listen to exhortations from old-
style Americans like myself, telling them *they* are the government and so can change it (underlying meassage: this bad society is what you dumb bastards deserve), they respond with the
only epithets they can think of, provided them for generations by
their masters: it's the Commies, pinkos, niggers, foreigners, it's
them who have somehow fucked up everything.

But the consumers still have no idea who the enemy *they* are,
no idea who really is tearing the place apart. No one has dared
tell them that the mysterious *they* are the rich who keep the consumers in their places, consuming things that are not good for
them, and doing jobs they detest. Witness, the boredom and fury
of the younger workers on the Detroit assembly lines; no doubt
made more furious—if not bored—by the recent mass firings, as
the depression deepens.

Not since Huey Long has a political leader come forward and
said we are going to redistribute the wealth of the country. We
are going to break up the great fortunes. We are going to have a
just society whose goal will be economic equality. And we can
do this without bloody revolution (although knowing the clever
resourcefulness of our rulers, I suspect it will be a terrible time—
Attica on a continental scale).

True revolution can only take place when things fall apart in
the wake of some catastrophe—a lost war, a collapsed economy.
We seem headed for the second. If so, then let us pray that that
somber, all-confining Bastille known as the consumer society will
fall, as the *first* American revolution begins. It is long overdue.

"Viable Solutions"

BY EDWIN NEWMAN

The day is not far off when someone about to join his family will excuse himself by saying that he does not want to keep his microcluster of structured role expectations waiting.

True, I came upon this gem of social-scientific jargon in London, but that only shows how far our influence has spread and how determined the British are to join the Americans at the kill when the English language finally is done to death. Asphyxiation will be the cause, with the lethal agent gas. This is the gas which, added to evidence, produces evidentiary material, and which, escaping from a Secret Service spokesman—how can you have a spokesman for a secret service?—turned President Ford and *his* microcluster of structured role expectations into protectees.

At that, protectee is better than a similar government word, escapee, which is used—misused—to mean somebody who escaped.

"To what do you attribute your escape?" (It is, by the way, becoming fashionable to say successful escape.)

"I am a fast runnee."

The chief current protectee of the Secret Service is not a gross offender—or offendee—against the language, and when he does offend, it is more often out of naïveté than self-importance. He has identified inflation as "the universal enemy of one hundred percent of our people" and has noted that in trying to deal with that enemy, we went through a "long process of economic sum-mit." Others less fortunately placed were going through a long process of economic valley.

Mr. Ford is enthusiastic about the virtues of dialogue. He has called for a new dialogue with the nations of Latin America, though most of those nations were not aware that the old dia-logue had ended, or even begun. In one of his first speeches as President, Mr. Ford said he wanted to have "a deepening dia-logue" with the nations of Latin America. Until then, I had thought that took place when two men talked to each other while digging a hole.

Last February, twelve senators and seventy representatives asked President Ford for a serious, unemotional dialogue on get-ting the United States out of Indochina. They should have asked for eighty-two dialogues.

It is curious, this devotion to dialogue. An Army officer in-volved in the amnesty program, Major General Eugene For-rester, was quoted as saying that he and his nineteen-year-old son had had an "extremely volatile dialogue over the war in Viet-nam." He evidently meant that they shouted at each other.

General Forrester, the eighty-two members of Congress and President Ford, bent on dialogue though they may be, might well blanch at the prospect of engaging in one with Alan Greenspan, chairman of the Council of Economic Advisers. How would anyone hold up his end after hearing Greenspan say this:

"Thus, once the inflation genie has been let out of the bottle, it is a very tricky policy problem to find the particular calibration and timing that would be appropriate to stem the acceleration in risk premiums created by falling income without prematurely aborting the decline in the inflation-generated risk premiums. This is clearly not an easy policy path to traverse, but it is the path that we must follow."

If that is the path that we must follow, I hope we are able to find it before it (another Greenspanism) obsoletes.

Greenspan was speaking in Washington, a city where a scar-city of money is routinely referred to as a tight resource environ-ment and where, after an experiment with fish in which all the fish died, the Atomic Energy Commission said that "The biota exhibited one hundred percent mortality response." There is a reason for this verbiage. In a tight resource environment, money is more likely to be forthcoming if whatever the money is wanted for can be made to sound abstruse and important. This is why money itself is rarely called money nowadays. It is called funding.

A reader sent me a report by the Youth Services Agency of the New York City Board of Education on the Board's summer program in 1974. The report concluded with the Y.S.A.'s opinion that the program should have more workers and more money, i.e., that it "should be considered for expanded allotments of enrollee personnel and more supportive measures from its own direct funding source."

The same report spoke of employees who had been held up after drawing their paychecks, listed precautions that had been taken, and concluded: "These precautions appeared to be quite successful in dissuading potential individuals with larcenous intent."

Now for a thrust:

"The major thrust of Y.S.A.'s recommendations to maximize the quality and efficiency of services rendered revolve around the necessity for more phone channels. Two additional phone channels would compensate greatly for both communicative and space difficulties and such implementation is strongly urged as an immediate necessity."

Revolve should be revolves, and such implementation also is urged as an immediate necessity, but no matter. A revolving major thrust is hard to match. Indeed, it is hard to find. However, the non-revolving species is spotted fairly often. It was seen at the 1975 convention of the American Booksellers Association, where a press release noted that the major thrust of the convention was (I ask myself whether this really happened) to "foster dialogue."

Major thrusts, unless met by major parries, may be fatal, but almost any thrust can be dangerous. A dean of a university department of home economics (no longer called home economics but family resources and consumer sciences) told an interviewer that in her previous job, in the Office of Education in Washington, most of her work had been in "conceptualizing new thrusts in programming." Beware the conceptualized thrust. There is a verified instance of one that went berserk. It took six strong men to hold it down.

Conceptualizing thrusts, or articulating them, is what we have come to expect from the social sciences. In that world, a sociologist will feel that he has advanced the cause of knowledge by classifying murder and assault as escalated interpersonal altercations; an applicant for a grant for technical training will write that "A quality void in technical capacity constrains achievement"; teachers who encourage children will be said to emit reinforcers; and an economist will be concerned about the adverse effect on the countercyclical dimension that would come from opening the Pandora's box of micro-goals.

It was a social scientist who wrote that knowledge that is transmitted from person to person *qua* knowledge is called intersubjectively transmissible knowledge or, for the sake of brevity, transmissible knowledge. Making knowledge something of a bridge over the river *qua*.

Words like funding, ongoing, constituency, thrust and viable can be worth millions in foundation grants. I received an appeal for money from an organization at Princeton University dedicated to finding viable solutions to international problems. We used to look for solutions and were pleasantly surprised on the rare occasions that we found them. Solutions are no longer sufficient. Viability is now required.

And if not viability, effectiveness. The Committee for Economic Development put out a statement of policy in which it said that a new generation of complex problems demanded fresh and effective solutions. A solution not effective would by definition not be a solution. Nor is there any reason that a solution must be fresh. Old solutions do the job and also have the advantage of experience.

But I stray. I recently came across a phrase that may be worth as much as funding, ongoing and viable put together. It was in a paper advocating the setting of behavioral objectives in schools. Behavioral objectives, so far as I can make out, mean nothing whatever, but it was claimed that they would enable teachers to "provide students with a pharmacy of learning alternatives matched to the objectives and tailored to the individual characteristics of each student." A pharmacy of learning alternatives. The proper reaction is wonder and veneration.

I do not wish to overlook the contribution of business to wrecking the language. B. Altman, in New York, has issued this

invitation: "Sparkle your table with Cape Cod classic glassware."
As it happened, I did not have time to sparkle my table because
I was busy following instructions given in another advertisement
and was accessorizing my spacious master bedroom with oil
paintings and, in the words of another advertisement that appeared in *The New Yorker,* "making beautiful happen to [my]
window treatments with Levolor Rivieras." Some days, I wish I
could just make clean happen to my window treatments.

Saks Fifth Avenue, also in New York, has offered to sell men a
magnificent—magnificent—glacé leather trench coat collared and
lined with natural muskrat. Unnatural muskrat is a muskrat of
doubtful sexual proclivities. An advertising executive I have
been told of wrote to a client: "This will enable us to direct the
most maximally impactful advertising toward the small and medium size dog owner."

I have seen advertisements for a recording of *Così Fan Tutte*
that was "totally complete," and for a California Riesling that
was "regretfully available only in very limited quantities." The
latter is the hopefully disease spreading, though no variation is
likely to approach the sheer majesty of the president of the
Green Bay Packers saying, when discussing the hiring of a new
coach, "We hope to have an announcement before the end of the
week, hopefully before that." The wine is regretfully available
only in limited quantities. You may have a vision of the Riesling
sobbing itself to sleep over its inadequacy.

The Chesapeake and Potomac Telephone Company has something called a single payment gift plan. Under the plan, the customer may pay for a year in advance, and then he receives no
other bills until the year is over. That's a gift. In Pompano
Beach, Florida, condominium apartments have been offered in
which the bedroom is a sleeping chamber, the kitchen is a culi-
nary center, and the dining room is the place de dinner. That last
would have been an appropriate place for a dish served at a
book-and-author luncheon sponsored in the Athens of America
by the Boston *Herald-American:* crepes a la seafood. Both the
Herald and the condominium promoters may have received advice from the Biltmore Hotel in New York which, for the benefit
of foreign visitors, has a sign outside a men's lavatory that reads
not only "Gentlemen" but "Monsieurs."

Let us return to Britain, where the locals—quick learners—are having major confrontations, consulting in depth, satisfying targets, giving the score situation instead of the score, flaunting instead of flouting, making an effort to try, calling for legislation that will galvanize a new sense of opportunity and partnership, and describing the way people talk as their conversation culture, and swimming pools and playing fields as leisure complexes.

Remnants of Britain's sturdy conversation culture do survive. At a meeting of shareholders of the British Leyland Motor Corporation, the chairman, Lord Stokes, explaining the disasters that had befallen the company, found his explanation being drowned out by slow handclapping.

Said Lord Stokes, sarcastically, "Well, thank you for your support."

Said one of the shareholders, "There is only one support you want because you are a bloody big rupture all the way through."

It was a little too long to be ideal, but it undoubtedly enlivened the dialogue situation.

The British, in any case, are not as resourceful as the Americans when it comes to making language mushy and boneless. The playwright William Douglas-Home, writing to *The Times* of London, said that the Conservative party "should be plugging, day in, day out, the true facts about taxation." True facts are, of course, the only kind of facts available, but see what a press release for an American television program does with them: "The facts hew to actuality." True facts. The facts hew to actuality. No contest.

But don't cheer, folks.

Soon, also, no language.

Boy Scouts

BY HAROLD BRODKEY

Sometimes in New York, I can create a zone of amusement and doubt around me by saying I was a Boy Scout.

I am forty-four years old now, bearded—I suppose I have a certain personal ambience which makes Boy Scout-hood unlikely.

I don't think it's my fault.

I was a Boy Scout in 1942. I was about five seven, newly grown from five two or three; I was temporarily deformed, with short squat legs and feet that were nearly square—the arches had grown but I still had a child's toes. I had other physical anomalies of that sort: big knees and sticklike thighs.

My balls had dropped; my prick had started to grow—it was about five inches, not particularly thin, large for a child—it was still growing.

I was by some standards of measurement the smartest child in the state of Missouri. I was, am, Jewish and had been very ugly and was still, as well as deformed, but I was slowly turning, slowly showing a pale, transparent physical quality which in the suburb where I lived at that time was called "cute"—it didn't mean cuddly: it meant interesting—I think. My ears stuck out: I had them pinned back when I was in college, grown tired of the problem posed when one's appearance lies about what one is like. My father had heart trouble and was something of an invalid: he dabbled in the black market—there was a war and rationing. My mother was mentally unwell. I mention these things because they made up my social position.

The Boy Scout troops I knew about were, each one, attached to a church—or a temple; I don't believe synagogues bothered. Each troop had a social rank according to the social rank of the church or temple that founded it.

It cost money to belong to a Reform temple: you have to have that extra money and be willing to enter on the confused clashing of social climbing and Anglo-Saxon mimicry and personal loneliness and religion as a set of tenets and questions about the secular, the fate of Jews, and the nature of guilt—such things as that—in the Middle West, among the cornfields. We had Sunday school and confirmation—nothing Jewish except the rabbi's nose: it was the boniest, largest, most hooked nose I ever saw, ever in my life; he also used his hands a lot when he talked. He was reputed to be "a good speaker," but I believe it was his nose and hands, his physical status as a Jew—I don't remember him ever making a religious remark or showing any interest in anything to do with the spirit—that enabled him to force a salary of twenty-five thousand dollars a year, in 1942, from the Russo-Jewish magnates—well-tailored, quick-eyed, bad-tempered, secretive, restless, and clever—who ran the temple.

The rabbi was so jealous of a book called *Peace of Mind* written by a Boston rabbi and which became a best seller that he wrote a book called *Peace of Soul*—he wanted very much to be famous—and he had it printed privately and mailed to every member of the congregation in a plain brown wrapper with a bill enclosed: a married couple would be sent two copies and two bills, each bill being for three dollars.

We were members of the temple because my mother's brother was on the board of directors. He was rich by local standards, and I was smart; and either he had a dim sense of community duty or else his two sons irritated him: he did not think his sons were smart. I thought they were smart enough. One wanted to be an artist and tried the arts, each in turn, and he insisted he was unhappy, which made his father very restless. My uncle was skinny. His other son was a perfect Anglo-Saxon except for a nose shaped like a peanut: that too displeased my uncle although this son was brave and athletic and likable enough; he did drink and spend a lot of money, and he wracked up the family Cadillac twice, once by crashing into the gatehouse that guarded the entrance to the enclave where my uncle had his house. Of that son, his mother said, "He's so brave: his jaw is wired shut and he never complains." My uncle said his son was meshuggeneh, and to irritate him and the other one as they irritated him, he would praise me and "do things" for me such as send me to Sunday school or finance my entry into the Boy Scouts: not only finance it but insist the troop pursue me since I didn't want to join. It seemed I owed it to Judaism and the war effort to be a Boy Scout.

The troop had a reputation for consisting of three types of boys—the refined, the would-be refined who would probably never get there (to refinement), and the wild ones, the crazy or tough ones, pugnacious or obsessive. I always thought refinement was a joke, all things considered, and do still, but some of those boys were very impressive, I thought: two of the older ones, who had remarkable, even tempers and never showed signs of cruelty or of pride except for expecting quietly to be dominant, spoke to each other only in Latin. Another boy knew entire Shakespearean plays by heart. And two of the boys would hum themes from a Brahms quintet—I couldn't do things like that. But I was famous locally, and they were not. I was powerful at school and could force a teacher to regive a test that was unfair or unclear—not for my sake, my grades were always high, my average was sometimes given as 101, but for the sake of my classmates. Then, too, because of my foul tongue and for other reasons, the working-class kids at school, a minority, accepted me: I was a point where the varying kinds of middle-class children, the few rich, and slightly more numerous poor, met. There were two or three other children of whom this was true (including two political girls), but they were fine children and had not read Thomas Mann. I was considered a fine child because of my parents' plight and the way I treated my parents, but there was something decidedly not fine about me, something anomalous and confusing; it is very unlikely but it is true that I was treated, on the whole, with respect; and so, fineness was ascribed to me to resolve the anomaly and strangeness.

In those days, fine or "distinguished" families had a decided moral tone: social climbing had a moral cast to it—as in how much you gave to charity and how much charitable work you did—and this moral tone was refined—it included euphemisms such as "passed on" or "passed away." It was my opinion as a child unable sometimes to crack the grown-ups' code of talk that if someone will lie about what to call a fuck, they'll lie about anything. Also, if you remember, eleven and twelve pre- and during puberty are particularly nasty, intellectual, realpolitik ages—at least for some kids, male and female. I had, decidedly, a moral rank, a high one, but it was not based on the right things; however, people did not keep track, and they would have some vague sense I *was* refined. Meanwhile, the war blazed. I had enormous maps with flags; and I fretted over strategy, the quality of Allied war matériel and leadership—Churchill was a complete bust militarily—the problems of courage and the daily and unremitting horror of what one translator of Proust calls "a bloody hedge of men constantly renewed."

If life were nice—well, nicer—one would have Einstein's katzenjammers, space and time for research, a number of anecdotes, nuances, but one is rushed. One has to forego discussing the names of ranks in Boy Scouts, from Tenderfoot to Eagle Scout, and the Merit Badges, and the costume partly designed to mimic the uniforms developed by the British during the Boer War. There is the subject of Anglophilia—where *is* the Anglophilia of yesteryear?—and the equipment: where did those sleeping bags and axes and knives come from in wartime? Perhaps everyone had an older brother.

In small towns, social class is comparatively simple: the line is between respectability and the rest—if the small-town rich are not respectable, they are excluded. It's more complicated in a city. The Scouts from the beginning had an origin in social class but with a built-in ambiguity: there were to be troops for poor boys to give them a chance at purity and so on; but the main thrust, I think, was to keep the middle class or upper middle class trained in outdoorsmanship for leadership in the Boer War. It was a junior paramilitary outfit designed to teach skills for guerrilla warfare in open plains—maybe in the woods. It was not up-to-date: the Scouts in my time were still doing Morse code and stuff with semaphores; and the walkie-talkie was already in use, and slang instead of codes (or so the papers said). Besides that, one *knew* about the Army and social class, that the poor and Southern red-necks made up the troops, and they shot incompetent, cruel, hysterical or snobbish officers in the back in battle—or so *I* was told—and how could we practice leadership if we had no red-necks, farmers, or working-class boys in the troop? These things worried me. I was told that as Jews we wouldn't be given a chance to lead usually anyway, not even in the quartermaster corps. It seemed our refinement, as a troop, was slightly warped by competition toward other troops and was actually an exercise in self-righteousness expended in a vacuum.

I think a third of the boys in the troop were quite mad—some with unfocused adolescent rage, some with confusions, others with purity. One boy, the son of an accountant and a very talkative mother, had a mania for Merit Badges, a silly giggle, acne on his back, large muscles from lifting weights, and a way of leaping from stillness into a walk like a two-legged horse that suggested to me considerable mental dislocation. Some boys were mad with slyness, some were already money mad, some were panic-stricken. There they were, lined up in the temple auditorium, in their khakis with axes in snap-on head holsters, or whatever, on their belts and sheathed knives and neckerchiefs and that damned sliding ring to hold the neckerchief.

I remember—not in great detail: this is not something I am going to present in the full panoply of reality—going on a fourteen-mile hike. Or was it a twelve-mile hike? I don't remember, but you had to do it to pass from some rank—Tenderfoot?—to another—Second Class? Maybe. (You had to pass other tests, too.) This hike came quite early in my brief Scouting career before I created the scandal and furor in the troop by insisting that for my outdoor-cooking test I be allowed to use premade biscuit dough from a can—like a real soldier. "Do you hate Scouting?" one of the men who ran the troop asked me. I don't think I did, but perhaps I did.

The hike had to be done within a certain length of time, and I think you had to run or jog twelve minutes and then walk twelve minutes, it was twelve somethings or other, twelve paces maybe (the injunction against self-abuse was on page four hundred and something of the manual). The route had been laid out on back roads in the country—roads built in the twenties for developments that weren't built because the Depression came. They were concrete, mostly, and cracked, and grass grew out of them in spots. I had a new pair of shoes paid for by the uncle whose doing all this was—Boy Scout Shoes. A slightly older boy—he was thirteen, probably, with a patch of pimples on one cheek, an exacerbated triangle of them, and then a few single ones on his forehead and chin—was to lead us, instruct us, keep us from cheating. Quiet-voiced, he bore the look of someone planed down and cautious from the skirmishes grown-ups wage, often for the sake of social climbing or in the name of happiness, in order to enforce what purity they can on their young. He had not yet outgrown his freakishness: he was too broad and short-legged and long-necked: he was less freakish than I was—I think he took on the final physical shape for the duration of his youth when he was fifteen. This boy's eyes were extraordinarily blank, as if he had found childhood and youth to be a long, long wait.

I can almost count us—five or seven boys were to make the march. Ah, memory—or research. I think there were five of us. The leader made six. The idea of seven comes to me because the five of us doing the march for the first time, the Tenderfoot, were dwarves. Two were still physically ten years old although they had turned twelve: they were bright and quick, brainy. No bodily growth dimmed their intellects or powers of vision.

Where did we gather? Someone's front lawn, I think. I remember we talked about how we were doing more than the statutory distance because of where we started. There were jokes about the humiliation of giving up. We clomped along. I don't remember the running—the alterations of running with walking: it seems to me some of the younger boys skipped; and we were of such different heights that we couldn't run with any order; and so we walked slowly for a while, and then faster, then slowly.

One boy had to give up or thought he did: he had a blister; he was one of the smaller boys—proud and temperamental, too. He didn't receive much sympathy, but he wasn't mocked either—we stared at him: I don't know why we didn't mock him: either because this was Scouting or we were well-bred Jews, you know, compassionate. It was one reason or the other. I remember him sitting by the side of the road in the weeds, an apple-checked kid small for his age. Do weeds survive pollution? Was he supposed to walk home or hitchhike: an occasional car did pass on this road but very occasionally. Hitchhiking wasn't considered dangerous in the county: you knew what a safe person looked like and smelled like: if they had the wrong eyes or smell, you said, "No, thank you," and if they persisted, you screamed. I don't remember grown-ups talking much about children being molested —we children spoke of it once in a while: it is strange to remember the essential panic and curiosity we felt day after day as we struggled to grow up.

Anyway, we left one child behind or was it two? Did we assign him a companion? We young ones did not know what was going on, and it would have been pushy, like usurping control of the hike to figure things out. Our leader had no interest in leadership: he had been made a leader against his will, I think; and he found it dull and had no particular talent for it: he would stare off into the sky or into the branches of trees—this was latish autumn, chilly and damp, a gray day—if you asked him a question. I think he had an older brother he was pretty much dependent on—not that it matters now.

We didn't know how to walk distances. We discussed how to carry yourself—we put our shoulders back—we rose up on our toes—but none of our particular group was coordinated physically yet, not even our leader; and we progressed clumsily, in haphazard effort, muscular effort; at times, two boys—it was usually by twos—would find a rhythm, find a way of walking, hip joint, spine, ankle, knee, and foot; and they would sail along, sail ahead, ahead even of the leader who clomped along at the side of the road, sad and dutiful. I had a nail in my shoe—I've never been lucky with equipment: I once had a pair of galoshes that leaked—the nail gouged my heel, and it was painful as all hell, but people were always worried about how sensitive I was —how much I noticed, what did I think of them, was I a sissy all in all, did intelligence make a coward of me: that sort of thing— and I was used to concealing pain: in this case I persuaded myself it was preparation for real war, but I hated the pain anyway as unnecessary and part of a fools' march.

The route was laid out like a rough figure eight, and when we came to where the two loops crossed, we saw some other boys coming down the far road at an angle to us. They were not dwarves. We knew them, but I don't recall if they were from our troop or merely from the county somewhere. I think they were richer Jews—maybe merely older, with real legs, real hands.

There was a twenty-mile hike, I think, for passing from some upper rank to one still higher; or maybe it was thirty miles.

The greetings echoed among the trees on that empty road. But were not really good-natured. There was some discussion between our leader and their leader—the other leader was not bored and had on at least three lanyards: the ends were tucked into his pleated pocket, but I would imagine he had a whistle, a pocketknife, and maybe a compass. I suppose the ill nature of the greetings came from mutual suspicion: we were outcasts, pre-pubic; but the other group was crazed and low with Scouting. One forgets how satiric children are just before puberty, how harsh in judgment; and how strange the ones seem who after puberty are cheerful or enthusiastic and not gloomy and secretive.

The older Scouts were on a rigorous schedule, and yet two of them joined us. The mysteries accumulate and suggest to me the mysteries of that day as I lived it, of being on a road I did not know, doing a faintly foolish thing, among boys I did not know.

Because of my reputation, I was more or less suffered to ask more questions than most younger children were allowed to ask, but I was not in a mood to use my privilege: I was being one of the bunch. The new boys were quite old and glamorous; one was skinny: in the end I did gravitate to the older boys and to the leader—I felt older than my age, and I was nosy, I believe. One of the newcomers noticed I was limping and I told him about the nail, but he didn't believe me. An entire lifetime of people saying *I don't believe you* suddenly weighs on me. Sighing, I sat down on a stone alongside the road and took off my shoe and showed him the blood on my sock; and then I took off my sock and showed him the wound. There was talk of tetanus from the nail, but one of the dwarves said his father was a doctor and the nail would have had to have been exposed to manure to be dangerous. I had been told swearing was lip filth, but I did it anyway. I said, "Well, I didn't shit in my shoe, so I'm probably all right." This was considered pretty charming and was looked on as revealing a real sense of humor—life was simpler then—and it made the leader like me and the two older boys and some of the dwarves: I had magically become a non-dwarf in the course of the hike, a big shot. Liking led to talk of sex: the boys were walking more or less in a circle around me—some of them walked backward—and told me about fucking. I had heard before, frequently, but I was one of the more latent boys: it had never really penetrated, but now it did; I was disbelieving. "My parents wouldn't do that," I said. They had to in order to have children, I was told. "Not my parents," I said, and then thought about my parents: "Well, they might do it in a closet," I said. One of the older boys said, "Don't you masturbate?" I did but wasn't sure how that related to sex, to fucking; the explanations I was offered were unclear to me. An older boy said, "Didn't you ever fool around with another boy?"

"What do you mean? We're fooling around now."

"It's called homosexuality," one of the younger boys said, "and it's a phase."

"It's all right until you're about sixteen, and then it has to be girls."

"How come?" I said.

"Let's go in the woods and look at each other's pricks," one of the younger boys said—one of the boys with no prick.

There was a sudden flurry of talk: did we have the time, and one boy had promised his parents he would never do anything dirty; and then we all went into the woods, the two newcomers, the older boys leading the way.

We crashed clumsily among twigs and bushes until we came to a clearing, a mud-floored glade. The older boys and some of the younger ones immediately took up positions showing experience—from summer camp or wherever—in a circle.

But there were two kinds of circle, clumped close together, the units I mean, and more spread out. Somehow without voting we settled on a spread-out circle or oval—we were about an arm's length from each other. I believe one of the older boys counted and then we all unbuttoned; and some boys revealed themselves at once; but some didn't; and the older boy counted again, and at the count of three we all displayed ourselves.

It was very quiet. I thought it was all very interesting, but I was a little blank-headed, almost sleepy: I wasn't sure why it was so interesting: but it was clear from the silence, the way the boys breathed and stood, from the whole atmosphere, that this was more interesting than the hike itself, this curious introduction to genital destiny.

Then it was decided we should all try to come—I think how it went was someone asked if I could come, and I wasn't sure—I wasn't sure what he meant: I really had an enormous gift for latency.

Some boys didn't know how to masturbate and were shown the gesture. But before we began, there was a ceremony of touching each other's pricks. No one in that glade was fully developed. The absence of cruelty became silently, by implication, an odd sort of stilled and limited tenderness.

Then the circle was re-formed—in the silent glade—and we all began to pull rhythmically—perhaps it was like rubbing at Aladdin's lamp; perhaps we are at the threshold of the reign of magic and death. The glad was shadowy and smelled vinegary—it also smelled of earth. A few boys came—a drop or two. We cleaned ourselves with leaves and with a Kleenex one boy divvied up.

The leader looked at his watch and said we were ten minutes behind schedule.

So then we hurried—we left the woods and went on with the hike.

There is no time for the rest of what I want to tell about the Boy Scouts.

Cornball

BY GERALD NACHMAN

If people simply had a fuller understanding of "corn," they would be a lot less frightened by it. In time, they might even come to love it, as I do, and be able to stand up before a large crowd like this and gobble it down openly.

Nobody treats corn seriously enough—or else they treat it too seriously and label it "camp," which is what happens to fine wholesome corn when it grows up and moves to New York. Camp is your fancy canned corn off the cob and I can't get it down any more without choking. Honest-to-gosh corn is a personal thing that pops up out of the ground organically—Steve and Eydie, say, to pick a prime example at the peak of perfection.

Steven and Eydie are twice as corny as Kansas in August, but what of it? The important thing is, do you really like them? At first, you may not like yourself for it, but once you get over that you'll have the proper healthy attitude toward corn and corn by-products.

Beware of cheap imitations like Carmen Miranda, who is campy and as safe to enjoy as Lena Horne. What I'd like to know is, do people truly like Carmen Miranda or are most of them faking it? Do they, deep down, really dig Steve and Eydie and secretly loathe Carmen Miranda?

At one time, during that fuzzy period when it wasn't yet chic to savor her, Carmen Miranda was mere corn. People probably liked her all along but didn't dare come out of the closet until the coast was clear. Someday, Steve and Eydie may be designated official camp, but right now they're still just good juicy lip-smackin' corn. This is the time to sink your teeth in.

A while back, Rona Barrett slid from high corn to low camp. Now, of course, everybody rolls his eyes and quite adores her, but try to wring a confession out of a single avid Robin Adams Sloan reader. It's getting tougher to tell the difference between private home-grown corn and the socially accepted plastic variety—soap operas, horror movies, beauty pageants, Nelson Eddy-Jeanette MacDonald musicals, etc. Lately, I notice a lot of bending over backward to embrace alien corn, dreadful stuff you don't enjoy at all but feel obliged to wink at—game shows, Spiderman, rock 'n' roll groups from the 1950s.

The only corn test is: Would you indulge in it all by yourself? I know I love barbershop quartets, because I once went out of my way to hear a regional competition, but I'm not so sure about parades. You have to like corn for its own sake, not because you're supposed to or it's cute. You must be scrupulously on the level about it.

For instance, I sincerely like Roy Rogers (and Dale—but *only* if she's with Roy), and part of it is that he's not ashamed of himself or defensive about Trigger or "kidding himself" like Dean Martin, Kate Smith and Liberace. Roy never swerves a foot from pure cowboy; it's all he knows and that's plenty for me. As a kid, I liked Roy (well, I was a pretty corny kid, too—I read *Archie* and *Little Lulu* rather than *Plastic Man* or *Wonder Woman*), which explains a basic appeal of corn. It's just a small part of you that won't go away or grow up. Roy's charm is, he has never gotten any older himself; he thinks he's Roy Rogers. I was worried when *The Village Voice* discovered Roy, but I doubt if it'll go to his head; he's just not the type to go campy on you all of a sudden.

I also love Peanuts dolls, I swear it. On my lunch hour, I'll kind of *casually* drop into a stationery store to see what's new at the "Peanuts Gallery," making believe I'm hunting for a get-well card, when in fact I'm wondering whether to buy a Lucy figurine. The thing is, see, I already *have* a Snoopy bank and a perfectly good Charlie Brown, so I don't really need a Lucy doll right now, but one day I may break loose and get it. (I won't buy just any Peanuts figurine; I'm fussy. If the saying is dumb, or the expression is a little off, I'll skip it.)

It took years for me to acknowledge that I am hip to Muzak. People go around maligning it carelessly, but there's good Muzak and lousy Muzak. Maybe there's a little too much of it around, but in the right lobby, at the proper moment, Muzak can sure set me humming; no wonder all those dairy cows tap their feet when they hear it. I'm unable to leave an elevator if an especially nice medley is playing, and once I went six floors past my office to hear a terrific banjo solo all the way through; it would have been rude just to walk out. In any case, as elevator listening goes, Muzak's an improvement over strangers asking me if it's started raining out yet.

I guess this is the place to divulge my long-term infatuation with Lawrence Welk's show, which I think is just grand and so does my grandmother and there's nothing wrong with her. She's the first to complain if Welk has had a "bum show," as she did once when there were too many songs she'd never heard of. I could understand that. I hate hearing songs I don't know, and Lawrence Welk plays fewer of them per square minute than any conductor this side of Guy Lombardo. Welk once said that if you wake up a jazzman at three A.M. he'll reveal he likes Welk. We've reached a darn sorry state in America when you have to go around knocking on doors in the middle of the night to rouse a few champagne-music lovers out of bed.

Were it not for Welk, what's more, there would be no Lennon Sisters, and what sort of a world would that be? Even people reluctant to say they watch Welk can be nudged into conceding that, yes, they, well, always kind of liked the Lennons. Why be shy about it? Can't we all be big enough to admit those were four adorable girls who sang yummy close harmony? It was like discovering a quartet that did Gregorian chants and was perky to boot. If the Lennon Sisters were the Andrews Sisters, everyone would be falling over each other in ecstasy. Just remember: Someday they *will* be the Andrews Sisters and then we'll see who eats crow.

Speaking of food, when I'm out on the town alone, with nobody around to see where I go, I'm almost sure to tiptoe past a massage parlor and instead slip quietly into a Steak & Brew or International House of Pancakes. Next to these, McDonald's and

Colonel Sanders are trivial dining experiences. McDonald's is where you go on your way home from something *else,* it is not the thing itself, unlike Steak & Brew or I.H.O.P., which require you to lay your plans early. You must find the courage to say, in a clearly audible voice: "Say, why don't we all go to the House of Pancakes for dinner Saturday night?" The reason, should any-one ask, is simply that dollar-size buttermilk hot cakes don't grow on trees and neither do German pancakes lolling in butter and lemon or Swedish babies with lingonberry jam.

The basic pull of Steak & Brew, needless to say, is the salad bar; I'm partial to *any* place with a salad bar and chilled plates. The top sirloin and all the beer I can drink are secondary. What I'm in there for, let's face it, is all the croutons I can sprinkle.

In the annals of cornography, there may be nothing more damaging than a frank admission that you are a blatant Jerry Vale fan. If you will bother to listen to him, however, it's quite appar-ent that Vale is one hell of a crooner, the last of our throbbing Italian singers who is not afraid to pull out the throttle on his tremolo all the way. Believe me, this man does not mess around with a love song.

I like Vale, but most of all I like Eddie Fisher. People laugh when I sit down to play my Fisher records, but it's only because they forget how just plain wonderful he sounds. If they'd stop snickering at me for a second and listen to a few bars of *I Need You Now* or *Tell Me Why,* I guarantee they would be a lot less smug, smiling indulgently and saying, "Oh-h-h, I used to like Eddie Fisher." Your hard-core Fisherphile can't dismiss him so easily and may still be found sneaking an old album off the shelf, pulling the shades and listening to him let loose on *Down-hearted.*

Most of the time, you like somebody who's considered "corny" and don't know why. It's nearly impossible to defend a heartfelt yearning for Steve and Eydie or Steak & Brew because it's pure passion and you can't discuss it without being reduced to bab-bling. God knows what I like about Billy Graham, but you can't deny the Rev. Billy is tops at it. I easily can understand why Richard Nixon wanted to have Graham around: If I were Presi-dent, I'd ask Billy over all the time myself just to hear him talk in that gorgeous North Carolina drawl. I've long been a Graham disciple but not until now have I been willing to get right up out of my seat—this very minute—and come forward.

Mind you, none of this is meant as an excuse for soft-core corn, which is something else and mustn't be tolerated. There's sweet corn and mushy corn. Overripe corn includes the Johnny Mann Singers, sad clowns and pussycats on black velvet, Ferrante & Teicher, polished redwood coffee tables, the *National Star*, Three Stooges comedies, candles shaped like banana splits, Doc Severinsen's wardrobe, abalone ashtrays, anything labeled "World's Greatest Mom," "Sue the Bastards" or "I Love You THIS Much" and Amtrak food. I mean, that's just ordinary horrible stuff and an insult to golden sun-kissed corn.

If you want the real thing, help yourself to any of these rich kernels of goodness spilling out of my cornucopia:

Ozzie and Harriet. The Nelsons lived in a corn-bread house, spoke corn-fed lines and did cornball things, yet what I wouldn't give for a crack at some reruns now. While everyone else loved Lucy, I found solace with Ozzie and Harriet. No show could duplicate their nifty dimension of life as art, but most of all, the Nelsons were just so damn *nice*, the soul of corn. It took a real effort not to like that family. Things came apart when Ricky got hold of a guitar and combed his hair forward, but that happens in even the best homes. Say what you will, the Nelsons were classic hot buttered corn.

Woolworth's. Here is another lunchtime diversion of mine: aimlessly wandering the aisles of this ancient corn palace, checking out the latest line of vegetable graters, bathtub toys and porcelain birds—plus, of course, a candy showcase featuring such hard-to-find items as orange marshmallow peanuts, cinnamon bears and Mexican hats. While Halloween and Valentine's Day are throw-away holidays, they're taken to heart at Woolworth's, and around mid-October and early February you can't get me out of there. The candy corn is in season.

Ice shows. Critics who set out to mock the frilly pants off ice shows always return to their typewriters chastened; as a veteran ice-show reviewer, I can vouch for this. The stupid things are absolutely superb; you just have to admire all that "wizardry over ice," as we call it. (Footnote: I also want to mention my fondness for ice-rink organ medleys, an underappreciated musical form.)

Arthur Godfrey. I liked him better before he was recycled as an ecologist, when it took some courage to tune him in and risk being marked for life as a little old lady; however, all lovers of corn are at least fifty percent little old lady (indeed, I have an unnatural appetite for tearooms and cafeterias and will take a first-rate cafeteria over a French restaurant any day). Godfrey is now an elder statesman of broadcasting and eminently revered, but there was a time when serious people just did *not* listen to Arthur Godfrey on the radio. Of course, your hard-core crowd found Godfrey too highbrow; our taste ran more to Don McNeill's *Breakfast Club.*

Paintings, posters, postcards and calendars depicting autumn leaves, snowy barns and crashing surf. If they're well done (or even if they're not particularly), I'm a terrible sucker for nature scenes. You can try disguising this fact by buying prints of the same stuff by Monet or Hopper, but you may as well recognize the fact that you have an innate taste for—well, pure corn oil.

The whole point is, there's nothing wrong with corn if only people would face it squarely instead of shuffling around and apologizing and changing the subject, or, even worse, giggling and saying, "I love Lawrence Welk's show—it's so awful," which is a very corny thing to say, by the way. If you think he's awful, don't go around liking him. I hate to see an accordionist patronized like that. When it comes to corn, it would be nice to see people holding their heads high (as an elephant's eye) rather than jabbing a toe in the ground and shucking their responsibilities.

Well, I'm going in now to put on some Eddie Fisher records while I thumb through this week's *People,* after which I may drop by Woolworth's to see if they have any new Peanuts dolls in or autumn scenes, then I'll probably just grab a bite at the House of Pancakes and finish this article on Billy Graham in the *Reader's Digest* or just catch a little good uninterrupted Muzak, but I want to leave in time to get home for a Steve and Eydie special with Roy Rogers and Jerry Vale (with any luck, he'll do *You Don't Know Me*).

And to hell with Carmen Miranda.

Commencement Address

BY JOHN STEINBECK

This letter was written in 1956 and first published in
Esquire *in 1975. It is addressed to James S. Pope, exec-*
utive editor of the Louisville, Kentucky, Courier-Jour-
nal, *for which Steinbeck covered the 1956 national po-*
litical conventions. Pope had mentioned that he was
obliged to prepare a commencement address for deliv-
ery at Emory University in Georgia, and the novelist
amused himself for the evening by dashing off a re-
sponse.

Sag Harbor
May 16, 1956

Dear Jim:

A letter from Alicia [Alicia Patterson, publisher of *Newsday*]
today enclosed an interview with Bill Faulkner which turns my
stomach. When those old writing boys get to talking about The
Artist, meaning themselves, I want to leave the profession. I
don't know whether the Nobel Prize does it or not, but if it does,
thank God I have not been so honored. They really get to living
up to themselves, wrapped and shellacked. Apparently they can't
have any human intercourse again. Bill said he only read Homer
and Cervantes, never his contemporaries, and then, by God, in
answer to the next question he stole a paragraph from an article
I wrote for the *Saturday Review* eight months ago. Hell, he's
better than Homer. Homer couldn't either read or write and the

old son of a gun was blind. And Cervantes was broke, a thing Bill never let happen to him while he could go to Hollywood and turn out the Egyptian. THE ARTIST—my ass! Sure he's a good writer but he's turning into a goddamned phony. I guess that got rid of my nastiness and Elaine [Steinbeck's wife] wouldn't approve of my saying it. That will teach her not to go away.

It's late but I'm not sleepy so I might as well write you a commencement speech, what the hell! Of course if I had to do it myself I'd cut my throat.

I see you sitting in the front row, robed in academic splendor. It is pretty hot and you are sweating under that cape. You sat on your back tassel and pulled it off and shoved it in your pocket and that got your robe caught in your pocket and you can't get it out so you yank at it and out come your keys and a handful of small change. You keep thinking the tassel of your mortarboard is a fly and you swat at it every time it swings in front of your eyes. You wish you hadn't worn nylon drawers. You itch.

Then you hear the president announce:

"And now, I have the honor to present our honored guest, William D. Pope, who has consented to address you."

As you stand up you try to work the nylon drawers out of your crevice by dragging against the little hard chair but it sticks. So you say to yourself, "The hell with it," and you try to get your notes out of your pocket under all the harness you are wearing and you realize that if you did manage to dig them out, you would have to throw your skirts over your head. So what do you do? You advance to the front of the stage and deliver the address I am about to write for you.

COMMENCEMENT ADDRESS BY JAMES S. BISHOP

"President Onassis," you begin. "Honorable regents, members of the faculty, without whose loving care this day could not happen [laughter], ladies and gentlemen":

(Now draw a big deep breath because it is the last one you are going to get as you become caught up in the fire and thunder of your address. And you don't really have to go to the bathroom. It is just your imagination.)

"I suppose you think I am going to give you one of those 'You are going out into the world' speeches. [Laughter and cries of 'Hear, hear.']

"Well, you are perfectly right. You are going out into the world and it is a mess, a frightened, neurotic, gibbering mess. And there isn't anyone out there to help you because all the people who are already out there are in a worse state than you are, because they have been there longer and a good number of them have given up.

"Yes, my young friends, you are going to take your bright and shining faces into a jungle, but a jungle where all the animals are insane. You are going from delinquency to desuetude without even an interlude of healthy vice. You haven't the strength for vice. That takes energy, and all the energy of this time is needed for fear. That takes energy too. And what energy is left over is needed for running down the rabbit holes of hatred to avoid thought. The rich hate the poor and taxes. The young hate the draft. The Democrats hate the Republicans and everybody hates the Russians. Children are shooting their parents and parents are drowning their children when they think they can get away with it. No one can plan one day ahead because all certainties are gone. War is now generally admitted to be not only unwinnable but actually suicidal and so we think of war and plan for war and design war and drain our nations of every extra penny of treasure to make the weapons which we admit will destroy us. Generals argue with Secretaries about how much *they*'ve got and how much *we*'ve got to fight the war that is admitted will be the end of all of us.

"And meanwhile there is no money for the dams and the schools and the highways and the housing and the streets for our clotted and festering traffic. That's what you are going out to. Going out? Hell, you've been in it for years. And you have to scrape the bottom to avoid thinking. Some of us hate niggers and some of us hate the people who hate niggers and it is all the same thing, anything to keep from thinking. Make money! Spend all of your time trying to avoid taxes, taxes for the sixty billion dollars for the weapons for the war that is unthinkable.

"Let's face it. We are using this war and this rumor of war to avoid thought. But if you work very hard and are lucky and have a good tax man, then when you are fifty, if your heart permits, you and your sagging wife can make a tired and bored but first-class trip to Europe to stare at the works of dead people who were not afraid. But you won't see it. You'll be too anxious to get home to your worrying. You'll want to get your blown prostate home in time for your thrombosis. The only exciting thing you can look forward to is a heart attack. And while you have been in Athens on the Acropolis not seeing the Parthenon, you have missed two murders and the nasty divorce of two people you do not know and are not likely to, but you hate to miss it.

"These are your lives, my darlings, if you avoid cancer, plane crashes and automobile accidents. Your lives! Love? A nervous ejaculation while drunk. Romance? An attempt to be mentioned in a column for having accompanied the Carrot Queen to a slaughterhouse. Fun? Electric canes at a convention. Art? A deep-seated wish to crash the Book-of-the-Month Club. Sport? A television set and a bottle of the proper beer. Ambition? A new automobile every year. Work? A slot in a corporate chain of command. Religion? A private verbal contract with a deity you don't believe in and a public front pew in your superior's church. Children? Maybe a psychiatrist can keep them out of the detention home.

"Am I boring you, you nervous sons of bitches? Am I keeping you from your moldy pleasures? And you, President Booker T. Talmadge, are you restless to get to your rare roast beef? Regents, are you lusting for the urinal? And you, Professors—are you cooking up some academic skulduggery for the Faculty Club?

"Now, you say hopelessly, he is going to give us his science lecture. And you are right again, but it is the last time you will be right.

"Your professors will squabble about how many millenniums ago it was when a man picked up fire and it burned him, and he picked it up again and it burned a forest and he brought it home and it burned his shelter and he threw it on a piles of bones and leaned to cook and he found a piece of shining metal under a bonfire and wore it for a while and then hammered it to a cutting edge. It took him hundreds of thousands of years to get used to fire. The very concept of fire so frightened him that he refused to think about it. He called it a god or the property of a god, and gradually over hundreds of thousands of years he reluctantly evolved a set of rules and techniques and mores for thinking about fire. Then he loved it finally and it was the first lord of the hearth, the center of his being, the symbol of his ease and safety.

Many more people got warm than got burned and so he gradually inspected this extension of himself, this power and found what made it do the things it does. But that was the end of the process, not the beginning. And meanwhile there must have been a good number of men who, seeing a forest burning, shrieked out that this devil would destroy the world.

"Do you know what is wrong with you? It isn't niggers or Democrats or Russians. The quantum theory tumbled your convictions about order, so you refused to think about it. The Expanding Universe blasted your homocentric galaxy, and then the fissionable atom ripped the last of your fire-minded world to ribbons. For the first time you have unlimited power and an unlimited future, the great drama of magic and alchemy. And are you glad? No, you go groveling to analysts to find out what is the matter with you. You will not inspect the new world that is upon you.

"Wouldn't it be wonderful if you could look at your world and say, and hear yourself, 'This was once true but it is no longer true. We must make new rules about this and this. We must abandon our dear war, which once had a purpose, and our hates which once served us.'

"You won't do it. It will have to slip up on you in the course of the generations. But wouldn't it be wonderful if you could greet the most wonderful time in the history of our world with wonder rather than with despair?"

Now you bow coldly and try to get out alive. The audience is silent and as you walk up the aisle working at your suffering crotch you hear whispered comments. "The old fart. Who does he think he is?" "Nigger lover." "Did you hear him say those Communists weren't dangerous? He must be one."

Say—I like that! I may make that speech myself—from a helicopter. But you may borrow it if you like. And invite me to hear you deliver it. I'll cover your exit and bring a few of the boys.

Oh, Elaine will be so mad at me!

yours
John

I told you I was a spastic writer.

The Private Eye

BY MARSHALL FRADY

At that smoky hour of a summer sundown out on the weedy south fringes of Atlanta, it seemed no more, from a distance, than a young man in a knit golf shirt, lingering outside a small auto-parts office, chatting with someone in a powder-blue station wagon. He was standing by the car with an easy slouch, lightly tossing something—keys, a lighter—in one hand, while late-afternoon traffic whisked by on the highway and neon signs began stammering on at a nearby shopping center.

In an olive-brown Impala parked alone in a far corner of that shopping center, a small thin man in blue jeans muttered, "Yeah, that's him." He lowered his binoculars for a moment, glanced around, then lifted them delicately for another long peer. "That's our boy. Sho is. I can tell just by the shape of how he stands—I know him by the way he holds his body. And that's her station wagon, too, by God. That's her in there for sure." Slumped behind the steering wheel, huddling behind the binoculars, he went on in the rapid, eager whisper of someone smuggling out an exotic confidence. "They definitely having some sort of confab. Notice those backlights—something's not settled, the way her foot's on that brake. No doubt about it, they deep into that screwing syndrome—she wants to get laid tonight, but he's telling her he can't, something's come up, and she's not a bit happy about it. It's heavy, man. Course, true love's always heavy." He suddenly dropped the binoculars to the seat and scuffled forward to snick on his car's ignition as, in the distance, the station wagon now began backing to turn into the highway. "Yes indeed, never so heavy as when it's got that extra tang of the illicit."

Few there are among us who have not at least fleetingly fancied that we might—God, what if!—be under such scrutiny. George Compton is, in fact, the man we feared was watching us. (Compton is disinclined to allow real names, including his own, to be used in this article. Consequently, all names have been changed.)

These moments of dim unease are, quite probably, about all that's left now of that old archaic dread, in another stauncher age and in our own lost Sunday-school childhoods, of the vigilant and unblinking gaze of the Lord, when not a sparrow fell without His notice, the very hairs of our heads were numbered, all our deeds were inked into the Big Ledger for a final accounting on the Day of Judgment. As one of Graham Greene's capsized clerics somewhere ponders, "There were no detective stories in the age of faith. . . . God used to be the only detective when people believed in Him." But George Compton and his myriad obscure colleagues—all the plumbers, political or personal—have become the inheritors, by default, of that old omniscient eye on high: the anonymous bookkeepers of the inner heart's most furtive secrets, the unseen recording angels of sin and guilt and retribution.

For fourteen years, Compton himself, like some attendant sprite of the illicit, has been the witness unawares, the secret sharer of countless assignations and mischiefs in south Florida motels, Memphis warehouses at midnight, even once a leprous resort along the lost wild cliff-coasts of Mexico ("runaway Junior League housewife, that one was, run away about as far as it's possible to get from all that. Found her barefooted, in beads, playing a flute among the flies"). Compared to the conventional dramatic pop image of his kind—such ponderously jaded knights-errant as, say, Gene Hackman in *Night Moves*—Compton suggests more some vagrant jockey. Or, in the black wool-knit dock-worker's cap that he affects with dark glasses, a slightly dissolute leprechaun. A wispy and boyish figure, bowlegged, with a ceaseless elfin energy in the eager scamper of his moves and banter, he is disposed to snug short-sleeved alligator shirts, pipe-stem denim trousers, straggle-lace tennis shoes, togs

in all reminiscent of a grammar-school playground. Indeed, he
has about him the slightly frayed innocence, the discreetly dam-
aged freshness of a choirboy gone truant, his glittering eyes only
a little elusive and murky now and then in the early glare of
morning, his hand only faintly trembling when he lights his cigarette, lifts his cup of coffee. He happens, though, to possess a
singularly canny and articulate insight into his particular place
in these times.

Snuggling on his dark glasses, he swung out into the traffic a
few cars behind the station wagon. "It's nothing but paranoia
that keeps me and nine tenths of all other detectives in business
these days—a mixed blessing, in a way, because it's gotten a lot
harder to work cases since whoever you're following is also
thinking along those lines. Everybody's seeing double now—in
fact, quadruple. It's like a fuddled television picture picked up
from a station a long way away, with all kinds of warped and
wavery ghosts around the figures—nobody knows which is real,
the ghosts or the actual image. The thing is, we just about been
turned by the megacorporations into one big coast-to-coast suburban office park and shopping center; it's all gonna be Los Angeles soon, and what that's brought us is a general case of the
Los Angeles dreads. Nobody's able to relate to anybody else any
longer. God's not around any more, and nobody knows what's
actually happening to 'em now, or who anybody else really is.
Everybody's living in their own sealed cellophane bag."

Compton says, "Just as sure as there was an age of faith and
an age of reason, what we into now, buddy, is the age of paranoia. I mean, goddamn, *every*body's fantasizing—I'll get a call
from some guy who wants to pay me twenty-five dollars to
watch his wife one night working at the car wash. A lady comes
to me who met her husband while they were both married to
someone else, and now six years later, she's convinced he's running around again. I ask why, and she says, 'Because suddenly
he's started acting just like he used to act when he was seeing
me. He's happy all the time.' Christ. People call you just crazy to
give you leads—got to where I was spending half the day on the
phone listening to breathless leads from the private hallucinations of strangers."

So epidemic and ferocious an avidity has it become, says
Compton, that for a while he had to resort to removing his name

from the Yellow Pages. "What I am, see, is that extra third eye they all want. They want me to give 'em that secret second sight on what's actually happening to them with their wives and business partners and their own children even—if they're really loved, if they're being made a fool of." He was once retained, Compton recalls, by a grand young landowner in south Georgia whose wife had confessed to a brief dalliance with the local Pontiac dealer. "She swore to him it had only happened twice, it had been a year ago, and it'd never happen again. But he had me trail that woman day and night for almost two months. She was completely clean, she was being totally straight with him. I finally had to tell him I just couldn't be wasting his money any longer, there just wasn't anything there. But somehow he still couldn't find it in his heart to believe her. And damn if he didn't wind up divorcing her anyway about six months later." Most often, Compton finds, "they don't want innocence. I mean, they just don't want to know it if it ain't what they wanted to know when they hired you. They want me to bring 'em guilt. They get downright mad sometimes if I come back and tell them there's nothing to their fantasies—almost want to fight."

On the whole, Compton has wound up with his own special vision of what the human species amounts to. And it's hardly the stuff of high literature. Rather, by his epiphanies, we are all made up of the pulp-novel truths of a Fannie Hurst soap opera, or at best, one of John O'Hara's lesser suburban melodramas. "The so-called universal human experience," he sniffs, "is nothing but a B movie." In fact, he has come to derive some purgative exaltation from watching, every Monday evening, the antic and elemental grotesqueries of human nature on *Let's Make a Deal*. "Hell, now, that speaks to me," he reports. "It's better than *Hamlet*."

In all this, Compton leads rather the precarious existence of a body collector in the midst of a medieval plague. "Paranoia, friend, is a condition as contagious as smallpox. You around it only a little while, you gonna start catching some of it. And it happens to be the staple I traffic in for a living. You almost need to be a celibate recluse, some kind of eunuch, to be safe from it all," he declares.

Asked what has kept him at it for fourteen years, Compton winces, then shrugs. "Hell, it's hard to explain. I guess one thing:

you're still as free as you were when you were a little boy playing alone in the backyard—you know, just you alone with your
own wits and imagination in your own world. It's probably a little bit what it's like for somebody writing stories and novels. I
like to see a case I'm working on change and develop, especially
one that's tricky where somebody's trying hard to throw me off.
It gives you sort of a feeling of being in complete control—it's a
bit of an ego trip, I admit."

He is, in a certain sense, the ultimate collector. "You wind up
being the world's greatest trivia expert after a while," he says.
Over the long course of his trackings, he has come by a sizable attic's accumulation of eclectic and incidental wisdom about the
vagaries of the race. "Like, the two rush seasons in this business
when you really run your ass off are around January and then
May to June—January because that's when folks turn loose with
all those parties, get drunk and hung over, and then take another
look at their lives and decide they want something else, their secretary or their best friend's husband or the paper boy, whatever.
In spring, it's just the weather warming up, the sap starts to rise
again, you know?"

More than anything else, what sustains and impels Compton is
sheer compulsive curiosity—the omnivorous curiosity of a six-
year-old which, in Compton, seems simply to have never sub-
sided. His obsession is working human crossword puzzles.
"Human nature ain't nothing but a matter of patterns, you can
depend on that. Like on this case where I been called to watch a
wife somebody's wondering about, I've gotten to where I can
usually tell about the second day whether I'm gonna find anything or not. She'll take on certain patterns if there's anything
going on. She'll circle the guy's business seven or eight times a
day, then cruise his home at night even if it's only been a half
hour since she left him. It's total concentration, man, when
you're in an affair, with everything you do from waking to sleeping focused right on it, and a complete abandon and recklessness
about consequences—kind of a quiet berserkness, kind of a de-
mentia, really. All of which, of course, only makes them more
vulnerable—delivers 'em right into my sack. A woman'll plunge
into something like that usually only once in her life, but men
are more sentimental in a way—might happen to them three or

four times. But the more passionate it is, the more strictly it's all going to be programed. Meeting the exact same time of the day, the same days every week—I don't know, maybe there's something about the regularity itself that turns 'em on, that systematic anticipation, sin on a schedule where they can just sort of give themselves up to a ritual and beat what's larger and beyond them, like fate. It all comes down to patterns. That's all human beings are about."

The particular crossword puzzle that had Compton now trailing the station wagon—first presented to him, as usual, in a call from an attorney—seemed conventional enough: a young husband, suddenly and unexpectedly sued for divorce by his wife, with rather clobbering demands in alimony and child support, was given, shortly, to grim speculations about some unknown Lothario poised just offstage. Compton had earlier stopped by the attorney's office in downtown Atlanta, emerging after a minute with a blank white envelope from which, once back in his car, he ruffled out his retainer check, then several color snapshots taken at cozy and idle moments back in the couple's oblivious simple days of wine-and-pizza happiness. A glimpse of the two of them cuddled together in a commodious black Naugahyde lounger in a glarish yellow pine-paneled den, him gazing at the camera flash with a vaguely startled grin which, considered now from the front seat of Compton's car, seemed to hint, already, at some dull uneasiness. She—perched in his lap, now the unsuspecting quarry—smiled mildly and musingly, some doe-like haziness about her, and the fresh dewy lambent face of numberless other supermarket madonnas of outer suburbia. "Her name's Judy," Compton said. "Sweet-looking little gal, actually. But I've found it's the ones who look so quiet and demure, those nice little Karen Valentine types, who'll throw themselves into the real hell-for-leather affairs. . . ."

Trailing several cars behind her now, Compton remarked, "Couldn't tell you how many station wagons I've followed over the years in this work—station wagons and Mercedes, thousands of 'em. Always seems to be one or the other, for some reason." She turned into a road, with Compton after her, that led down into one of those instant mazed subdivisions of the New South's self-reconstitution into one vast San Fernando Valley—a fathomless curlicueing of culs-de-sac with Disneyland-tidy toy houses imitating Spanish villas and Aspen chalets ranked in endless and fiercely geometric reduplication across a moonscape of gullied red clay and scanty jack pines, all bare to a blank unblinking sky: a neighborhood that seemed finally some zone beyond all time and place, without past or memory, part of that single monolithic anonymous American suburbia where all the little family scenes in the television commercials take place. "Yeah, what I figured from the way they were talking back there —she's heading back to her house," Compton said. "This is the limbo, man, out here where she lives. Whole new class of people we invented, living out in these subdivisions—been manufactured out of thin air by the real-estate developers and the savings-and-loan folks. Hell, ten years ago they were just good ole boys driving bread trucks and running filling stations, living in dumpy little frame houses with geraniums growing in those half tires in their front yards. Now, they living almost like the doctors and bankers—they got them split-levels with charcoal grills on the patio and automatic garage doors."

Pausing at a stop sign, Compton quickly lit a cigarette. ". . . and the cases I get out of these suburbs now has increased out of sight. It's not the folks suddenly going haywire when they start approaching middle-age crisis, like you might think—it's the young marrieds, people in their middle thirties living out in places like this, just beginning to achieve some stability in their businesses, got a family and a purty little house. What it is is boredom. Like that song of Peggy Lee's sometime back, *Is That All There Is?* Our little girl here, she's just a bored housewife in a cul-de-sac. That, and mobility. Can you imagine back, say, in the days of the frontier, the problems you'd have carrying on an affair like Judy's doing now? No more. We in the TV-dinner age of affairs—instant and disposable."

It had been on a preliminary cruise through the neighborhood the Saturday before that Compton, scanning the geography and checking addresses after the attorney's call, happened to fall in behind Judy's station wagon as she was pulling out of her driveway. He followed her on to a nearby warren of apartments where "damn if I didn't hop right on top of 'em." To his surprised delight, she parked before one of the apartments and disappeared inside. After only a few minutes, a yellow Dodge Charger with black racing stripes pulled up beside her station wagon, a youngish man climbed out, clad in a maroon jumpsuit, and went in after her. "That just don't happen often, you make a strike like that the very first time out," Compton later recounted jubilantly. "The guy didn't come back out until around nine-thirty that night, and she followed him a few minutes later and drove back to her house. That was their hole. You ever find their hole, then you got 'em. You got it licked—they gonna be in that hole whenever they're together, 'cause that's the only place they feel safe. All it is is fox hunting."

Returning the next afternoon, Sunday, Compton found her station wagon again parked in front of the apartment, its back to the curb. "That's so nobody can see her license plate, I guess," he snorted. "That's just one step above Edgar Allan Poe, ain't it?" Then, as he was easing past for a close squint, she suddenly emerged from the door with her two small children—no more, for that instant, than ten feet from Compton, he merely emitting, at this abrupt startling ambush of immediate and intimate adjacency, a low light suppressed, "Umh. Um-hummh. . . ." She seemed to pause a moment on the steps—a tall and luxuriously tapered figure with long lank black hair, in pale jeans and a lime terry-cloth sweater—regarding the slow passage of Compton's car with a calm inscrutable flat gaze of dark glasses as she stood mute and composed and somehow briefly exposed, defenseless in the brilliant sunlight.

"She sure got a look," Compton muttered as he turned at the far end of the parking lot. "I'm not too crazy about that. Don't like for that to happen more'n once or twice." He then parked his Impala around the corner of another apartment unit. "Let's just set here a few minutes. Wouldn't do for her to spot us cruising right back by." Snatching down the bill of his train-engineer cap and settling back in the seat, his elbow slung out the window, he shortly fell to ruminating. "Damn pleasant-looking lady. Makes you wonder what happened. I did find out who the guy is—fella name of Larry Roy, Larry Roy Telfair, owns him a little auto-parts store. Just happens to turn out ole Larry Roy's in the middle of getting himself a divorce, too. Seems the two of them first met about two years ago in a Sunday-school class for young marrieds at the Baptist church. No way of telling yet how long this thing's been going on, but that would have meant she was pregnant when they first eyed each other. But of course, a lot of these things happen right soon after a woman's had a baby—you know, the first fella who comes along and pays her a lot of attention and makes her feel she's desirable again as a woman, before you know it she's seeing him in a room at the Ramada Inn every Monday and Thursday afternoon. Hell. . . ." He fastidiously spit out a small speck of something from his front tooth.

"But my people don't really want to take this thing to court, they just want some cards to play when the lawyers sit down to talk. Nothing but one big continuous poker game I'm involved in with this work. All it is. It makes these cases a lot easier, too, since you don't need that hard-core evidence any longer, just circumstantial enough for reasonable presumption of sinning. So all we really after on this one are some of those negotiables, you know what I mean?"

Pulling out finally to take another leisurely pass by the apartment, Compton drove to the entrance to the main road, then mumbled furiously, "Lookahere, lookahere," as, directly in front of his car, a yellow Charger turned into the apartment drive and swept by him, the face behind the steering wheel heavy and blunt and sun-scorched with fine ink-black coiffured hair, the eyes rheumy with some blur of pool chlorine or whiskey, giving Compton in that instant only a quick bland glance in which there may have been the briefest glint of wariness. "Godamighty-damn," Compton murmured, "we bumping into 'em ever which direction here. This is like getting caught in the middle of a pinball game." He pulled on out into the road and drove a distance to the first side street, then hastily backed around and headed toward the apartments again. But, approaching the entrance, he found the station wagon and Charger both leaving, turning in separate directions. "That's funny," he said, his voice a bit thin and light. "They seem to be acting sort of restless all of a sudden. Can't believe they've sniffed they being watched. Well, shit, we already way ahead of the game, I don't want to press 'em too close. I'll just let it float loose for another night."

Now, this Monday dusk, the third day of his surveillance, Compton tagged after Judy's station wagon as it curled on through the streets of her neighborhood, past empty sidewalks scattered with tricycles and foot scooters, living-room windows already dimly tinted with the blue gloom of television suppers inside. "You know, it looks like she's just driving around here

aimlessly," Compton said after a while. "It's like she'll do anything to avoid having to go back to that house in that cul-de-sac.
That house is a setting of her past." Then he said, "You know,
she doesn't have those children with her tonight, which is
strange. Hell, could it be she's not actually going back to her
house at all?" Presently, the station wagon swung into a corner
hamburger drive-in. On Compton's second pass, it was swinging
back out. And after following her through a few more turns,
Compton suddenly barked, "Be damn. Know what? She's heading straight back for those apartments now. Sure as hell." He
softly chattered as he accelerated on after her. "All right. All
right. I think we gonna be getting us some of those negotiables
this evening, by God. This is turning out to be a dream, like I
figured—like stealing candy it's so easy. By God, I *knew* I had
this thing pegged as a pattern case."

Compton himself dwells with his second wife, Brenda, and
their two small children in a leafy sedate Norman Rockwell
neighborhood nestled just off Atlanta's fabled Peachtree Street.
It is a simple and inconspicuous frame house, painted moss
green, with a meagerly furnished front room, drawn curtains and
wan lighting. Through a narrow door to the right is Compton's
small spare office, paneled in an orange-lacquered pine. He and
Brenda—a sleek girl with pale sunny hair and a pleasant
freckled prettiness, quiet and measured of word, whom he found
at a quarter-horse show in Indiana six years ago—seldom ven-
ture out for any social gatherings. Through the long months of
spring and summer, if he isn't on the road, Compton will pass
the blue cool of the evenings alone in his fenced backyard, tend-
ing his patch of a vegetable garden—tomatoes, squash, collard
greens. His neighbors for the most part are not quite certain of
his profession. "It makes 'em wonder when they see me coming
out of the house in the middle of the morning to get the mail.
People get a little uneasy these days with any unknown quantity
in their midst."

Compton has one consuming extra-professional enthusiasm—
turtles. Sitting alone in his dark car along outback roads, he is
given to collecting any he spies moseying over the pavement,
bumbling along the weedy edges of ditches—bringing them on
back to his house, where, at times, he will have a whole congre-

gation of them, named for the parties in the case he was on, shuffling and bumping in washtubs around his yard. He seems to have found some special mystic communion with them, patient and impassive creatures, solitary and enduring, moving with discreet deliberation, as ancient as Eden and The Fall. "When I was a little boy," Compton declared one evening as he was driving to a stakeout, "I used to watch 'em all night long out my bedroom window, moving around out there in the backyard. May not think it, but a turtle's got a personality, you sit there watching it long enough. And they so fuckin' tough. You can find one all mangled on the side of the road, been hit by a tractor and missing three fourths its parts, but by God after a little while you see that mutha starting to move again across the pavement. They just keep on truckin'. But nobody yet really knows anything about 'em. All you can find is just a paragraph or two in these musty ole books. They still a goddamn enigma, common as they are."

Occasionally, in the cavernous green faery glooms of Atlanta twilights, Compton and Brenda will have a certain few friends over for bourbon and steaks on the cement patio just outside his basement recreation room. Most of these visitors tend to have a touch of the ravaged and refugee about them: a writer somewhat sour and moldering with angst, a derelict and weedy young architect, who arrives usually walloping drunk and commences to play the piano with galactic splendor. Toward the end of one such evening, Compton (reposing well sloshed himself in a plastic-mesh lawn lounger) began to discourse: "Naw, not too many people last long in this business. It can be hell on a marriage. Psychologically, the mortality rate's pretty high. You got to have a kind of perverse love for it to last any while—got to be goddamn *called*, in a way. Want to know what separates the artists from the hacks? The good ones, you can throw him on a rock and he can scramble—something he was just born with, like a cat. It takes some real delicacy sometimes. You working these things without any vested authority at all—just those primeval damn instincts when you out there on that nether edge with people. You can't just slam 'em up on the side of the head. If you do, you become a cop. Working any case is ninety percent a matter of patiently letting somebody's character develop before you. It's all a game of chasing glimmers. You hanging, waiting for that one quick little accidental glimmer in a situation, and then you dive into it, and it opens up the whole picture pattern."

In truth, Compton's craft is not without its own intuitive and existential graces, and by all indications Compton himself is one of the virtuosos of the medium. "I don't believe in sitting still," he allows. "You can get out of the natural pitch and rhythm of real life like that." He has a discomfort with the elaborate mechanical and electronic equipage employed by many investigators, confining himself instead to minimal props such as a pair of binoculars, a Nikon, a vintage 8mm movie camera. "You start relying on all that technology and gadgetry, it'll dull your instincts. You can lose your art in a hurry like that."

Compton was to his art peculiarly born and nurtured. His father, who now desultorily occupies himself with a general store outside a musty Georgia junction near Atlanta, in fact happened to be a professional gambler through most of his son's boyhood. To Compton growing up, his father was seldom seen and mythic, and Compton still insists, "I'd rather be around professional gamblers than just about anybody else I know. Best company in the world, nobody funnier and smarter about fate and folly and the real metaphysics of life than gamblers. They exist totally out there on that windy edge, man."

Compton, in his teens, wound up working four years on the night shift at the Atlanta Greyhound Bus Terminal, fetching baggage, answering phones, sweeping the tile floors. "Best job I ever had," he fondly reminisces. "Damn place has never had its doors closed since it was built, and something was always happening. It was like being in a carnival that just went on forever."

It was in college that Compton, more or less as a petty-cash expedient, sidled into a few incidental investigative chores for Retail Credit. "It was strictly Class D ball, but I knew the minute I was into it that I was home. I was there." He was then only twenty. From that, he paced through the next six years as an agent for such interests as Mutual of Omaha, at last peeling off from a large private investigative firm in Atlanta and, with an elder from that firm, a still fitfully ambulatory seventy-four-year-old detective named Nelson Brantley, opened up his own shop: Brantley & Compton. "I was ready to fly, man."

Compton recalls, "I was totally and surgically detached on a case. I wasn't much more than a hunting machine." Indeed, photographs of Compton from those years are like barely recognizable glimpses of him in some alien incarnation, ruthlessly sober in horn-rimmed glasses and neat dark blazers and collegiate-stripe ties. "I could of gone straight, without a blink, right on into the F.B.I. or C.I.A.," he says. But then in the late sixties, with a sudden swarm of commissions to track down runaways, Compton began moving more and more into the inner rainbowed Dionysian region of the counterculture—and, as it turned out, never emerged again. In his tarryings among communes of gentle young subterraneans in San Francisco basements and out on New Mexico mesas, he underwent an aurora borealis Zen dawning of consciousness that worked on him an almost corporal transfiguration. "It was like Lazarus waking up," he remembers. It became his suspicion that the American corporate estate, which he was continuing to serve as an agent in personnel and credit investigations, in fact comprised the superstructure of totalitarianism. The enlightenment left Compton an imperfect changeling, hung in some arrested middle stage of metamorphosis between two profoundly different sensibilities. "Like when the banks call me to check out suspected homosexuals in their personnel—and I mean, banks are still just crazy about queers. I happen to have liberated ideas on queers now, too, but do you think I'm gonna tell the bank president that? Hell, no, I just become a cop again."

It has become Compton's lot now to live in an abiding disquiet about the implicit indecency of what he is doing. "I mean, really," he will grumble periodically, "why the hell should I be watching and reporting on some poor lonely housewife who's just trying to get some pleasure in her life? She's probably got every right to want it." But at the same time, Compton remains extravagantly testy to the faintest suggestion, from anyone else, of the same sort of contempt. Returning from a morning's conference with one woman considering contracting his services, Compton snapped, "No, it didn't work out, and I'm glad of it. I didn't like her attitude at all toward me. I was just a little distasteful to her, you know. To hell with the bitch, I don't need that from anybody." One reason he and Brenda rarely range beyond the comfortable seclusion of their life at home is that, almost always at any party or large soiree, Compton has learned he can depend on someone finally accosting him with the demand, "I wonder, how can you really live with yourself, doing what you do, rummaging into other people's privacy?" To which Compton will blush red as a radish, a small muscle flickering along his jaw, and briskly inquire, "And who do you work for, you work for a bank or law firm here? Oh, yeah, them, they called me just a couple weeks ago to check out one of their people."

Privately, though, Compton is engaged in an endless ragged skirmish with his own nicer sensibilities—a disconcertment considerably complicated by the fact that now "it's gotten to where I'll wind up identifying more with who I'm following than who hired me to follow them. That ain't too good in this business. I pass in and out of schizophrenia about four times on a case. I'm not any better than these people I'm following, we really the same. Hell, I'm the whore in all this, I know that. But I can only deal from where I am—I'm just the hired hand, but at least I know who I am, and if you lose that, then where are you? In the beginning, I never felt any connection at all, but over the last several years, I've begun to find there's just no way to spend a week shadowing somebody, copying every single move in their life, without there growing this strange kind of closeness and intimacy between me and them."

Compton's facility for being a psychic chameleon is both his special art and special uneasiness now. "I'll have me an alias—another identity—that gets to be so natural on a case, I think if somebody jumped up and started hitting me on the head with a stick, I'd blurt out that name before my own. That's the best disguise of all, being that comfortable in a role. But you worry sometimes that, passing by a mirror, you won't see any reflection at all, just a room full of furniture."

But the world in which Compton dwells is itself largely one of mirages. In the late lost hours of one Wednesday night, Compton sat blearily hunched over a bourbon and water in the narrow dank cave of a bar long miles away from Atlanta and home—one of those Shangri-la lounges in the patent-brand motels that have clamorously collected along all the interstates blazed on now into the South's last primeval outbacks. Over a swimming swoon of liquid guitars from the jukebox, with ole boys from nearby scanty little towns now roosting gawkily around him in cranberry blazers and diamond-patterned dress shirts, Compton confessed, "It's all a bedlam, man. Half the time, the realities turn out to be more Byzantine than the paranoias—some woman comes to me absolutely convinced her husband is seeing another gal, so I check it out, and it's a totally ridiculous notion, nothing like that at all. He's running around with another man. Damn right, it's Chinatown. Also, most of the time when I get into a case, I realize right away the wrong person's being followed—it ought to have been the person who hired me. Hell, it's like trying to find your way through a maze of trick windows. It's all shadows—nothing but shadows."

For all his frets of conscience, Compton finally remains the ultimate outsider—living in a kind of free float out on the edge of the great nihilistic void, in a twilight of limitless possibility just beyond all the common orderly gravities of truth and good and evil. And every few months, with Brenda, he simply flees it all—that chaos of appearances and fantasies, innocence and guilt—to Las Vegas and rapt forty-eight-hour communions at the crap tables. There at least, on calm green surfaces of felt pooled in quiet hooded glows, it is all reduced and contained in the design and sacramental ceremonies of a game, a formal metaphor of limitless possibility abstracted out of the furies and heat—pure pattern. "When I'm over those crap tables out there," he says, "I've never known such peace. It's like paradise."

On his way that Monday for the last evening's surveillance of the young housewife in south Atlanta, Compton declared, "Once a year, maybe, you'll get one that actually interests you. Big criminal case or missing person, something like that—the kind that'll give you those blood rushes. They'll make you over again. But after that, I just run on automatic pilot. Naw, it just don't happen in petty domestic shit like this. This is the kind of thing that just keeps the shoes on the baby." But as he headed south again, there seemed some irrepressible rising giddiness in the car. And about an hour later, after staking out the auto-parts shop and then trailing her station wagon on through her neighborhood, as he picked her up again as she wheeled out of the hamburger drive-in he murmured almost amorously, "All right. She's heading straight back for those apartments now. We gonna get it all in focus tonight."

From several cars behind, he watched her station wagon now

curving down the hill toward the apartment entrance—and then right on past it. Compton blinked. He was silent for a long minute as he dangled along after her in abrupt uncertainty. "Weird. She's just not going to cooperate, is she?" He began feverishly shuffling through the deck of possibilities: "I don't know, it could be a totally different case now, 'cause we informed the client this morning what was happening. You never know what they'll do once you let 'em in on the story, they can mess the whole thing up good. Course, you'd think these two'd naturally be a little spooky in their situation, but then the thing to remember, anybody involved in this sort of thing, nothing's ever gonna happen to you. They could have actually made me, though. Sho could. There was just a little bit too much brushing past each other in that apartment lot yesterday. I doubt it, but they could have. Course, one thing about them making you, they never know how long you actually been on 'em, and lots of times they just give up right there. Still, I don't think . . ."

Ahead of Compton, the station wagon now slowed and pulled into a curb market. "God*damn*," Compton whined. He floated past her, down the road and around a curve, then back around in the parking lot of a bank. "That's the thing about them stopping on you like that, every time you gotta go through your setups again. And it's still just a little too bright and clear—summer's the worst for this kind of surveillance with those long afternoons going on until nine o'clock. I prefer that overcast winter weather."

From a parking lot across the road, Compton stood waiting under the aluminum-slat awning of a television showroom, watching behind dark glasses until the station wagon backed out, swerved around and then headed toward the apartments. "I'm almost afraid to say anything," Compton murmured, as he pulled swiftly out into the road after her. Then, drifting on down the hill, Compton breathed, "There she goes—she's turning. She's in the hole. She's in the hole. I got her. You just have to wait long enough, see. He's probably already in there waiting for her. This is the way I like it, now."

Driving a short distance past the apartment entrance, Compton looped back and turned in after her—but the station wagon had somehow, inexplicably, vanished. "Strange, optical slip here —I could have sworn—damn, I can't believe she's made me. But

that was awfully foxy, turning in there and then right back out
again. Unless she was checking to see if he . . ." He paused.
"That's what it was. Bet you. That's the pattern, too, cruising by
when you can't actually be with 'em. That was her strike on him,
was what. But what the hell, we got the other end of the stick if
he's still back there at his auto-parts store."

On the way there, suddenly, at no more than an instant's blur
of a car passing in the other direction, Compton snapped, "There
he is, there he is—and that's her in there with him." Turning in a
vast fuming of dust, Compton crooned, "That's what this game's
all about, buddy—you notice I ain't met any of 'em from the
back." Surging after them, he leaned back luxuriously with one
arm stretched out straight against the wheel, his other hand
lighting a cigarette with a snick of his Zippo. "Yessir. It's not
only patience, it's that sixth sense of thinking like they're thinking, *feeling like they feeling*—you just happen to be at the right
place at the right time. Yeah, there they go, by God, they turning
down that road to the apartments." Compton, turning after
them, then slowed. "We'll just hang back here a little bit, give
'em a chance to get settled in without our booming right in there
behind them."

But again, when Compton eased on into the entrance drive,
the curb in front of the apartment was blank. They had simply
disappeared like swallows in the nightfall. "I tell you, I'm getting
a stink off this case. Breaking patterns like that is hardly ever
done unless you're trying to shake somebody. But it's usually the
older ones who're cool like that, because they aren't obsessive,
it's not their whole life—they can be tough as a snake. But these
two, they just too young to be pros."

He drove back to her neighborhood, where he found her house
empty, but with all its rooms brightly lit. "This is getting awfully
strange. It looks more occupied now than it ever has. Hell, I'm
gonna check his place—nobody's been there for the past two
weeks, but it's just down the road." Larry Roy's house was also il-
luminated, with the yellow Charger parked in the driveway.
"Sonuvabitch. Know what? I bet that wasn't Judy at all in his
car—it was his wife. That's what the whole problem was between them tonight—he couldn't see her 'cause he had to come
back here with his wife for that last little ritual of divvying up
the spoils before the divorce." Then, coasting back down past the

house, he considered again, "Or, of course, he could be having second thoughts about the whole thing. I can see this thing from several sides of the prism. This little arrangement could of actually been going on for a long time now, and we could be coming in just as it's playing out. It may have all already happened. Now that it's down to the crunch, he might have started thinking about trying it over again with his wife. That's the pattern a lot of times, too."

Then, taking another pass by Judy's house, he found it lightless. "What the hell's going on?" He drove back to Larry Roy's house. It, too, was now dark, deserted, the driveway empty. "Goddamn," Compton said, "I almost get the feeling I'm being played with." Heading back once more to the apartments, he began to fret: "Damn, all I'm seeing on the road now is blue station wagons and Dodge Chargers, seems like. This ain't no work of art, that's for damn sure. I *knew* it was coming together too quick and neat." The curb in front of the apartment was still vacant, the windows black. "Well, the hell with it. My people have already got their ace—they know about her staying in there with him the other night for four hours. When the lawyers sit down to talk at the conference tomorrow morning, it'll be like a game of seven-card stud—they can raise on that ace showing, and if the other side ain't holding one, too, they won it."

Nevertheless, at ten o'clock, when he had been instructed to turn it loose if nothing had developed by then, Compton was still making swoops past Judy's house, Larry Roy's, the apartment, the auto-parts shop. "Just say I'm off the clock now. I'm just curious what the hell's actually going on out here. They got to be around here somewhere."

It wasn't until after midnight, in fact, that he at last gave it up. On the way home, he stopped off at a lounge in a motel just off the expressway, plopping himself with a scrub of his jeans on the maroon velveteen nap, then proceeded to bolt down rapid successive bourbons. He fumed. "Well, fuck 'em, they'll both be married to somebody else six months from now anyway. Or maybe shoot each other in a couple of weeks. You think I really empathize with any of 'em on these cases? No more than a dog does a rabbit. You think I'll actually be talking about this scumbag situation even a week from now? I couldn't give less of a shit what happens to those people. You won't ever know, and you can drive yourself crazy if you let yourself get involved like that—like an endless series of coitus interruptus, one after another. Hell, I just hit my lick and move on to the next one. No other way you can make it in this business. You got to keep on moving."

The next morning, in a call from the attorney who had hired him, Compton was left with the somewhat amorphous denouement of the lawyers' negotiations, which he reported later as, "Well, we played our ace, and they must not've been holding any of their own, 'cause they folded right there. No alimony, not even two thirds the child support she was demanding. I still wouldn't mind knowing what the story really is down there. It began to get damn strange there with his wife in it suddenly, all that running around, those lights going on and off. Christ, who knows, it could have been that—but you never gonna know what was really happening. And that's all it ever really comes to, anyway."

That night, Compton flew with Brenda to Las Vegas.

Bourbon

BY WALKER PERCY

This is not written by a connoisseur of bourbon. Ninety-nine percent of bourbon drinkers know more about bourbon than I do.
It is about the aesthetic of bourbon drinking in general and in
particular of knocking it back neat.

I can hardly tell one bourbon from another, unless the other is
very bad. Some bad bourbons are even more memorable than
good ones. For example, I can recall being broke with some
friends in Tennessee and deciding to have a party and being
able to afford only two fifths of a $1.75 bourbon called Two Nat-
ural, whose label showed dice coming up five and two. Its taste
was memorable. The psychological effect was also notable. After
knocking back two or three shots over a period of half an hour,
the three male drinkers looked at each other and said in a single
voice: "Where are the women?"

I have not been able to locate this remarkable bourbon since.

Not only should connoisseurs of bourbon not read this article.
Neither should persons preoccupied with the perils of alcohol-
ism, cirrhosis, esophageal hemorrhage, cancer of the palate, and
so forth—all real enough dangers. I, too, deplore these afflictions.
But, as between these evils and the aesthetic of bourbon drinking, that is, the use of bourbon to warm the heart, to reduce the
anomie of the late twentieth century, to cut the cold phlegm of
Wednesday afternoons, I choose the aesthetic. What, after all, is
the use of not having cancer, cirrhosis, and such, if a man comes

home from work every day at five-thirty to the exurbs of
Montclair or Memphis and there is the grass growing and the little family looking not quite at him but just past the side of his
head, and there's Cronkite on the tube and the smell of pot roast
in the living room, and inside the house and outside in the pretty
exurb has settled the noxious particles and the sadness of the old
dying Western World, and him thinking: Jesus, is this it? Listening to Cronkite and the grass growing?

If I should appear to be suggesting that such a man proceed as
quickly as possible to anesthetize his cerebral cortex by ingesting
ethyl alcohol, the point is being missed. Or part of the point. The
joy of bourbon drinking is not the pharmacological effect of
C_2H_5OH on the cortex but rather the instant of the whiskey
being knocked back and the little explosion of Kentucky U.S.A.
sunshine in the cavity of the nasopharynx and the hot bosky
bite of Tennessee summertime—aesthetic considerations to
which the effect of the alcohol is, if not dispensable, at least secondary.

By contrast, scotch: for me (not, I presume, for a Scot), drinking scotch is like looking at a picture of Noel Coward. The whiskey assaults the nasopharynx with all the excitement of pare-
goric. Scotch drinkers (not all, of course) I think of as
upward-mobile Americans, Houston and New Orleans busi-
nessmen who graduate from bourbon about the same time they
shed seersuckers for Lilly slacks. Of course, by now these same
folk may have gone back to bourbon and seersucker for the same
reason, because too many Houston oilmen drink scotch.

Nothing, therefore, will be said about the fine points of sour
mash, straights, blends, bonded, except a general preference for
the lower proofs. It is a matter of the arithmetic of aesthetics. If
one drives the same pleasure from knocking back 80-proof bourbon as 100-proof, the formula is both as simple as $2+2=4$ and as
incredible as non-Euclidean geometry. Consider. One knocks
back five one-ounce shots of 80-proof Early Times or four shots
of 100-proof Old Fitzgerald. The alcohol ingestion is the same:

$$5\times40\%=2$$
$$4\times50\%=2$$

Yet in the case of the Early Times, one has obtained an extra
quantum of joy without cost to liver, brain, or gastric mucosa. A

bonus, pure and simple, an aesthetic gain as incredible as two parallel lines meeting at infinity.

An apology to the reader is in order, nevertheless, for it has just occurred to me that this is the most unedifying and even maleficent piece I ever wrote—if it should encourage potential alcoholics to start knocking back bourbon neat. It is also the unfairest. Because I am, happily and unhappily, endowed with a bad GI tract, diverticulosis, neurotic colon, and a mild recurring nausea, which make it less likely for me to become an alcoholic than my healthier fellow Americans. I can hear the reader now: Who is he kidding? If this joker has to knock back five shots of bourbon every afternoon just to stand the twentieth century, he's already an alcoholic. Very well. I submit to this or any semantic. All I am saying is that if I drink much more than this I will get sick as a dog for two days and the very sight and smell of whiskey will bring on the heaves. Readers beware, therefore, save only those who have stronger wills or as bad a gut as I.

The pleasure of knocking back bourbon lies in the plane of the aesthetic but at an opposite pole from connoisseurship. My preference for the former is or is not deplorable depending on one's value system—that is to say, how one balances out the Epicurean virtues of cultivating one's sensory end organs with the greatest discrimination and at least cost to one's health, against the virtue of evocation of time and memory and of the recovery of self and the past from the fogged-in disoriented Western World. In Kierkegaardian terms, the use of bourbon to such an end is a kind of aestheticized religious mode of existence, whereas connoisseurship, the discriminating but single-minded stimulation of sensory end organs, is the aesthetic of damnation.

Two exemplars of the two aesthetics come to mind:

Imagine Clifton Webb, scarf at throat, sitting at Cap d'Antibes on a perfect day, the little wavelets of the Mediterranean sparkling in the sunlight, and he is savoring a 1959 Mouton Rothschild.

Then imagine William Faulkner, having finished *Absalom, Absalom!*, drained, written out, pissed-off, feeling himself over the edge and out of it, nowhere, but he goes somewhere, his favorite hunting place in the Delta wilderness of the Big Sunflower River and, still feeling bad with his hunting cronies and maybe even a little phony, which he was, what with him trying to pretend that he was one of them, a farmer, hunkered down in the cold and rain after the hunt, after honorably passing up the does and seeing no bucks, shivering and snot-nosed, takes out a flat pint of any bourbon at all and flatfoots about a third of it. He shivers again but not from the cold.

Bourbon does for me what the piece of cake did for Proust.

1926: as a child watching my father in Birmingham, in the exurbs, living next to number-six fairway of the New Country Club, him disdaining both the bathtub gin and white lightning of the time, aging his own bourbon in a charcoal keg, on his hands and knees in the basement sucking on a siphon, a matter of gravity requiring cheek pressed against cement floor, the siphon getting going, the decanter ready, the first hot spurt into his mouth not spat out.

1933: my uncle's sun parlor in the Mississippi Delta and toddies on a Sunday afternoon, the prolonged and meditative tinkle of silver spoon against crystal to dissolve the sugar; talk, tinkle, talk; the talk mostly political: Roosevelt is doing a good job; no, the son of a bitch is betraying his class.

1934: drinking at a Delta dance, the boys in biswing jackets and tab collars, tough-talking and profane and also scared of the girls and therefore safe in the men's room. Somebody passes around bootleg bourbon in a Coke bottle. It's awful. Tears start from eyes, faces turn red. "Hot damn, that's good!"

1935: drinking at a football game in college. U.N.C. vs. Duke. One has a blind date. One is lucky. She is beautiful. Her clothes are the color of the fall leaves and her face turns up like a flower. But what to *say* to her, let alone what to do, and whether she is "nice" or "hot"—a distinction made in those days. But what to *say?* Take a drink, by now from a proper concave hip flask (a long way from the Delta Coke bottle) with a hinged top. Will she have a drink? No. But it's all right. The taste of the bourbon (Cream of Kentucky) and the smell of her fuse with the brilliant Carolina fall and the sounds of the crowd and the hit of the linemen in a single synesthesia.

1941: drinking mint juleps, famed southern bourbon drink, though in the Deep South not really drunk much. In fact they are drunk so seldom that when, say, on Derby Day somebody gives a julep party, people drink them like cocktails, forgetting that a good julep holds at least five ounces of bourbon. Men fall face-down unconscious, women wander in the woods disconsolate and amnesiac, full of thoughts of Kahlil Gibran and the limberlost.

Would you believe the first mint julep I had I was sitting not on a columned porch but in the Boo Snooker bar of the New Yorker Hotel with a Bellevue nurse in 1941? The nurse, a nice upstate girl, head floor nurse, brisk, swift, good-looking; Bellevue nurses, the best in the world and this one the best of Bellevue, at least the best looking. The julep, an atrocity, a heavy syrupy bourbon and water in a small glass clotted with ice. But good!

How could two women be more different than the beautiful languid Carolina girl and this swift handsome girl from Utica, best Dutch stock? One thing was sure. Each was to be courted, loved, drunk with, with bourbon. I should have stuck with bourbon. We changed to gin fizzes because the bartender said he came from New Orleans and could make good ones. He could and did. They were delicious. What I didn't know was that they were made with raw egg albumen and I was allergic to it. Driving her home to Brooklyn and being in love! What a lovely fine strapping smart girl! And thinking of being invited into her apartment where she lived alone and of her offering to cook a little supper and of the many kisses and the sweet love that already existed between us and was bound to grow apace, when on the Brooklyn Bridge itself my upper lip began to swell and little sparks of light flew past the corner of my eye like St. Elmo's fire. In the space of thirty seconds my lip stuck out a full three-quarter inch, like a shelf, like Mortimer Snerd. Not only was kissing out of the question but my eyes swelled shut. I made it across the bridge, pulled over to the curb and fainted. Whereupon this noble nurse drove me back to Bellevue, gave me a shot and put me to bed.

Anybody who monkeys around with gin and egg white deserves what he gets. I should have stuck with bourbon and have from that day to this.

The Car

BY HARRY CREWS

The other day, there arrived in the mail a clipping sent by a friend of mine. It had been cut from a Long Beach, California, newspaper and dealt with a young man who had eluded police for fifty-five minutes while he raced over freeways and through city streets at speeds up to 130 miles per hour. During the entire time, he ripped his clothes off and threw them out the window bit by bit. It finally took twenty-five patrol cars and a helicopter to catch him. When they did, he said that God had given him the car, and that he had "found God."

I don't want to hit too hard on a young man who obviously has his own troubles, maybe even is a little sick with it all, but when I read that he had found God in the car, my response was: *So say we all.* We have found God in cars, or if not the true God, one so satisfying, so powerful and awe-inspiring that the distinction is too fine to matter. Except perhaps ultimately, but pray we must not think too much on that.

The operative word in all this is *we.* It will not do for me to maintain that I have been above it all, that somehow I've managed to remain aloof from the national love affair with cars. It is true that I got a late start. I did not learn to drive until I was twenty-one; my brother was twenty-five before he learned. The reason is simple enough. In Bacon County, Georgia, where I grew up, many families had nothing with a motor in it. Ours was one such family. But starting as late as I did, I still had my share, and I've remembered them all, the cars I've owned. I remember them in just the concrete specific way you remember anything that changed your life. Especially I remember the early ones.

The first car I ever owned was a 1938 Ford coupe. It had no low gear and the door on the passenger side wouldn't open. I eventually put a low gear in it, but I never did get the door to work. One hot summer night on a clay road a young lady whom I'll never forget had herself braced and ready with one foot on the rearview mirror and the other foot on the wind vent. In the first few lovely frantic moments, she pushed out the wing vent, broke off the rearview mirror and left her little footprints all over the ceiling. The memory of it was so affecting that I could never bring myself to repair the vent or replace the headliner she had walked all over upside down.

Eight months later I lost the car on a rain-slick road between Folkston, Georgia, and Waycross. I'd just stopped to buy a stalk of bananas (to a boy raised in the hookworm and rickets belt of the South, bananas will always remain an incredibly exotic fruit, causing him to buy whole stalks at a time), and back on the road again I was only going about fifty in a misting rain when I looked over to say something to my buddy, whose nickname was Bonehead and who was half drunk in the seat beside me. For some reason I'll never understand, I felt the back end of the car get loose and start to come up on us in the other lane. Not having driven very long, I overcorrected and stepped on the brake. We turned over four times. Bonehead flew out of the car and shot down a muddy ditch about forty yards before he stopped, sober and unhurt. I ended up under the front seat, thinking I was covered with gouts of blood. As it turned out, I didn't have much wrong with me and what I was covered with was gouts of mashed banana.

The second car I had was a 1940 Buick, square, impossibly heavy, built like a Sherman tank, but it had a '52 engine in it. Even though it took about ten miles to get her open full bore, she'd do over a hundred miles an hour on flat ground. It was so big inside that in an emergency it could sleep six. I tended to live in that Buick for almost a year and no telling how long I would have kept it if a boy who was not a friend of mine and who owned an International Harvester pickup truck hadn't said in mixed company that he could make the run from New Lacy in Coffee County, Georgia, to Jacksonville, Florida, quicker than I could. He lost the bet, but I wrung the speedometer off the Buick, and also—since the run was made on a blistering day in July—melted four inner tubes, causing them to fuse with the tires, which were already slick when the run started. Four new tires and tubes cost more than I had or expected to have anytime soon, so I sadly put that old honey up on blocks until I could sell it to a boy who lived up toward Macon.

After the Buick, I owned a 1953 Mercury with three-inch lowering blocks, fender skirts, twin aerials, and custom upholstering made of rolled Naugahyde. Staring into the bathroom mirror for long periods of time I practiced expressions to drive it with. It was that kind of car. It looked mean, and it was mean. Consequently, it had to be handled with a certain style. One-handing it through a ninety-degree turn on city streets in a power slide where you were in danger of losing your ass as well as the car, you were obligated to have your left arm hanging half out the window and a very *bored* expression on your face. That kind of thing.

Those were the sweetest cars I was ever to know because they were my first. I remember them like people—like long-ago lovers —their idiosyncrasies, what they liked and what they didn't. With my hands deep in crankcases, I was initiated into their warm greasy mysteries. Nothing in the world was more satisfying than winching the front end up under the shade of a chinaberry tree and sliding under the chassis on a burlap sack with a few tools to see if the car would not yield to me and my expert ways.

The only thing that approached working on a car was talking about one. We'd stand about for hours, hustling our balls and spitting, telling stories about how it had been somewhere, sometime, with the car we were driving. It gave our lives a little focus and our talk a little credibility, if only because we could point to the evidence.

"But, hell, don't it rain in with that wing vent broke out like that?"

"Don't mean nothing to me. Soon's Shirley kicked it out, I known I was in love. I ain't about to put it back."

Usually we met to talk at night behind the A&W Root Beer

stand, with the air heavy with the smell of grease and just a hint
of burned French fries and burned hamburgers and burned hot
dogs. It remains one of the most sensuous, erotic smells in my
memory because through it, their tight little asses ticking like
clocks, walked the sweetest softest short-skirted carhops in the
world. I knew what it was to stand for hours with my buddies,
leaning nonchalant as hell on a fender, pretending not to look at
the carhops, and saying things like: "This little baby don't look
like much, but she'll git rubber in three gears." And when I said
it, it was somehow my own body I was talking about. It was *my*
speed and *my* strength that got rubber in three gears. In the
mystery of that love affair, the car and I merged.

But, like many another love affair, it has soured considerably.
Maybe it would have been different if I had known cars sooner. I
was already out of the Marine Corps and twenty-two years old
before I could stand behind the A&W Root Beer and lean on the
fender of a 1938 coupe. That seems pretty old to me to be talking about getting rubber in three gears, and I'm certain it is *very*
old to feel your own muscle tingle and flush with blood when
you say it. As is obvious, I was what used to be charitably called
a late bloomer. But at some point I did become just perceptive
enough to recognize bullshit when I was neck deep in it.

The 1953 Mercury was responsible for my ultimate disen-
chantment with cars. I had already bored and stroked the engine
and contrived to place a six-speaker sound system in it when I
finally started to paint it. I spent the better half of a year painting that car. A friend of mine owned a body shop and he let me
use the shops on weekends. I sanded the Mercury down to raw
metal, primed it, and painted it. Then I painted it again. And
again. And then again. I went a little nuts, as I am prone to do,
because I'm the kind of guy who if he can't have too much of a
thing doesn't want any at all. So one day I came out of the house
(I was in college then) and saw it, the '53 Mercury, the car upon
which I had heaped more attention and time and love
than I had ever given a human being. It sat at the curb, its black
surface a shimmering of the air, like hundreds of mirrors turned
to catch the sun. It had twenty-seven coats of paint, each coat
laboriously hand-rubbed. It seemed to glow, not with reflected
light, but with some internal light of its own.

I stood staring, and it turned into one of those great scary rare moments when you are privileged to see into your own predicament. Clearly, there were two ways I could go. I could sell the car, or I could keep on painting it for the rest of my life. If twenty-seven coats of paint, why not a hundred and twenty-seven? The moment was brief and I understand it better now than I did then, but I did realize, if imperfectly, that something was dreadfully wrong, that the car owned me much more than I would ever own the car, no matter how long I kept it. The next day I drove to Jacksonville and left the Mercury on a used-car lot. It was an easy thing to do.

Since that day, I've never confused myself with a car, a confusion common everywhere about us—or so it seems to me. I have a car now, but I use it like a beast, the way I've used all cars since the Mercury, like a beast unlovely and unlikable but necessary. True as all that is, though, God knows I'm in the car's debt for that blistering winning July run to Jacksonville, and the pushed-out wing vent, and finally for that greasy air heavy with the odor of burned meat and potatoes there behind the A&W Root Beer. I'll never smell anything that good again.

TV

BY ANDY WARHOL

Television is so important to my life I watch two color sets at the same time, doubling my pleasure, always in bed, usually while I'm talking on the phone to somebody who's watching the same thing. Sometimes I switch from color to black and white for a few seconds. That's very nice.

I am never bothered by reruns. During the summer you can watch whatever you didn't watch during the winter and tell yourself you're watching something new. I like really old reruns because the people stay young forever. On the other hand, it's fascinating to study people getting old on up-to-the-minute TV. I have watched Barbara Walters get older and, do you know, she has another crow's-foot. I've been counting.

I mainly watch the major networks, as well as the movies on the local stations. I hate PBS because it is too intellectual and gets me depressed. PBS tries to make you feel guilty for watching their stations without paying. I would rather have someone trying to sell me something than someone trying to make me feel obligated. Moreover, commercials are pick-me-ups; programing becomes too intense if there aren't enough commercials in between. Whenever I watch a show "without commercial interruption" I get itchy.

At the beginning of each week I take a TV schedule and circle anything and everything that might be good for me, even if it comes on at an hour I've never been up in my life. For a year now I've been circling *Modern Farmer* and *Agriculture U.S.A.* and haven't caught them once. But I know some morning a police car will siren by and I'll wake up, reaching for the *TV Guide,* and I'll see *Modern Farmer* right there, circled.

Now I would like to list my twelve favorite television offerings:

1. The ABC MORNING MOVIE. Ten A.M. weekdays is a great TV time for me because it's ladies'-movie time. You start off on Monday with *A Certain Smile,* and then Tuesday you'll get *Breakfast at Tiffany's,* or maybe it's John Saxon Week or Sandra Dee Week or Pat Boone Week—lots of Lanas, lots of Deborah Kerrs, lots of John Gavins—*Back Street* is big—everything that makes you cry at ten in the morning while you're ironing or cleaning. And while I've got the morning movie on, I never watch game shows on the other set—I hate them—but at eleven A.M. I make sure I've got. . . .

2. I LOVE LUCY on the other set. I love watching Lucy's two personalities: sometimes she's very up there, high-class and fashionable, talking on the phone saying, "This is Mrs. Ricardo at 623 East Sixty-eighth Street," and the next minute she'll be hanging out the window. Everybody wants to know girls like Lucy and Ethel. Lucy does the two-personality comedy routines better than anyone else who's ever tried, and Vivian Vance plays her Ethel comedy perfectly. And the idea of putting those two incongruous couples, the Mertzes and the Ricardos, together as landlords/tenants and best friends was great.

3. The TODAY show. I love the way you can see Barbara Walters' mind working, who she wants to have lunch with later on, the way she talks with her eyes to tell you something "means" something. And I love the way she gets controversial by saying, "But don't you think there's another side to it?" I like to jot down the questions she asks and use them when I go to interview people myself. The *Today* show is the beat of the world; I love it, even if the second hour is a repeat.

4. KATHRYN KUHLMAN the faith healer is someone I never like to miss on Saturday morning. She's a positive thinker; it's all up-up-

up with her. I know her from my childhood because she did her first entertainments forty years ago in the Pittsburgh area. (Something else I never miss on Saturday is *Abbott and Costello*. I love them. I'm never sure if I'm watching the same one I saw the week before, but then it doesn't matter—they're all the same and they're all great.)

5. I watch STAR TREK faithfully because the *Enterprise* crew is full of people you can count on. And the concept of *Star Trek* is reassuring because it assumes that we've made it through all of the problems we have now. It's comforting to imagine we never had a complete holocaust. I also like *Star Trek* because it made obsolete the boring television "chase scene": almost every TV adventure shows ends with some kind of a chase scene—in elevators, down highways, over cliffs, across airports. But the *Star Trek* people substituted the "bounce scene" for the "chase scene" —when the *Enterprise* is in trouble, it just bounces and everybody lurches across the control panel and that's it.

6. KOJAK fascinates me because it solves all the real crime stories on the news. It's hard to believe that nobody ever sues Kojak, but then you wouldn't sue him any more than you'd sue the Godfather: when you're very big or very little nobody sues you; but when you're medium big you really have to worry.

7. SATURDAY-MORNING TELEVISION is nice because you get all of the thriller-chiller and sci-fi movies. I also watch the dance shows—*Party* on WPIX, *Soul Train* on WNEW, and *American Bandstand* on ABC.

8. I love all the spin-offs—GOOD TIMES, THE JEFFERSONS, and especially RHODA. Rhoda is incredible—what other girl would have the nerve to leave a steady job as a *window dresser* in Minneapolis to try to crash the all-male New York window-dressing world? I guess that after she got here, even Rhoda decided not to push it—she knew she'd have to wrestle one of the boys for his staple gun in the window of Bonwit's if she wanted to get anywhere. She decided to become a "wife" instead. I really think, though, that they rushed the Rhoda/Joe marriage and lost

a lot of good episodes in which she could have been dating. She should have married Joe *this* year. I love Rhoda's whole family and I hope her sister spins off soon. As a matter of fact, I even hope Joe spins off if the marriage doesn't work out.

9. I love SANFORD AND SON and THAT'S MY MAMA and most of all ALL IN THE FAMILY because it's great to see working people and people working. I guess *The Life of Riley* was a forerunner of Archie Bunker, with William Bendix working at the "plant"— Cunningham Aircraft—while most of the other TV men in the fifties worked in "firms" like Honeywell & Todd or sold insurance. I love shows in which you get to see real people—the kind who write letters to the New York *Daily News* when they're mad.

10. THE TONIGHT SHOW is always good simply because you never have to get embarrassed for Johnny Carson; he has TV magic, is always cool, clever and American. Johnny doesn't care about "issues"—he wants to make things easy but entertaining, and he does that night after night. When you look at him you never have to worry that he has a problem—you know he won't fall apart. I probably would have enjoyed Dick Cavett's shows more if he hadn't stopped off at Yale on his way from Nebraska to New York. I got too involved with Dick's shows because they were so good, and I don't want to get involved—I just want to watch. One thing I always wonder about talk shows is why they don't have tight close-ups—they never do.

11. NEWSCENTER 4 (NBC's New York news) is really computerized TV news. I love it. You get the buhp buhp buhp buhp buhp and you see in the computerized writing what's going to be on minute by minute:

5:03 Betty Furness tells about cheap cigarettes in North Carolina.

5:07 Pia Lindstrom on the East Side talking to so-and-so.

I love it when they try out new restaurants around town. Robert Potts went to an Indian restaurant on Lexington Avenue where everything they showed him to eat in the store was a ball and was made out of white flour, milk, and sugar. You knew from looking at his face while he tried it that it was no good because if he likes something he really slurps it up.

12. The CATHERINE DENEUVE AD FOR CHANEL. This is one of the best ads I've ever seen, and it shows that if you really spend the money and get the right celebrity, you get your money's worth. The difference between getting Catherine Deneuve and a less expensive look-alike is the difference between getting a real Chanel suit and a copy. Catherine Deneuve really makes you want to be Catherine Deneuve, and if you have to eat blueberries and wear Chanel No. 5 to do it, fine.

Fried Chicken

BY JIM VILLAS

When it comes to fried chicken, let's not beat around the bush
for one second. To know about fried chicken you have to have
been weaned and reared on it in the South. Period. The French
know absolutely nothing about it, and Julia Child and James
Beard very little. Craig Claiborne knows plenty. He's from Mississippi. And to set the record straight before bringing on regional and possible national holocaust over the correct preparation of this classic dish, let me emphasize and reemphasize
the fact that I'm a Southerner, born, bred, and chicken-fried for
all times. Now, I don't know exactly why we Southerners love
and eat at least ten times more fried chicken than anyone else,
but we do and always have and always will. Maybe we have a
hidden craw in our throats or oversize pulley bones or . . . oh, I
don't know what we have, and it doesn't matter. What does matter is that we take our fried chicken very very seriously, having
singled it out years ago as not only the most important staple
worthy of heated and complex debate but also as the dish that
non-Southerners have never really had any knack for. Others
just plain down don't *understand* fried chicken, and, to tell the
truth, there're lots of Southerners who don't know as much as
they think they know. Naturally everybody everywhere in the
country is convinced he or she can cook or identify great fried
chicken as well as any ornery reb (including all the fancy cookbook writers), but the truth remains that once you've eaten real

chicken fried by an expert chicken fryer in the South there are simply no grounds for contest.

As far as I'm concerned, all debate over how to prepare fried chicken has ended forever, for recently I fried up exactly twenty-one and a half chickens (or 215 pieces) using every imaginable technique, piece of equipment, and type of oil for the sole purpose of establishing once and for all the right to fix great fried chicken. In a minute I'll tell you what's wrong with most of the Kentucky-fried, Maryland-fried, oven-fried, deep-fried, cre-ole-fried, and all those other classified varieties of Southern-fried chicken people like to go on about. But first *my* chicken, which I call simply Fried Chicken and which I guarantee will start you lapping:

Equipment (no substitutes):
A sharp chef's or butcher's knife 12 to 13 in. long
A large wooden cutting board
A small stockpot half filled with water (for chicken soup)
A large glass salad bowl
A heavy 12-in. cast-iron skillet with lid
Long-handled tweezer tongs
1 roll paper towels
2 brown paper bags
1 empty coffee can
A serving platter
A wire whisk
A home fire extinguisher

Ingredients (to serve 4):
3 cups whole milk
½ fresh lemon
1½ lbs. (3 cups) top-quality shortening
4 Tb rendered bacon grease
1 whole freshly killed 3½- to 4-lb. chicken
1½ cups plus 2 Tb flour
3 tsp salt
Freshly ground black pepper

To prepare chicken for frying:
Remove giblets and drop in stockpot with neck. (This is for a

good chicken soup to be eaten at another time.) Cut off and pull out any undesirable fat at neck and tail. Placing whole chicken in center of cutting board (breast-side up, neck toward you), grab leg on left firmly, pull outward and down toward board, and begin slashing down through skin toward thigh joint, keeping knife close to thigh. Crack back thigh joint as far as possible, find joint with fingers, then cut straight through to remove (taking care not to pull skin from breast). Turn bird around and repeat procedure on other thigh. To separate thigh from leg, grasp one end in each hand, pull against tension of joint, find joint, and sever. Follow same procedure to remove wings. Cut off wing tips and add to stockpot.

To remove pulley bone (or wishbone to non-Southerners), find protruding knob toward neck end of breast, trace with fingers to locate small indentation just forward of knob, slash horizontally downward across indentation, then begin cutting carefully away from indentation and downward toward neck till forked pulley-bone piece is fully severed. Turn chicken backside up, locate two hidden small pinbones on either side below neck toward middle of back, and cut through skin to expose ends of bones. Put two fingers of each hand into neck cavity and separate breast from back by pulling forcefully till the two pry apart. (If necessary, sever stubborn tendons and skin with knife.) Cut back in half, reserving lower portion (tail end) for frying, and tossing upper portion (rib cage) into stockpot. Place breast skin-side down, ram tip of knife down through center cartilage, and cut breast in half.

(**Hint:** Level cutting edge of knife along cartilage, then slam blade through with heel of hand.)

Rinse the ten pieces of chicken thoroughly under cold running water, dry with paper towels, and salt and pepper lightly. Pour milk into bowl, squeeze lemon into milk, add chicken to soak, cover, and refrigerate at least two hours and preferably overnight.

To fry chicken:

Remove chicken from refrigerator and allow to return to room temperature (about 70°). While melting the pound and a half of shortening over high heat to measure ½ inch in skillet, pour flour, remaining salt and pepper to taste into paper bag. Remove dark pieces of chicken from milk, drain each momentarily over bowl, drop in paper bag, shake vigorously to coat, and add bacon grease to skillet. When small bubbles appear on surface, reduce heat slightly. Remove dark pieces of chicken from bag one by one, shake off excess flour, and, using tongs, lower gently into fat, skin-side down. Quickly repeat all procedures with white pieces; reserve milk, arrange chicken in skillet so it cooks evenly, reduce heat to medium, and cover. Fry exactly 17 minutes. Lower heat, turn pieces with tongs and fry 17 minutes longer uncovered. With paper towels wipe grease continuously from exposed surfaces as it spatters. Chicken should be almost mahogany brown.

Drain thoroughly on second brown paper bag, transfer to serving platter *without* reheating in oven, and serve hot or at room temperature with any of the following items: mashed potatoes and cream gravy*, potato salad, green beans, turnip greens, sliced homegrown tomatoes, stewed okra, fresh corn bread, iced tea, beer, homemade peach ice cream, or watermelon.

*To make cream gravy:

Discard in coffee can all but one tablespoon fat from skillet, making sure not to pour off brown drippings. Over high heat, add two remaining tablespoons flour to fat and stir constantly with wire whisk till roux browns. Gradually pour 1¾ cups reserved milk from bowl and continue stirring till gravy comes to a boil, thickens slightly, and is smooth. Reduce heat, simmer two minutes, and check salt and pepper seasoning. Serve in gravy boat.

Now that's the right way, the only way, to deal with fried chicken. Crisp, juicy on the inside, full of flavor, not greasy and sloppy, fabulous. Of course one reason my recipe works so well is it's full of important subtleties that are rarely indicated in cookbooks but that help to make the difference between impeccable fried chicken and all the junk served up everywhere today. And just to illustrate this point, I cite a recipe for "Perfect Fried Chicken" that recently appeared in *Ladies' Home Journal*.

1. Rinse cut-up 2½- to 3-lb. broiler-fryer and pat dry.
2. Pour 1 in. vegetable oil in skillet, heat to 375°. Combine ½

cup flour, 2 tsp salt, dash of pepper in a bag. Coat a few pieces at a time.

3. Preheat oven to 250°. Place paper towels in shallow baking pan.

4. Fry thighs and drumsticks, turning occasionally, for 12 minutes until golden. Pierce with fork to see if juices run clear. Remove to baking pan and place in heated oven. Fry remaining pieces for 7 or 8 minutes. Serves four.

Snap! That's it. A real quicky. Fast fried chicken that promises to be perfect. Bull! It tastes like hell, and if you don't believe me, try it yourself. The pitfalls of the recipe are staggering but typical. First of all, nobody in his right mind fries a skinny two-and-a-half-pound chicken for four people, not unless everyone's on some absurd diet or enjoys sucking bones. Second, the recipe takes for granted you're going to buy a plastic-wrapped chicken that's been so hacked and splintered by a meat cleaver that blood from the bones saturates the package. What help is offered if the chicken you happen to have on hand is whole or only partially cut up? Third, what type of skillet, and what size, for heaven's sake? If the pan's too light the chicken will burn on the bottom, and if you pour one full inch of oil in an eight-inch skillet, you'll end up with deep-fried chicken. And as for sticking forks in seared chicken to release those delicious juices, or putting fried chicken in the oven to get it disgustingly soggy, or serving a half-raw thick breast that's cooked only seven or eight minutes—well, I refuse to get overheated.

Without question the most important secret to any great fried chicken is the quality of the chicken itself, and without question most of the three billion pullets marketed annually in the U.S. have about as much flavor as tennis balls. But, after all, what can you expect of battery birds whose feet never touch the dirty filthy earth, whose diet includes weight-building fats, fish flours, and factory-fresh chemicals, and whose life expectancy is a pitiful seven weeks? Tastelessness, that's what, the same disgraceful tastelessness that characterizes the eggs we're forced to consume. How many people in this country remember the rich flavor of a good old barnyard chicken, a nearly extinct species that pecked around the yard for a good fifteen weeks, digested plenty of barley-and-milk mash, bran, grain, and beer, got big and fat, and never sent one solitary soul to the hospital with contamination?

I remember, believe you me, and how I pity the millions who, blissfully unconscious of what they missed and sadly addicted to the chicken passed out by Colonel Sanders, will never taste a truly luscious piece of fried chicken unless they're first shown how to get their hands on a real chicken. Of course, what you see in supermarkets are technically real chickens fit for consumption, but anyone who's sunk teeth into a gorgeous, plump barnyard variety (not to mention an inimitable French *poularde de Bresse*) would agree that to compare the scrawny, bland, mass-produced bird with the one God intended us to eat is something more than ludicrous.

I originally intended to tell you how to raise, kill, draw, and prepare your own chickens. Then I came to my senses and faced the reality that unless you were brought up wringing chickens' necks, bleeding them, searching for the craws where food is stored, and pulling out their innards with your hands—well, it can be a pretty nauseating mess that makes you gag if you're not used to it. Besides, there's really no need to slaughter your own chickens, not, that is, if you're willing to take time and make the effort to locate either a good chicken raiser who feeds and exercises his chickens properly (on terra firma) or a reliable merchant who gets his chickens fresh from the farm. They do exist, still, be their number ever so dwindling. If you live in a rural area, simply get to know a farmer who raises chickens, start buying eggs from him and then tell him you'll pay him any amount to kill and prepare for you a nice 3½- to 4-pound pullet. He will, and probably with pride. If you're in a large city, the fastest method is to study the Yellow Pages of the phone book, search under "Poultry—Retail" for the words "Fresh poultry and eggs" or "Custom poultry" or "Strictly kosher poultry," and proceed from there. Even in huge metropolitan centers, it's not as hard as you think to find a nice barnyard chicken. Philadelphians have easy access in their stores to the fresh poultry brought in from the Pennsylvania Dutch region. In San Francisco, there's no problem finding barnyard birds in Chinatown, and even in New York's Chinatown the markets are full of fine, healthy chickens raised on special farms over in New Jersey. (Interestingly enough, the Chinese seem to be the most discriminating consumers when it comes to chicken.) Of course, real Manhattan chicken lovers think nothing of making the tiresome drive to East Hampton,

Long Island, for the sole purpose of picking up a couple of freshly killed (and expensive) meaty birds at Iacono Farms, reported by many (myself included) as having the fattest, juiciest, best-tasting old-fashioned chickens on the Eastern Seaboard. Nor is it out of the question to go chicken hunting at the Saturday morning flea market in Englishtown, New Jersey.

Next in importance to the quality of the fowl is the cutting-up procedure, a subject rarely even touched upon in cookbooks. I suppose most cooks just don't like to be bothered cutting up their own chickens, but again, if you're determined to have the best possible, you must get into the habit of buying only whole chickens and doing the job yourself. And the reasons are logical. First, as any fried chicken expert knows, the way commercial birds are rapidly hacked apart today in supermarkets, it's a wonder people aren't dead from swallowing splintered bones (a possibility Southerners have feared for generations). Second, unless care is taken to separate parts at the joints and cut evenly through the skin, you end up with bloody pieces of chicken with half the flavorful skin ripped off. Third, the only way on God's green earth to get ten pieces from a chicken (including the lower back and pulley bone) is to cut them yourself. Why the back portion and pulley bone? Well, not only does the former contain that delectable morsel of meat known only to Southerners as the oyster, but by cutting away the tender pulley-bone piece you reduce the size of the two breasts and thus allow for greater space flexibility in the skillet. Besides, eating fried chicken is just not eating fried chicken without the age-old ceremony of two chicken eaters pulling on the pulley bone for good luck (the one with the long end getting to make the wish).

From this point on, argumentation over fixing fried chicken becomes hotly outrageous, and since I've already implied I have no intention of batting my brains out defending each and every step of what I'm inalterably and forevermore convinced is the fail-proof recipe, I'll explain one-two-three only the most essential features while occasionally making reference to all those other varieties of fried chicken I mentioned.

The skillet: I can't overemphasize the importance of frying chicken in a heavy cast-iron skillet that's well seasoned and black as tar from long use. All expert chicken fryers agree. Not only does

cast iron heat slowly, evenly, and maintain heat well (all of
which are essential when shallow-frying many pieces); it also
yields gravy-making drippings like no other cookware. If you
don't own this skillet, buy one (at a hardware store), wash it
thoroughly, rub the bottom and sides with unsalted oil, and heat
it slowly in the oven at 275° for at least one hour to season it. I
find enameled cast iron a weak substitute.

Seasoning and batter: Real fried chicken should be seasoned with
nothing more than salt, fresh pepper, a touch of lemon juice, and
a few tablespoons of bacon grease added to the cooking fat.
Some people like to add paprika, cayenne, and anything else they
can sprinkle on; others dump on soy sauce and Worcestershire;
and creole-fried chicken can contain anything from garlic to
thyme to Tabasco. All of which are wrong if what you're looking
for is classic fried chicken.

One reason Maryland-fried chicken (which even old Escoffier
included in his cookbook, *Ma Cuisine,* with, mind you, a
béchamel sauce!) never seems to be quite crisp enough on the
outside is it's not coated with a well-seasoned batter before frying. (The other reason is that people glop gravy all over the
chicken—which is wrong—instead of pouring it in the center of
a mound of mashed potatoes—which is right.) Lots of recipes
for Kentucky-fried indicate an egg-milk (or egg-cream) batter,
while in the Deep South it's not unusual to find chicken dipped
in buttermilk before flouring. The first possibility is out of the
question since the egg absorbs too much grease. The second, I
must say, makes for pretty good eating if you don't mind a
slightly sweet taste to your chicken. Overall, I still prefer a
seasoned whole-milk batter, and I'm absolutely convinced that
soaking the chicken for at least a few hours before dredging not
only allows the seasoning to penetrate the meat to the bone but
also gives it a nice, moist texture.

Cooking oil: This is the area in which most people really make a
mess of things, either out of ignorance or carelessness or just plain
laziness. Cookbook writers, in particular, almost consistently offer
you the option of lard or shortening, or lard or vegetable oil.
That's sloppy teaching. The one and only thing to use is a bland,
high-grade shortening (Crisco is best) that holds up well over

intense heat. Lard, which is animal fat, not only breaks down quickly but also overwhelms the natural flavor of the chicken. Bottled corn oil stinks, literally, and even the odor of hot vegetable oil makes me nauseated. Now, I don't know why those very very healthy polyunsaturates smell and taste so bad, but they do, and I wouldn't drop even a wing in a single ounce. Nor would I ever consider frying chicken in peanut or olive oil, both of which are too heavy in flavor. As for adding butter to the shortening (as even some Southerners do), I'm also against that, for the simple reason that it makes the chicken taste like some fancy, rich French dish. Classic fried chicken is neither fancy nor rich, and this is why butter-basted oven-fried chicken is not fried chicken. Don't get me wrong about butter, no sir, not for one minute, for I normally use it for everything but bathing. Butter is great for soothing grease-spatter skin burns, but chicken sautéed in butter is soft and golden on the outside, while true fried chicken is so crisp and brown it crumbles almost like a croissant when bitten into. Both are superlative, but the two just aren't kin.

Frying: The first rule in frying chicken is never to allow more than one half inch of grease in the skillet. If you add any more, you'll end up with deep-fried chicken, or something that resembles the atrocities served at greasy spoons. The same principle explains why, contrary to what the books say, the pieces should be arranged fairly close to one another, allowing the bottoms to brown without the grease bubbling too far up the sides. Whether or not to cover the skillet has always been a major point of debate, and I suspect the true reason many people keep a lid on throughout the process is to keep grease from spattering all over God's creation—which is, of course, stupid. After frying my twenty-one and a half chickens, I concluded that covering the skillet during the first seventeen minutes helps the upper sides of the pieces to retain moisture, which is later sealed in when you turn the chicken. During the next seventeen minutes, the lid should be removed so the upper browned portion absorbs no more moisture and remains crisp on the outside. Never turn fried chicken more than once, never, and don't fiddle with the drumsticks. They'll cook properly without being rolled all around. Please note that my frying time is for a chicken three and a half pounds or larger. If your bird is smaller (which it really shouldn't be) you'll have to reduce the time.

The paper bag: Nothing in heaven or on earth (not even a sponge or Kleenex) absorbs chicken grease like a brown paper bag. Again, I don't know exactly why this is true, but if you don't have a paper bag on hand, forget about frying chicken till you do. Paper towels just don't do the job. Still again, I don't know why, but I do know when you pick up a piece of fried chicken that's been draining on paper towels, the chicken is, for some reason, still greasy on the bottom. Some experts use the same bag for both dredging and draining, and sometimes that works just fine. But flour tends to sneak through the folds of most paper bags, so unless you don't mind a little white dust on your chicken (I do), it's a good idea to have a clean bag for draining.

Now, if you think I take my fried chicken a little too seriously, you haven't seen anything till you attend the National Chicken Cooking Contest held annually in early summer at different locations throughout the country. Created in 1949, the festival has a Poultry Princess; vintage motorcar displays; a flea market; a ten-feet-by-eight-inch skillet that fries up seven and a half tons of chicken; ten thousand chicken-loving contestants cooking for cash prizes amounting to over $25,000; and big-name judges who are chosen from among the nation's top newspaper, magazine, and television food editors. It's a big to-do. Of course, I personally have no intention whatsoever of ever entering any chicken contest that's not made up exclusively of Southerners, and of course you understand my principle. This, however, should not necessarily affect your now going to the National and showing the multitudes what real fried chicken is all about. A few years back, a young lady irreverently dipped some chicken in oil flavored with soy sauce, rolled it in crushed chow mein noodles, fried it up, and walked away with top honors and a few grand for her Cock-a-Noodle-Do. Without doubt she was a sweetheart of a gal, but you know, the people who judged that fried chicken need help.

Acid Indigestion

BY ART BUCHWALD

America is an abundant land that seems to have more of every-thing than anybody else. And if one were to ask what we have the most of the answer would be acid indigestion.

No country can touch us when it comes to heartburn and upset stomachs. This nation, under God, with liberty and justice for all, neutralizes more stomach acid in one day than the Soviet Union does in a year. We give more relief from discomfort of the intestinal tract than China and Japan combined.

They can say what they will about us, but we Americans know what to do with our excess gas.

It is no accident that the United States became the largest producer of acid indigestion in the world. When the first settlers came to the New World they found their lives fraught with dan-ger. First they had to worry about Indians, then they had to worry about their crops. Afterward they had to worry about witches. This played hell with everyone's stomach and the early settlers realized if they ever hoped to survive they would have to come up with a cure for acid indigestion.

Providence was on their side, because amongst the early set-tlers were two brothers, Alka and Bromo Seltzer. They were both chemists who had experimented with various potions that had been given to them by the Indians.

One potion was a white powder that the Indians used for ath-lete's foot. Why, asked the Seltzer brothers, couldn't the same powder be used for upset stomachs. Al was neater than Bromo and rolled his powder into a tablet which he then dropped into a mug of water where it immediately fizzed. Bromo said it was too expensive to make tablets, and it was much easier just to dump the powder into the water, which would produce the same effect.

The brothers split in anger, and Al put out his product under the name Alka-Seltzer, while Bromo put his out as Bromo-Seltzer. Fortunately for the country, both methods worked, and as soon as the cure for acid indigestion had been concocted the New World could be settled once and for all.

You would think that after we killed all the Indians and won the West and became a large industrial nation Americans would have stopped having queasy stomachs. But the truth is we suffer more from the blaahhs now than we ever did before. Some of it still comes from fear, some of it comes from ambition, and some of it comes from eating the whole thing.

As a people who strive for the best we must accept the fact that it takes a cup of acid for every step we take up the ladder of success. It is no accident that the men and women who run our corporations and our advertising agencies and our networks and our government are the same people who keep the Maalox, Pepto-Bismol, Bisodol tum and Rolaid companies alive.

Show me a man who has to drink milk instead of wine with his meals and I'll show you a titan of American industry.

For years other nations have tried to catch up with us when it came to sour stomachs and heartburn. But they never had the drive to produce a good case of acid indigestion. They never understood what it takes to keep up with the Joneses or outdo the Smiths. They don't realize that in order to live in the best of all possible worlds you have to have a certain amount of stomach discomfort to go with it.

If there is anything that shows up our system to that of the Communist nations, it is that we Americans can not only live with acid indigestion but we have three thousand different remedies to give us relief. In a Communist society the state decides what you should coat your digestive tract with, and if it doesn't soothe you, the state couldn't care less if you burp all night long.

Acid indigestion is as American as Mom's apple pie (which is one of the reasons we get it) and as long as there is enough heartburn to go around, we, as a great nation, will survive.

The Movie Star Cowboy

BY MARK GOODMAN

Long before your friendly neighborhood theater began showing
Gravel Pit Grovel and *A Roman Springs on Mrs. Stone,* American movie schedules were as healthy and predictable as a Betty
Crocker menu. Saturday night through Tuesday was generally a
musical starring Betty Hutton or a bobbed-haired ingenue
named Doris Day. Wednesday through Friday meant adventure,
either a black-and-white Humphrey Bogart or a gold-red-green-
silver Robert Taylor. And Saturday afternoon belonged to Roy
Rogers.

First the Republic eagle flashed on the screen. Then Roy
would appear, lean and hard, with patented squinched eyes that
bespoke desert sun and a Choctaw strain. He rode the golden
palomino Trigger, more precious (quite literally) than the Aga
Khan's proudest stallion. Behind him rode Gabby Hayes, win-
somely septic, with the juice of good American chawin' tobacco
dribbling into his hoary beard, and Dale Evans, with her knee-
high boots (then considered wholesome) and bee-stung lips. You
cheered lustily as Roy galloped across the sage in *Under Nevada
Skies,* as he blasted the .44 out of a wrongo's hand in *Billy the
Kid Returns,* as he lassoed a whole passel of wrongos in *South of
Santa Fe*. And at the end, when the town or ranch or universe
was secure, Roy and Dale sang *Happy Trails to You* and you just
plumb *knew* that God was in His heaven, and all was right with
the world.

Art Rush, Roy Rogers' agent and manager for the past thirty-three years, says it all: "Roy Rogers, after all, is a living legend!"

In the native tongue of Los Angeles, "a living legend" means "he died but he won't fall down." Also, if the legend is still vigorous, it can mean handsome profit.

It would be unfair to blame Roy Rogers for making a Western at sixty-three (or for not dying); or to castigate the producers for luring the living legend out of the security of his rodeos and his Roy Rogers Family Restaurants and his Apple Valley, California, museum and his battalion of children and grandchildren and his God. But it is with some sadness that one notes that Roy Rogers, the quintessential Western hero, accurately billed for three decades as "America's favorite cowboy," the man who rode through 188 theater and TV films, who sang his way into the nation's hearts with more than one hundred songs of prairie and prayer, the man whose clean, sharp features adorned more than four hundred Sears, Roebuck cowboy appurtenances, the world's most celebrated adoptive parent, is coming out of semi-retirement to star in a movie entitled *Mackintosh and T.J.*, to be released soon. It is Roy's first picture since he made *Son of Paleface* with his buddies Bob Hope and Jane Russell back in the second ice age (1952). Now, for the first time, Roy Rogers will not play Roy Rogers. He'll play Mackintosh, a cowpoke who roams the Texas prairie in a pickup truck.

Snuff Garrett, a merchant of musical packages (including Roy's latest album, *Happy Trails to You*), first went to Al Ruddy, producer of *The Godfather*, with the notion of Roy's resurrection. Ruddy, thinking he had found a good thing, enthusiastically observed: "If we can pull off a high degree of quality and integrity, we can have a smash film." But the idea of Roy playing a modern-day Texas Ranger failed to impress Paramount and the other major producers. Ruddy dropped out of the picture, and a Fort Worth independent producer, Tim Penland, dropped in. Penland's prior film experience was making commercials for Radio Shack International. It so happened that Radio Shack's owner, Mrs. Charles Tandy, also owns one of the largest ranches in West Texas, The 6666. Penland decided it was high time he broke into feature films and what better way to do it than on Mrs. Tandy's ranch with the most famous Western star in history? He sold Roy on the idea, then hired Marvin Chomsky, director of *Live a Little, Steal a Lot,* to direct and Paul Savage of *Gunsmoke* fame to create a script around the living legend. So, although Roy regrettably will not sing *Happy Trails,* he will at least ride one again.

I take the long trail to Apply Valley with Art Rush, who has spent these thirty-three years managing Roy without a contract. Like everyone connected with Roy, Art is family, a gentle, gangling ex-basketball player who also brought you Nelson Eddy and Mario Lanza. As we pull out of Burbank and head for the Mojave, Art begins his agent litany.

"Back in 1946–47, Roy set the all-time Madison Square Garden record of one hundred nineteen thousand dollars gross in one day. Why, he grossed more that day than Sinatra did all that week at the Paramount. He's done practically every state fair in the country and definitely every major rodeo. In '58–'59 he made four hundred eighty-seven thousand dollars on the circuit. I can only think of three, four times he didn't set an all-time record at a state fair. We did Europe in 1954—oh, they loved him *there*. Sixty-five sold-out shows.

"All those products we merchandised through Sears? We averaged thirty million dollars retail annually. We've had a comic-book contract with Western Printing going back to the thirties. We averaged twenty-two, twenty-eight million copies per year. Roy's TV show ran six and a half years on NBC, then it was syndicated for two and a half years, then spent four years on CBS in the mornings. Those and all the Republic films have also been dubbed all around the world." (I can verify that. Once, in a *brauhaus* in Bad Kreuznach, I looked up at the TV and saw an Indian ride up to Roy, raise his hand and shriek, *"Achtung, Herr Rogers!"*)

Art assures me that's amusing. Then: "You know, Roy's picture has been on the cover of two and half billion boxes of Post cereal? And restaurants? We made a deal with Marriott Hotels six years ago; now he has about two hundred family restaurants in the U.S. and twelve in Canada. We're pretty remote from city life out here," he interjects, as we pass Mel's Mobile Homes and the Mamma Mia Pizzeria.

We pass Rogers' unpretentious ranch house alongside the

highway and pull into the museum parking lot. Roy's red and black Honda rests under the porte cochere; on the roof stands a life-size plastic replica of Trigger I.

I shake hands with the living legend. He is alive all right, and the fittest sixty-three-year-old I've ever seen. He stands five feet eleven inches and weighs little more than his old hundred-sixty-five-pound riding weight. The face betrays his years somewhat. People with accipitrine features can go two ways when they age; either their faces become cadaverous or they thicken, fade and blur. Roy Rogers falls into the second class; he looks rather like an old photograph.

Roy is friendly, firm handshake, the big crinkle-eyed smile that I figure I saw, one way or another, practically every day of my first twelve years. He is tightly wound—after forty-four years in show business, personal interviews still make him extremely nervous. H. Allen Smith once wrote in a *Life* cover story that Rogers was wont to take a Scotch and soda before an interview, and I suspect he still does. We sit down in a room rimmed with animal horns and family pictures, including two of his race-horses, Triggairo and Run, Trigger, Run. A stuffed owl is perched over my head, and a mounted bobcat snarls at me from the corner. I try to avoid its malevolence and concentrate on this most extraordinary tale of an ordinary man who sidled into fame.

Little Leonard Slye was born on November 5, 1912, in that rootinest, tootinest of two-gun frontier towns, Cincinnati, Ohio. "They bulldozed over my house when they built Riverfront Stadium," he says in his flat twang. "I like to tell people my first home is now second base.

"Anyway, Dad worked in a shoe factory all his life. When I was little he and his brother built a houseboat on the Ohio, and we took it upriver to Portsmouth. We lived on that for six years, with Dad coming home once every couple of weeks. Then he bought us a little farm up in Duck Run, and I became a bona fide country boy. My life was a dog and a slingshot and a barlow knife."

Not to mention a mandolin guitar, which both of his parents could play. Roy, it turned out, was a pickin' fool. "Mom and Dad and I and my three sisters, we used to get together with some of the neighbors on Saturday night and have some mighty fine square dances." Headiest moment in his early youth was a trip to Columbus with the pig that had won him a 4-H Club first prize at the Scioto County Fair. Yes, it was a sky-blue, Booth Tarkington boyhood, untainted by cigarettes and self-abuse.

Despite his touch with string and hog, Leonard nurtured a curious ambition: he wanted to be a dentist. In fact, were it not for Leonard's father, ole Doc Slye might be peering into your mouth this very moment saying, "Rinse, please." But Dad sold the farm, and Leonard left school to work beside him in the shoe factory.

"One morning," Roy recalls, "Dad said to me, 'Let's quit our jobs and go see your sister in California.' So we drove out, stayed four months, and then came back." But how're you gonna keep 'em? Roy hitched back to California a few months later and set out to make his mark.

But how, in the teeth of the Depression? "It was rough going," he remembers. "You couldn't even buy a job, and the breadlines were a mile long." He picked peaches with the Okies, drove a gravel truck, anything. "I read *The Grapes of Wrath* once," he says. "That's about the way it was."

He managed to wedge in a bit of pickin' and singin' on a radio show in Glendale called *Saturday Night Jamboree*, and soon joined a group called The Rocky Mountaineers. They toured the trailer camps and honky-tonks of the Southwest. Says Roy, "We ate most every cottontail and jackrabbit between here and Roswell." They did get some decent home cooking in Roswell from the Wilkins family, whose daughter Arlene blushed like a prairie flower at young Slye's slim good looks. Arlene and Leonard were married in 1936 while he was working in a Hollywood radio station with a ragtag group called The Sons of the Pioneers.

One day, Leonard went into a Glendale shop to pick up his only hat, which was being cleaned, "I was just gettin' it when this ole boy came in the size of John Wayne. He told the man he had to have his hat right away for a screen test the next morning. When I asked what test, he said, 'Out at Republic. They're looking for a new singing cowboy.'"

The studio, it seems, had been squabbling with its star, Gene Autry, and wanted to make sure it had someone to fill his filigreed boots in case Gene up and walked. "So the next morning," Roy continues, "I saddled up my guitar and went out to the

Republic lot, but I couldn't get in. I hung around all morning till people came back from lunch, and I just scooted in with them. Pretty soon a hand fell on my shoulder. It was Sol Siegel, the big Western producer. He recognized me from a few Gene Autry backgrounds I did. He said, 'Get your guitar,' so I ran all the way to the car and back. I was puffing too hard to sing, but I yodeled for a while and finally sang some straight stuff. Siegel said, 'That's just what we're looking for,' and as soon as I got my friend Pat Brady to take my place on The Sons of the Pioneers, I signed with Republic." Thus Leonard Slye became Dick Weston, who became Roy Rogers.

Roy's first starring role came in 1938 as a young congressman in *Under Western Stars*. It was an instant success. Roy was not to be confused with any of the Barrymores, but his homespun sincerity, his message that purity and perseverance could triumph over any evil be it a Black Bart or a Depression, struck heartland heartstrings. That year he ranked number three in Western box office, and when Gene Autry greenly went to war, Roy became number one and remained there as long as the genre rode tall.

Picture by boffo picture, Roy built his little family. He was joined in the Republic corral by The Sons of the Pioneers, then by a coot from central casting named Gabby Hayes. "Ole Gabby wasn't a bit like his screen image in real life," Roy is fond of saying. "He walked straight and tall, and dressed in the finest tweeds. Once he even shaved his beard off. He called me long-distance and said, 'Roy, I'm the worst-looking thing you ever saw,' and he went into the desert like a hermit for six weeks till it grew back in."

It was Gabby's job to be repulsive and to snigger behind the horse trough in the last reel when Roy did not kiss the girl. One of the many girls he did not kiss was a bosomy young songstress named Dale Evans.

Dale came along just before Roy, by then an established star, was to undergo the first round of his lifelong scrap with tragedy. He and Arlene had adopted one little girl; then, to their surprise, they had a girl of their own. But when Roy Jr. was born, Arlene died six days later.

Dale had not had an easy time with her career until she met Roy. The former Frances Smith had come a piece from Uvalde,

Texas, but found that the going was mighty rough for a twenty-eight-year-old mare with a thirteen-year-old colt from a previous marriage. But Dale had the kind of apostolic tenacity one would expect of a woman who, by now, at sixty-three, has been mother to nine children and written eleven inspirational books. She and Roy melded beautifully, on and off the screen. They were married on an Oklahoma ranch on New Year's Eve, 1947, and went coon hunting the following night.

Dale and the kids and Gabby and Pat Brady and the Pioneers were merely the human elements of the Rogers family. First and foremost, the family member who will endure long after the others are gone (and I mean that literally since, although they josh about it, I doubt seriously that Roy and Dale will ultimately have one another stuffed) is Trigger, the golden palomino Roy picked out of a horse-rental lot one day.

Like so many Hollywood stars, Trigger was rich, talented, ego-centric and spoiled. He could count to twenty-five, drink milk from a bottle and sign his "X" on a hotel register with a pencil in his teeth. He could observe civilized convention. Trigger was allowed in all the better places because he was (in all likelihood) the world's only housebroken horse.

Not that his life was entirely a bed of new-mown hay—little fans delighted in plucking souvenirs from his posterior. Also, he and his master had more than one set-to over his penchant for scene stealing. After one such episode at the Earle Theater in Washington, Roy stormed off the stage and announced, "Someday I'm going to shoot that goddamn horse right between the eyes."

Surprised to hear Roy blaspheme? Roy has done that more than once, especially in the old days. He was also known to have a few drinks with the boys (but never in a public bar), and only gave up cigarettes ten years ago. Also, by his own admission, "I wasn't particularly religious back then. But I came to feel the responsibility for my family and my responsibility to millions of kids. They felt you were their hero, and their mothers expected me to be their Saturday-afternoon baby-sitter."

Roy worked hard to live up to that image. "I didn't mind," he says. "I enjoyed success like a kid with a new toy." Still, it couldn't have been all that easy. He wore cowboy clothes every waking moment, gave up what little wastreling he did, and became a pillar of the Presbyterian church. He also became the most stalwart Christian soldier in the battle for celluloid decency. Hear him on the subject of film censorship.

"I think we have more freedom in this country than in any other place in the world. If you don't believe in censorship then you don't have a family or don't care about it and don't care about your country and if you break the back of the American family, then you're going to break the back of this country!" The veins on Roy's neck are bulging now. "I walked down Broadway one day a few years ago and thought I'd go see a cowboy movie. So I stopped in to see *Midnight Cowboy.*

"That was sickening." He says it quietly, but his voice begins to build. "That was the most sick thing ever in an American movie. Whoever made that movie doesn't give a hoot about the public or the family or the nation. When that boy started going down on that guy, I was slidin' farther and farther down in my seat and that was *sickening* . . . SICK!"

Roy pauses to catch his breath. "I'm not a prude; I've been around some in my day. But there are things that are sacred in American life. What are we supposed to do, just go . . . FUCK?"

He is shouting again, with the frustration of the good, simple, inarticulate man watching his values sink into the Babylonian mire. He does not know what has happened to his white-hatted world, and I believe that is one of the reasons he has secluded himself and his family in Apple Valley.

Children and a decent environment for them form one of the dominant themes in Roy's life; death is the other. Three times the two have tragically intertwined. Roy and Dale's one natural child, Robin, was a Mongoloid who eventually died. Two adopted children died in senseless accidents: a little Korean girl in a bus crash, a sickly lad from asphyxiation (he had drunk heavily and vomited the night he made Army Pfc).

Those are not the only deaths to touch Roy's life. Eighteen years ago his former stand-in Spade Cooley, by then a TV Western star in his own right, brutally murdered his wife, then accused Roy of having had an affair with her. Roy was flabbergasted, then furious when the press played the story up. He was innocent; in fact, Spade called for him from his prison-hospital deathbed to apologize, but died before Roy could reach him.

Roy Rogers, a man with a short temper and long memory, has kept the press at arm's length since then.

Roy and Dale bear up under tragedy with such good Christian grace, and shoulder other people's misery so well that the infirm seem to gravitate to them, to find a comfortable place to die in Apple Valley. First Roy's mother, then his father, in between various friends. Gabby Hayes came to them as soon as his wife died and cried at their dinner table. . . .

But, enough. Roy has his bowling league this night, and I am left free to wander through the museum. In it are:

Roy's and Dale's first boots (bronzed), and scores of pictures of the two of them in various films and with their family. A special memorial section for the three children who died and for Roy's mother, featuring the dolls he brought her from his travels; a $55,000 exhibition saddle studded with fourteen hundred rubies; a scroll and fez proclaiming Roy a thirty-second degree Mason and the Rogers honorary doctor of humanities degree from Bethany College in West Virginia; a special display corner entitled "Our Religious Heritage"; the keys to a thousand cities and a plaque making Roy an honorary Kentucky colonel and badges of honorary sheriffdom everywhere. There are mementos from fans (handmade covered wagons and stagecoaches and cowboys and Indians) and a family table built for them by actor George Montgomery; Nellybelle, the Jeep from his TV series; and pictures of Roy with Max Baer, Jack Dempsey, Johnny Mack Brown, Babe Ruth, Joe Martin, Walter Brennan, Connie Mack, Alfalfa (a hunting partner), Clark Gable (another hunting partner), Bill Stern, Louella Parsons, Paul Whiteman, Billy Graham. . . .

There are awards for twelve straight years as the number-one Western box-office attraction; a plaque reading, "To Roy, Many Thanks," from General William Westmoreland for the thirty-four shows he did in seventeen days in Vietnam; and an automatic rifle taken from one of the six Vietcong captured while standing at the edge of the jungle watching Roy perform. Beyond that, there are enough guns to outfit the Bolivian Army, screen guns, hunting guns, rifles, shotguns, handguns. Roy Rogers, who would never kill a man on the screen, has slain just about everything else that walks, flies or crawls: lion, elephant, Cape buffalo, hippo, koodoo, antelope, wolves, foxes, grizzly bear, California brown bear, even a polar bear. There is his record-holding award

from the world-famous "One Shot Antelope Hunt" in Wyoming
(to which dukes and princes and tycoons are invited once in
their lifetime to stalk and shoot an antelope. Roy's record performance: one shot through the heart at two hundred and fifty
yards after a sixteen-minute stalk).

And, in a separate case, Trigger, mounted, his hooves raised
on high, with Bullet the stuffed Wonder Dog gazing up from the
corner. There is nothing comic to behold, only the echo of Roy's
remark: "I just couldn't put the old fellow in the ground."

That night, Roy is in high spirits at the Victor Bowl. He and
his five-man bowling team are resplendent in turquoise bowling
shirts bearing the legend ROY ROGERS MUSEUM on the back. Roy
uses a marbled red, white and blue bowling ball. His hyper-
tension shows through on the lanes; he jumps up and down
excitedly, giving it a rousing "Attaboy, Bubba!" when one of his
teammates fires a strike. Three times he drags me over to the bul-
letin board to show me his team's enviable record: five straight
league titles.

The next morning he takes me out to the site where the new,
enlarged Roy Rogers Museum may someday stand. I ask him
again why he is making this movie. He decided to make this
movie, he says, "because I've raised six children, and they've
given me fifteen grandchildren, and now I've got an itch to do
something. I gotta keep on the go all the time, and there's
nothing I like better than getting out and meeting the public."
Fair enough. Even an ole homebody like Roy can miss the roar
of the greasepaint.

We shake hands good-bye, and Art and I start back up the
long trail to L.A. He talks quiet, soothing, living-legend talk; it's
all very nice, but I somehow can't rid myself of the notion that
there is something peculiar about a man who not only keeps a
dead horse hanging around, but builds a split-rail cathedral to it
to boot.

So, what the hell. In his lifetime he has given more than six
thousand benefit performances—nearly all for children. He has
brought health and happiness to millions of youngsters in an age
when world leaders indifferently dispense hurt and misery
among their young. So if Roy wants to ride again in something
called *Mackintosh and T.J.*, I say he's damn well earned the
right.

Happy trails, Roy.

Dad

BY JOHN LEONARD

The following news item appeared, in its entirety, in the *International Herald Tribune* on Thursday, July 17, 1975:

SPERM BANK'S LOSS IS STERILE MAN'S LAWSUIT

SAN FRANCISCO, July 16 (AP)—*A man who stored a sample of his semen at a sperm bank and then had a vasectomy has filed a $5,000,000 lawsuit against the bank for accidentally destroying the specimen.*

Gregory Marton said in his suit filed yesterday in Superior Court that he has suffered "emotional and mental anguish" because of an apparent equipment failure at the Chartered International Cryo-Bank at Cathedral Hill Medical Center here.

Mr. Marton said that when he contracted with the bank in January, its president told him that his sperm deposit was "fully protected against destruction" by two "fail-safe" monitoring systems.

After being sterilized by the vasectomy operation, Mr. Marton said that, on June 22, he received a letter from the sperm bank saying that his semen had been destroyed in a possible equipment failure.

As it happens, the original of this news item was eaten by a goat in the Jardin d'Acclimatation, Bois de Boulogne, Paris,

France, where I had taken a small boy in order that he might humiliate me at miniature golf. The boy did not belong to me; he had been rented for the occasion. No American would visit the Bois without a child, even if the baboons *have* gone to the South of France for the summer. We lunched, among fat fish, listless fowl and the goats, at a restaurant called La Ferme du Golf. Such is the charm of La Ferme du Golf that each table comes provisioned with a stick. I assumed these truncheons were there for French families to use on their children. *Tant pis.* They were actually there for patrons to beat off the disreputable goats, who clomped into the restaurant and attacked us in our *jambon.* Denied ham sandwiches, the goats lunged into our laps, toppled the Alsatian beer, and gobbled up the *serviettes* and the French money with the pretty pictures of Voltaire and Berlioz on it and the July 17 edition of the *International Herald Tribune.*

Sad-making. Certainly we want to know more of Gregory Marton. Is he married? Has he children? What does he *do*—bail bondsman, astronaut, grape picker, wunderkind of corn chips, teacher of Berlitz? And yet, more information might injure him in his typicalness. I believe Gregory Marton to be the representative American male. He is practical, with yearnings. He is well-intentioned, and a hedger. He is a semi-hero sandwich. His passion for immortality (my chromosomes, my karma) and his impulse to cooperate in helping to fix things up (the population explosion, the energy crisis) have been grafted like transistor radios onto either side of his brain, a headset, one to each ear and each tuned to a different station. Free will and technology are his Muzak. He chooses to be vasectomized, but somewhere in a bank his sperm will be fail-safe, on ice, an investment of capital. When the monitoring systems dysfunction, he will appeal to the state for redress of biological and metaphysical grievance. Amazingly, he will assess the damage to his existential self at $5,000,000. And characteristically, as an American father apologizing to posterity, he will seek to blame whatever did or didn't happen on a "possible equipment failure." It had to be somebody else's fault, beyond the control of Daddy. Maybe money—a materialization of energy, the only mass known to the American male—will prove his innocence and compensate for the drying up of his gene pool.

Gregory Marton, a romantic, would not be appreciated in

France, this most bourgeois of nations, a kind of haughty Holland. The Frenchman is romantic, God knows why, about his war-making and his love-making, which is to say he is romantic about himself. He is not romantic about his children. I have been watching the way the French treat their children. It is roughly the way they treat their dogs. In the city, they lock their dogs in their cars. In the country, they keep their dogs on chains. All day, every day, everywhere in France, children hear three things from their parents: *assieds-toi, tais-toi,* and *ne touche pas* (sit down, shut up, don't touch). They are more important, of course, than dogs, but less important than furniture and the statues of generals. They are as unwelcome in most restaurants as they are on the grass of the public parks. Their education seems a deliberate attempt to keep them in their place, like the Portuguese maids and the Algerian street sweepers; to smother any spontaneity that might have been sparked by the friction of their rubbing against their peers. Perhaps this accounts for the fact that when they reach adolescence, when they form motorbike gangs, when they sit around café tables at, say, the Place de la Bastille or across the street from the Merovingians at St. Germain-en-Laye, wearing blue jeans and T-shirts printed with the names of American universities, drinking Cokes and blowing smoke into each other's eyes and trying to look menacing, they lack conviction. They are not persuasive. They have borrowed their behavior from the movies they go to incessantly.

To be sure, the traditional role of the American father has been to tell his children to sit down, shut up, don't touch, Daddy's driving. But it is equally traditional for him to feel guilty about it, as the French do not. (The only man in France who appears to feel guilty about anything is Marcel Ophuls.) Why should he feel guilty? Because the chief value of American culture is happiness, as the chief value of French culture is glory. When Americans are not happy, they feel guilty. And the American father is certainly not happy when most of his communication with his children consists of telling them to shut up. Neither, for that matter, are his children. This hurts. If, as is probably the case, the American father has not found happiness in his marriage, his work, his possessions, then surely it must reside in his children. When it does not—when his children, grow-

ing up surly, come more and more to resemble a tribunal, a
hanging judge with acne, and he is in the dock precisely for not
having made them happy—he begins to brood. It is another
difference between the two cultures. An American fails to
achieve happiness, feels guilty and begins to brood; a Frenchman fails to achieve glory, feels shame, denies it strenuously, and
takes a mistress.

Actually, happiness is just as silly as glory for a chief cultural
value, and the pursuit of it should never have been put into the
Declaration of Independence to make American fathers feel that
they have let their country down by being sad. Why Americans
feel guilty about being unhappy is something that political scien-
tists and investigative reporters ought to look into; it may be a
plot by psychoanalysts to keep their couches crowded. One
should feel guilty about failing to behave virtuously, not about
failing to be happy. Somehow, Americans have managed to
make happiness into a virtue. In no way does it correspond to
any definition of virtue I can find in the *Oxford English Dictionary,* from "the power or operative influence inherent in a super-
natural or divine being" to "conformity of life and conduct with
the principles of morality" to "a particular moral excellence."
Whether or not I am happy in La Ferme du Golf with a small
boy, a stick and the goats is a matter of personal interest to me
but is totally without moral, political or cultural significance.

I'm reminded of a story told by the novelist Dan Wakefield.
Wakefield, accompanied by another novelist, Kurt Vonnegut, Jr.,
and their publisher, Seymour Lawrence, ventured out one day to
inspect a rural New England commune run by the erstwhile radical Ray Mungo and his friends. Mungo showed them around
and then explained that his group was turning over the commune to younger people. His group would go farther north, toward the wilds of Canada, where the conditions were "really
primitive." Taming the "really primitive" appealed to them, said
Mungo, because "we want to be the last people living on the
earth." The novelists contemplated this ambition for a while in
silence. Then Vonnegut, many times a father, asked with a
frown: "Isn't that a kind of stuck-up thing to want to be?" Stuck-
up—the perfect fifties synonym for "conceited." When you are
accused of being stuck-up, you are likely to blush. It isn't a criminal offense; it is a social embarrassment, as failing to be happy is

a private embarrassment. I think that people who confuse their personal happiness with public virtue and cultural value are stuck-up. That goes for nations, too.

Nevertheless, the American father *is* unhappy, guilty, embarrassed. He believes he has tried hard. Life hasn't worked out the way it was supposed to. There should be, but there isn't, a machine to fix things up, or a pill. Somebody has to accept the responsibility for its not working out, and who else is there? Not all of us have the Chartered International Cryo-Bank around to sue for equipment failure.

I have written on this subject before, but I am going to repeat myself because the relative silence continues to amaze me. Why have so few of our established male novelists written about their children, their American fatherhood—especially those novelists who are principally concerned with manners and morals instead of the inadequacy of language and the cunning of the id? John Updike tries on occasion, as does Saul Bellow at a distance, always a chilly distance. Vonnegut flirts. Norman Mailer and Bernard Malamud and Philip Roth have so far avoided the subject. Henry James died amid subterfuges. Mark Twain turned the subject on its head. Melville was silent. Hemingway—with the exception of his last, posthumously published and pretty bad book—and Fitzgerald were their own bright little boys to the end: there's room in the nursery for just one of us. Faulkner violently engaged the generations, but his children were flowering curses, clocks wired to bombs; they proved a thesis. The male American novelist has usually been too busy killing his father to contemplate being one.

There are two exceptions, and they speak to my gloomy point. Allowing for extravagant differences in style, John Cheever's *Bullet Park* and Joseph Heller's *Something Happened* are remarkably similar in theme. Both novels deal with the inability of American fathers to protect the children we love. Both protagonists, Eliot Nailles and Bob Slocum, hold down dispiriting jobs in New York City and commute to those jobs from homes in suburban Connecticut, where they have removed their families—their emotional capital—to spare the children the anger, the dangerous chance, of the streets. In both books, what Cheever calls "that sense of sanctuary that is the essence of love" is violated. Neither Nailles nor Slocum is able to protect his son from the invasion of evil, anarchy, chance, father. Nailles, unconvincingly, epiphanizes; Slocum, helplessly, destroys.

I suspect most American fathers are acquainted with that helplessness; it is our nightmare, of wanting desperately to protect our children, not least of all from ourselves. The American father lives inside the discrepancy between what he hopes for his children and what he does to them. What he hopes is that they will be happy and approve of his trusteeship. What he does is to betray them, as he always expected he would. A stranger to any other virtue except "happiness," he will betray them by his absence, by accident, inadequacy, anger, vanity, the pursuit of his own vaguely defined and seldom secured peace of mind. Not on purpose, but because his own ecstasies and wearinesses have a larger claim on his attention than the need of his children to be preserved in aspic. He may even resent their need. After all, they cannot save him from death. Why should he be expected to save them from pain?

Still, he loves them. There is reciprocity in everything. If they don't recognize his helplessness, he remembers theirs. His mind is a revolving door of albums, snapshots. Once upon a time, when they were infants, when they burned like fierce little furnaces, when there was a hole in the tops of their heads, just membrane where the sections of skull hadn't grown together yet, he had held them—scared witness then, for them and him, giving them up to their mother before he might hurt them. He recalls as well the various strollers, apartments, fevers, teeth, parks, toys, their eagerness to pin life down and break its arm, the winsomeness of their inexperience and vulnerability, the skin like sand and the eyes like aquariums in which all light swam, every thought was a guppy, a trout. His awkwardness oppressed him; he was an accident waiting for them. When, exactly, had he wandered off into his own anxieties, leaving everything to their mother? I am tired, busy, disappointed, having an affair. He would die for them. No, he has to die for himself. Dying is privacy, another American virtue.

Thinking this way, he will try to prove his love. He will go on binges, elephant-gun bursts of no-I'm-not-too-busy-to-straighten-your-handlebars-correct-your-homework. He will mow down the guarded expectations of these wards, these hostages. Because he is not very inventive, he will have to rely on memory. American fathers are big on repeating what once worked, on institutionalizing *neat things* they did with their kids when everybody was too young to know any better. So he will read to them or wrestle with them, buy them dolls or electric trains, take them to circuses or ball games. He will accompany them on safaris to bag tacos or tennis sneakers. He will volunteer a game of crazy eights or Monopoly or miniature golf. He will admire their finger-painting, clarinet-playing, report cards, cootie-catchers, cavities, leotards, confections of hair lotion and raw shrimp, bad puns repeated for the tenth time. They will, as always, defer to him, almost imperial in their caution, as though prepared for the worst but willing to be pleasantly surprised. He is profoundly clumsy. Is that why they suspect him? Or perhaps they feel that his binge of love is just as arbitrary as his don't-touches and his shut-ups, a papal bull of intimacy, not to be trusted. He comes to bid good-night. They are absorbed in *The Waltons* or Horatio Hornblower or rock music. They look up, as if expecting equally a cuff or a kiss. They are as Arab refugees, lost in their music or their drugs or their dreams of vengeance. Even the music repudiates him. According to Rilke, music was supposed to be a breathing of statues, space grown from our hearts. These children have reversed Rilke like a raincoat. Transistorized, their music seems to have turned them into statues in the rooms of his own home; space grows *in* their hearts, and it's empty. They make of sullenness almost an abstract art; he isn't expected, he isn't intended, to understand. It's unfair. He will feel insufficiently approved of, having made such a special effort to curry their favor.

In this, the two cultures of America and France are one, given as much to self-pity as the rest of the adult male world, except perhaps China where, we are informed, nothing imperfect is permitted to happen.

I think most American fathers secretly do not believe in Father's Day. It is a joke played on us. It may not be necessary much longer. If the genetic engineers and the radical feminists get together, we will no longer be needed. After all, Dr. Daniele Petrucci kept *something* alive for twenty-nine days in a glass. When they get to the point, and they will, where life can be synthesized in the laboratory, where we can all be cloned from a single cell asexually, what then happens to Oedipus? Who'll take the rap? That will be a relief. Imagine a sperm bank on every corner, like a Parisian café; artificial wombs, eliminating the need for pregnancy; consenting adults shopping at a commissary where frozen one-day-old embryos are stacked like packages of flower seeds, selecting one, dropping it off at the bottling works on their way to a meeting, picking it up whenever it's hatched, then farming it out to the appropriate commune on two-year contracts, options to renew on both sides, for a very extended family life. Rent-a-child, like leasing a TV set: no blood, no birth, no death, no love, no failure. It is important, you see, to reduce the number of times we are obliged to fail, to minimize the number of things for which we can be held accountable.

Obviously, we will need more than two fail-safe monitoring systems.

Why is it that the American father doesn't know how to behave with his children? Why is it that he expects from the beginning to fail them, that his betrayals have an almost gratifying quality—at last, the bad dream come true? It is simply that he is born, he is raised and he will die in a culture that hasn't given a single serious thought to fathering, for all its baby books and marriage contracts and consciousness-raising bull sessions. The women will take care of the children. It is the business of the man to. . . .

To what? We are no longer hunters, warriors, Fisher Kings. Nor are we detectives or pioneers or spies or Texas Rangers. According to the movies, once upon a time we were supposed to be Judge Hardy; then we were asked to be Gregory Peck in *To Kill a Mockingbird;* now to be a father is to be Charles Bronson in *Death Wish.* According to the novelists, we are Eliot Nailles and Robert Slocum. According to the theater, we are Dagwood. According to television, we are now and always have been jerks, from *Ozzie and Harriet* and *My Little Margie* and *The Life of Riley* to *All in the Family* and *Sanford and Son* and *The Jeffersons,* regardless of race, creed or class. On TV, we can't even tie our shoes without falling on our faces. Only a dog would trust us to go to the grocery store without a name tag or a stamped, self-addressed return envelope. Some of us are so incompetent that the ordinary, everyday heroic wife and mother is insufficient for our needs; we have to have cute witches and magical nannies. Of course, there's Charles "Pa" Ingalls, but that was back in the nineteenth century. And there's John Walton, but that was back in the Depression. At best, the modern American father on TV is Dick Van Dyke, who is charming even as he trips over his own couch. Most of the time, though, we are either Desi Arnaz or Danny Thomas: there is contempt in their love for us. The women, as usual, will clean up the mess we've made.

The culture expects us to fail, and we oblige the culture.

I am sitting now at a typewriter near a window which looks out on the rue des Beaux-Arts, where, down at the end of the street, there is a Vietnamese restaurant that accepts American Express credit cards. My children aren't with me; I have rushed headlong into another future, rather astonished that there are still choices to be made and the energy, for good or ill, to make them. Somewhere, lawyers are deciding on visitation rights. Of course, I feel guilty for wanting to be happy and for making others unhappy. It seems that I have been having a mid-life crisis since I was seven years old. In a moment, I will take a train to Versailles where, I am told, the Sun King had a pretty good interior decorator, although it is said that some of the rooms are a little busy. I wonder if it is stuck-up to have a mid-life crisis. Perhaps I should rent another small boy to accompany me to Versailles. There is really no happy way to end this article.

The Stand-up Comic

BY ROBERT ALAN AURTHUR

It's as simple as this: There are some performers who have given you so much pleasure that, above and beyond paying the price of admission to theaters or clubs, or tuning in to television appearances and buying sponsors' products, you owe them. And when the opportunity arises, you pay off a little. For me, Milton Berle is such a performer. For nearly thirty years he has made me laugh harder, more, and more often than any other artist of our time; and with the publication of his book, *Milton Berle, An Autobiography* (with Haskel Frankel), I can now urge every reader with the slightest interest in show business to speedily make way to wherever books are sold and get a copy. Or borrow it from your local library. Or wait for the paperback. But read the book; because Milton Berle, showing his usual top form, has produced with writer Frankel perhaps the best book ever written about a performer. Not the least of the virtues of Milton's autobiography is that from its pages his mother, the ubiquitous Sandra, emerges as a monster of such dread proportions that in contrast Mrs. Portnoy becomes your favorite aunt. Still proclaiming love for her memory Milton has tried, painfully, through the process of telling his story, to come to terms with the woman who crippled him from birth. And made him a star, rich and famous.

On the day I read the book, at once deciding to write about it, I tried to call Berle in California only to learn that just the night

before he had gone to a Los Angeles hospital to have an operation. Ulcers. What a commonplace irony. Such a cliché. One of
the greatest stars of his time; a millionaire; a celebrity with a
hot-selling book as the latest success in a terrific career; and
three days after he is feted in New York by some of his peers,
and many lesser lights, at a giant Friars Club roast, at age sixty-
six he checks in for the ulcer operation. Berle has had the ulcers,
I am told, since he was fifteen years old. A commonplace story,
yes, in a business where the great star, a winner in the American
Dream contest, finds himself center stage alone, a headliner in an
emotional Tap City. Milton would like us to think about this.

Yet, waiting to hear the outcome of his operation, I prefer to
think of all the times I've seen Berle perform, starting with the
fabled appearance in 1946 at New York's Carnival Room. The
first time I'd ever been in such a nightclub. So funny it was painful. Customers screamed and fell from their chairs. When Milton
leaped out to join the super-square Ben Yost Vikings, yes, in the
baggy pants, the plastered-down hair, the blacked-out teeth, I
believe I cracked four ribs. Never before or since has there been
such comic hysteria. And all the times since then, lacking only
the shock of surprise, but nonetheless hilarious: Miami; Las
Vegas; Chicago; Cherry Hill, New Jersey; Westbury, Long Island; and Boston, in a huge, depressing barn of a club half filled
with mostly hostile drunks. That night in Boston my wife and I
took Agnes de Mille, who claimed that she had never before seen
Milton anywhere. Miss de Mille is not a big laugher (sometimes
a cool smile), but while Berle was on I think she went into some
kind of paralysis from pleasure.

There are those who do not think Milton Berle is funny, and
some who dismiss him as just a baggy-pants comic. We will ignore these minority groups to remember that Milton Berle was
the first and perhaps greatest of all television stars. In the United
States, starting in September 1948, Tuesday night at eight o'clock
belonged to Berle. Theaters, movie houses, and restaurants were
deserts. He had a Nielsen rating of 83.9. For seven and a half
seasons, about forty weeks a year, he produced, directed, helped
write, and starred in a *live* show, and in those seven and a half
years, figuring conservatively, he entertained some ten million
people a week. Fassa, fassa, fassa . . . if I can multiply right

that's three billion viewers, which is more than the number of people in the whole world at the time.

There are also those who believe that Berle's public image of brashness, even vulgarity, is all there is, but the facts are different. With Milton still hospitalized and unavailable, I speak to the publicist at his publisher's; she has been handling press on the book, accompanied Milton on his publicity hustle. "I guess I expected some kind of wild person," she says, "but I found him to be extraordinary. A lovely gentleman." Yes, and kind and generous. In a later phone call with writer Hank Frankel we talk about Milton's beneficence toward younger talents. I tell Frankel how I was once with Woody Allen when we ran into Berle in a restaurant. Straight out Milton told Woody what a fan he was; and then, learning that Woody was a magic freak, insisted on making a date to take him to a shop on Broadway where Milton would reveal all the great tricks. Berle's expertise with cards, by the way, is legendary. Somewhat stunned by the attention, and extremely grateful, Woody later reported that in the shop Milton had done about an hour of incredible material.

To me Frankel recalls a night spent with Berle in a dismal club in Springfield, Massachusetts. "There was a black comic whom Milton remembered from Fifty-second Street," Frankel says. "After the show Milton got the guy to run down his act, editing, adding jokes, giving him shtick. It was obvious the man was going nowhere, but Milton was fantastically kind."

The book was written, Frankel tells me, over a period of some two and a half years during which Berle made about five hundred hours of tape. I ask whether Milton tried to entertain him throughout the process. "Never when we were alone," Frankel says, "but the minute someone came in—a waiter, anybody— then he'd be on."

(One of the great evenings for me was about ten years ago when I was invited to a birthday party Ruth Berle gave for Milton in a rented house in Holmby Hills. There were many funny people there, but for a long while the evening was merely quiet and pleasant. And then someone, maybe Ernie Kovacs, recited a funny limerick, and everyone laughed. Instantly Berle leaped up and recited all the limericks he happened to know, perhaps three. *No one* laughed. Facing death, Milton became manic and began to improvise wild, crazy, mostly dirty limericks, which made no sense but did rhyme. He jumped up onto chairs, vaulted couches, tried to climb the mantel. Soon, everyone was laughing at the nutty infant screaming for attention, everyone but Jack Benny, who from deep in an overstuffed chair, completely solemn-faced, said, "What will you do for a finish, Milton?" Berle had the answer: He dropped his pants. Benny laughed.)

"It's surprising," Hank Frankel tells me, "that we went through all that and came out good friends." When Frankel felt that Berle seemed to be hiding too much, the writer sent him a copy of a show-biz autobiography where all the names and many of the facts had been changed. "Milton read it and was enraged," Frankel says, "because he knew the person and knew how dishonest the book was. The next time we met he kept saying, 'We've got to be honest . . . we've just got to be honest!'" And when I comment on the treatment of Sandra Berle: "That was the toughest part," say Frankel. "Through the taping he was always protective of her. You know, Milton has never been to a psychiatrist, but because of the book and as a result of a lot of subsequent interviews I think Milton is finding out that it's all right to hate his mother." Frankel is pleased, and perhaps surprised, that when Berle read the final manuscript he asked for nothing to be deleted or changed. "Not even the part about his mother pimping for him. I expected him to find that objectionable, but there was not a word. He took nothing out."

When Milton is released from the hospital, I call him at his home in Beverly Hills. He's pleased that I like his book. "It's honest, it's dramatic," he admits. There is not much we can say over a long-distance wire; he sounds tired, enervated, but I do ask who among the younger comedians makes him laugh these days. "It's very difficult for me," he says. "I can't see a performer without watching and analyzing techniques. It's impossible for me simply to be an audience. I like character comedy, juxtaposed comedy, the comedy of opposites. Though I'm a stand-up comic, and I like what I do, when it comes to watching someone else I prefer comedians to comics. I'm still a Woody Allen fan. Wild, funny switches coming from that serious little man; that's what I mean about opposites. And I wish Nichols and May would come back. I'm a Mort Sahl fan, too. I'm impressed by easy, sharp, sophisticated work." A quick, almost apologetic laugh. "Not exactly what you would expect from me."

Knowing that Milton failed to convert Lenny Bruce to a path of righteousness, I ask him whether he's seen Bob Fosse's film *Lenny*, where in a minute of devastating mimicry Gary Morton plays Milton Berle trying to affect Dustin Hoffman as Bruce. "Yes, I saw it," Milton says, "and off the record—no, on the record, who gives a goddamn—I didn't like it much. Sure, I was the one who told Lenny he didn't need all the obscenity, because he was too sharp, too funny. I became . . . I guess you could say I was his nemesis. But the picture never really goes into the sick drug thing, the *why*. I knew Sally Marr, I knew all those people, but from the movie you never know what made it happen."

To a significant degree Milton's book is his own attempt to find out the *why*. "My life," Berle says on page sixteen, "runs on guilt and adrenaline." And much later, sitting in his darkened Beverly Hills den, "still searching for an answer, still running to the next show . . ." Milton says, "People with homes and regulated lives make me nervous . . . I don't understand their lives, because I've never had what they've got. The idea of approaching tomorrow with peace because you know it will be like today is something I've never known."

Here is the closest that Berle, sometimes a sentimentalist, comes to a moment of self-pity. He agonizes over the fact that he's miserable; it doesn't figure. After all, he's *made it!* Starting among the poorest of the poor, through a combination of talent, drive and creativity, he became the greatest clown of his time; he picked up all the gold on his block; he hit the top and stayed there; he realized the American Dream; he even had an affair with Marilyn Monroe, for crissake! It just doesn't figure to feel rotten after all that. But because this part of Berle's story is so commonplace, shared by so many others in his business—the suicides, the drunks, the drug addicts, the crazies—maybe Milton is saner and luckier than most. After all, he's alive, he doesn't drink, God forbid he should even walk into a room where pot is being smoked, and he has a splendid wife and son to come home to. Too bad that's not enough.

And yet. . . . "Milton had a great title suggestion for the book," Haskel Frankel told me. "He wanted to call it *Love Me, Love Me, Love Me, Love Me* . . . big letters getting smaller and smaller, covering the jacket right into infinity. But the publisher rejected it." That figures.

Baseball

BY TOM WICKER

One hot night in the summer of 1949, I climbed to my usual
perch in the cramped press box above the wooden stands of the
baseball park in Lumberton, North Carolina. As telegraph editor, general reporter and all-around handyman for the afternoon
Robesonian of that city, I had appointed myself sports editor,
also, and regularly covered the home games of the Lumberton
Auctioneers, a farm club of the Chicago Cubs playing in the
Class D Tobacco State League. *The Robesonian* paid me not a
cent more for spending my summer evenings keeping notes and
score, but *The News and Observer* of Raleigh, the state-capital
daily, paid me three dollars a game—as I recall it—for filing
each night's box score by phone to its sports pages.

The '49 Auctioneers were undistinguished by anything, including success, except a locally famous first baseman named Turkey
Tyson. A stoop-shouldered slap hitter with a reputation for zani-
ness and getting on base, Tyson derived his nickname from a
gobblerlike sound of derision he made when he pulled up at first
after one of the frequent singles he poked through opposing
infields. The Turkey had played with more minor-league teams
than probably exist today and was at the end of the line in Class
D; his future was ten seasons behind him and he was old enough
to be the father of most of the post-high-school kids he played
with and against.

One exception—I recall only that his first name was Mike—

was a burly, blue-bearded outfielder the Auks (as I labeled them in the headlines over my stories) had obtained somewhere in mid-season. He could play ball, or something resembling it, when infrequently sober, had traveled the minor leagues from coast to coast, and although younger than Tyson was also down and about to be out in Class D. (Neither got much closer to the majors than the Game of the Day on radio.) Mike had some difficulty handling the ball, except at the plate; he swung a bat the size of one of the telephone poles that held up the dim lights in the outfield. When he connected he could hit the ball over those lights. More often, he took three mighty swings and hurried back to the bench for a quick swig.

I had noticed a little something about Mike and that morning in *The Robesonian* had unburdened myself of some inside dope for the avid readers, I liked to imagine. Mike, I told them, was a first-pitch swinger, and the other Tobacco State League clubs were onto him; if he'd lay off that first pitch, I suggested, and wait for *his* pitch, his average would go up and so would the Auks'.

There was a good crowd on hand that night and in the first inning Turkey Tyson rewarded his fans with his specialty—a ground single about two inches out of reach of a flat-footed second baseman who was probably getting eighty dollars a month and meal money and might someday make it to the Piedmont League, Class B. *Gobble-gobble* went the Turkey triumphantly from first, and Auks fans cheered. But that was nothing to the roar that went up when barrel-chested Mike, batting cleanup, strode to the plate, thumped his telephone pole twice upon it, then turned his back to the pitcher and pointed that huge bat straight up at the press box and me.

I can only imagine what it was he yelled at me, but I learned one thing—those fans had read my article in *The Robesonian.* That roar told me everyone in the park knew Mike would defy my first-pitch edict. I prayed for the pitcher to throw him the deepest-breaking curve or the fanciest knuckle ball in the history of Abner Doubleday's cow-pasture creation. But somehow I knew, and the crowd knew—as Mike turned back to the plate, hunched over it, waved his war club menacingly, and waggled his rump at the world—exactly what was going to happen.

It did. That pitcher came in with a fast ball that would have

bounced off a windowpane. I can still see that mighty swing,
hear the crack of the bat connecting, watch the ball soar into
outer darkness. As one of the Auks said later, "Mike just disappeared it."

I can still hear that crowd, too, roaring not just for Mike but *at*
me, isolated as I was under the single light bulb in my press-box
perch. In the open stands down the first- and third-base lines,
they stood and pointed upward and howled with glee, as Mike
showboated around the bases behind Turkey Tyson and reached
the plate again, jumped on it with both feet and bowed low to
the press box. Cowering above him in that naked light, I did the
only thing I could do; I stood up and bowed, too, and the crowd
howled some more. I thought there must be for Mike, in that
moment of defiance and triumph, a certain compensation for all
those long bus rides through the minor leagues, that long decline
of hope and youth down to the smelly locker rooms of Class D.
And I *knew* I was never going to make a sportswriter.

And I didn't, although I later did an unavoidable hitch in the
sports department of the Winston-Salem *Journal* before I could
escape to politics. I don't even see many baseball games these
days.

Some idle evenings, I may pick up an inning or two on television, but that's not really baseball on the screen—only part of a
reasonable facsimile of the sport I've loved all my life. Maybe I'll
get out to Shea Stadium two or three times a season, but somehow that doesn't seem like the real thing either.

It's not just that the game, at least the way a fan sees it, has
changed. It has, but it's not fundamentally different from Turkey
Tyson's game, or Babe Ruth's, for that matter. All the old symmetry is there—the innings and outs in their orderly multiples of
threes, the foul lines radiating out to the stands, the diamond in
its classic dimensions, the exact sixty feet and six inches between
the pitching rubber and home plate. The ageless rituals seem
never to change—the ball tossed around after an infield out, the
coaches waggling and patting their impenetrable signals, the
pitcher's sidewise stance with a man on first, the dash and whirl
of the pregame infield practice, that solemn conclave of managers and umpires at the plate just before *The Star-Spangled
Banner*.

Astroturf, designated hitters, Disneyland scoreboards, salad-bowl stadiums, and Batting Glove Day can't change all that. Nothing seems really to change the game itself: the spectacular individual effort on which it depends; the lack of violence but the sense of menace in the thrown ball, the slashing spikes, the swinging bat; the sudden splendid bursts of action—a runner going from first to third, or even home, on a single, sliding in inches ahead of or behind a perfect peg; the suspense of pitcher vs. hitter in a late-inning rally, with the winning runs on base; all the straight-faced exchanges of "strategy" between managers pulling the same hoary maneuvers John McGraw did, or Connie Mack; the power and the glory of an overwhelming pitcher in his prime; the art and cunning of an experienced pitcher past his prime; the swagger of a big hitter at the plate.

All that is still there for the seeing, even in stadiums like Shea or Chavez Ravine, where the players look like pygmies on a foreign field—even on Astroturf, which senselessly abolishes the clay crescent of the infield, which should be as much a part of the game as knee pants and billed caps.

No, the reason I don't see much baseball today has little to do with the game itself. The problem is that all that's really left is the big leagues and the Little League, and I don't trace back to either. I go back to small-town baseball before television and the suburbs. I loved the game on the vacant lots of childhood, with pickup teams from the neighborhood, someone's dime-store ball coming apart at the seams, and—in the railroad town where I grew up—sometimes a brake stick for a bat.

Later, in high school and the unending hot summer days of youth, baseball in the dust of skinned infields was life itself to me. Catching for my high-school team, I took a throw from the outfield and put the tag on a runner coming in spikes up, but not before he ripped my thigh open for six inches above the knee. I lay on the ground by the plate while they poured iodine or something on me and it didn't hurt much, because I knew that runner was out and I hadn't ducked away from his spikes. And then I saw my father leaning over me, down from the stands to check on his little boy's wounds, and for the first time in my life I cursed him, told him to go away. I thought I was no kid to be fretted over. That was the spring of '44 and before the year was over one of my teammates was dead in the Battle of the Bulge.

After school was out, we shifted annually to American Legion

Junior Baseball, on the same skinned infields, before the same wooden grandstands, in the concession stands of which the ladies of the American Legion Auxiliary sold icy Cokes and peanuts and "bellywashers"—the local name for Royal Crown Cola. The first time I played baseball under lights it was with the Richmond County American Legion Juniors. We played a preseason game in Greensboro, a big city to Richmond County kids, and got stomped; I remember Coach Bill Haltiwanger taking out his fourth pitcher of the night, a rawboned left-hander out of the cotton mills, who had just given up something like five runs after striking out the first batter he faced.

"Well, Lefty," Coach Haltiwanger said, taking the ball from him, "you almost had 'em."

Later on, I tried out for college baseball and got cut the first day of practice. No arm. Even later, I tried to stage a comeback in the Peach Belt League, a semipro circuit in North Carolina, but I didn't last long. Still no arm, and that was a pretty fast league. I remember one elderly Peach Belt pitcher, about Turkey Tyson's vintage, who had been knocking around the semipro and mill-town leagues as long as I'd been living. He had one pitch, a jug-handle curve that came in from the general direction of third base, and he could throw it through a keyhole at about the speed of ice melting. I've seen husky young men who could have broken him in two break their backs instead, trying to hit that jug-handle. He would stand out there and spit tobacco juice, not infrequently on the ball, and throw it past them for nine innings, or as long as the game went on. And I'd have sold my soul just to be able to throw out a runner at second maybe once or twice a game.

We were not, of course, unaware in those days of the major leagues, although we got a lot more news about the Charlotte Hornets of the Piedmont League, a Washington Senators farm club. I pored daily over the box scores from the big leagues, particularly the Dodgers and the Giants, and never missed a Game of the Day if I could help it. Other forms of life stopped during the World Series, while people huddled at the radio. In the main, however, the big leagues were far away and second fiddle to the American Legion Juniors—although I had seen a major-league game from the bleachers of old Griffith Stadium once when my family made a tourist trip to Washington. Dutch

Leonard pitched and a good ole Georgia boy, Cecil Travis, got a couple of hits. Most of life has been downhill since that day.

So baseball for a lot of people is the memory of Joe DiMaggio in center field, or the Gashouse Gang, or Lou Gehrig's farewell to Yankee Stadium, or all those Dodger-Yankee Series of the fifties (those magic names! Gionfriddo, Podres, Mantle, the Duke, Berra, Robinson, Campanella, Ford). I remember all that, too. I remember Bobby Thomson's home run, and the first televised Series I saw—Durocher's Giants swept Cleveland. I remember Don Larsen's perfect game and Ernie Lombardi's swoon and I have a dim memory of my father boasting about somebody he called The Goose—Goslin, of course, of the Senators. I hit Hubbell's screwball in my dreams.

But all that is secondhand to me, baseball once removed, the perfect baseball I never really saw or knew. Maybe it's age, maybe it's change, maybe it's wounds deeper than the one that left the scar I still bear on my thigh; but baseball to *me* is the skinned infield of my youth, the wooden grandstands, the despair of being washed up with no arm at age twenty-one, the recollection of a fast-ball pitcher who was throwing it past me until I choked the bat, stepped forward in the box and put it almost down his throat, just over second for a single. Baseball to me is the remembered taste of an ice-cold bellywasher sneaked between innings, against all rules. The railroad embankment was just beyond right field and the trains went by, whistling us on. It was always summer, and this season we were solid up the middle, we could win it all.

I like to think that thirty years ago baseball in America was something we had to hold on to, to hold us together—solid, changeless, universal, at one and the same time peculiarly *ours* and yet part of the great world beyond us. You pulled off the double play the same way for the Richmond County Juniors, the Auks or the White Sox. When I was in the press box in Lumberton or dying with shame when they stole second on me five times in Carthage, baseball was a common denominator; it had rules, symmetry, a beginning and an end, it challenged and rewarded, you could play or watch, it was the same one day as the next, in one town as in another.

But now the minor leagues and the semipros and country baseball are all but gone, and in the suburbs they put kids of ten and twelve in expensive Little League uniforms to play on perfectly proportioned fields and in the smaller cities the old lopsided parks have been torn down for housing developments and shopping centers. If anything holds us together now, our hometown teams playing in surrounding leagues, those leagues part of the widening circle of all the leagues—if anything holds us together that way now, it isn't baseball, concentrated as it is in the major leagues, the Chavez Ravines of this amortized world, concerned as it is with tax shelters and reserve clauses and player strikes and anti-trust, relying as it does on Bat Days and boom-boom superstars with salaries triple their batting averages. It isn't baseball that holds us together in 1976—not baseball in the Astrodome, on artificial grass, foreshortened by television, enlivened by organ music and computerized scoreboards that can simulate fireworks and joy.

The game may be the same, but it's been taken away from the country and the towns and given to the accountants and the TV producers and the high rollers. Turkey Tyson and Mike, the home-run hitter of the Auks, couldn't find a place to play today. Class D doesn't exist. To me, Shea Stadium is a poor substitute.

The Neighborhood Grocery Store

BY EUDORA WELTY

Two blocks away from the Mississippi State Capitol, and on the same street with it, where our house was when I was a child growing up in Jackson, it was possible to have a little pasture behind your backyard where you could keep a Jersey cow, which we did. My mother herself milked her. A thrifty homemaker, wife, mother of three, she also did all her own cooking. And as far as I can recall, she never set foot inside a grocery store. It wasn't necessary.

For her regular needs, she stood at the telephone in our front hall and consulted with Mr. Lemly, of Lemly's Market and Grocery downtown, who took her order and sent it out on his next delivery. And since Jackson at the heart of it was still within very near reach of the open country, the blackberry lady clanged on her bucket with a quart measure at your front door in June without fail, the watermelon man rolled up to your house exactly on time for the Fourth of July, and down through the summer, the quiet of the early morning streets was pierced by the calls of farmers driving in with their plenty. One brought his with a song, so plaintive we would sing it with him:

> "Milk, milk,
> Butter milk,
> Snap beans—butter beans—
> Tender okra—fresh greens . . .
> And buttermilk."

My mother considered herself pretty well prepared in her kitchen and pantry for any emergency that, in her words, might choose to present itself. But if she should, all of a sudden, need another lemon, or find she was out of bread, all she had to do was call out, "Quick! Who'd like to run to the Little Store for me?"

I would.

She'd count out the change into my hand and I was away. I'll bet the nickel that would be left that all over the country, for those of my day, the neighborhood grocery played a similar part in our growing up.

Our store had its name—it was that of the grocer who owned it, whom I'll call Mr. Sessions—but "the Little Store" is what we called it at home. It was a block down our street toward the Capitol and half a block farther, around the corner, toward the cemetery. I knew even the sidewalk to it as well as I knew my own skin. I'd skipped my jumping rope up and down it, hopped its length through mazes of hopscotch, played jacks in its islands of shade, serpentined along it on my Princess bicycle, skated it backward and forward. In the twilight, I had dragged my steamboat by its string (this was homemade out of every new shoe box, with a candle in the bottom lighted and shining through colored tissue paper pasted over windows scissored out in the shapes of the sun, moon and stars) across every crack of the walk without letting it bump or catch fire. I'd "played out" on that street after supper with my brothers and friends as long as "first dark" lasted, I'd caught its lightning bugs. On the first Armistice Day (and this will set the time I'm speaking of), we made our own parade down that walk on a single velocipede— my brother pedaling, our little brother riding the handlebars, and myself standing on the back, all with arms wide, flying flags in each hand. (My father snapped that picture as we raced by. It came out blurred.)

As I set forth for the Little Store, a tune would float toward me from the house where there lived three sisters, girls in their teens, who ratted their hair over their ears, wore headbands like gladiators, and were considered to be very popular. They practiced for this in the daytime; they'd wind up the Victrola, leave the same record on they'd played before, and you'd see them bobbing past their dining-room windows while they danced with each other. Being three, they could go all day, cutting in:

> "Everybody ought to know-oh
> How to do the tickle-toe
> (how to do the tickle-toe)."

They sang it and danced to it, and as I went by to the same song, I believed it.

A little farther on, across the street, was the house where the principal of our grade school lived—lived on even while we were having vacation. What if she would come out? She would halt me in my tracks—she had a very carrying and well-known voice in Jackson, where she'd taught almost everybody, saying: "Eudora Alice Welty, spell OBLIGE." OBLIGE was the word that she of course knew had kept me from making 100 on my spelling exam. She'd make me miss it again now, by boring her eyes through me from across the street. This was my vacation fantasy, one good way to scare myself on the way to the store.

Down near the corner waited the house of a little boy named Lindsey. The sidewalk here was old brick, which the roots of a giant chinaberry tree had humped up and tilted this way and that. On skates, you took it fast, in a series of skittering hops, trying not to touch ground anywhere. If the chinaberries had fallen and rolled in the cracks, it was like skating through a whole shooting match of marbles. I crossed my fingers that Lindsey wouldn't be looking.

During the big flu epidemic, he and I, as it happened, were being nursed through our sieges at the same time. I'd hear my father and mother murmuring to each other, at the end of a long day, "And I wonder how poor little *Lindsey* got along today?" Just as, down the street, he no doubt would have to hear his family saying, "And I wonder how is poor *Eudora* by now?" I got the idea that a choice was going to be made soon between poor little Lindsey and poor Eudora, and I came up with a funny poem. I wasn't prepared for it when my father told me it wasn't funny and my mother cried that if I couldn't be ashamed for myself she'd have to be ashamed for me:

There was a little boy and his name
    was Lindsey.
He went to Heaven with the
    influinzy.

He didn't, he survived it, poem and all, the same as I did. But his chinaberries could have brought me down in my skates in a flying act of contrition before his eyes, looking pretty funny myself, right in front of his house.

Setting out in his world, a child feels so indelible. He only comes to find out later that it's all the others along his way who are making themselves indelible to him.

Our Little Store rose right up from the sidewalk; standing in a street of family houses, it alone hadn't any yard in front, any tree or flower bed. It was a plain frame building covered over with brick. Above the door, a little railed porch ran across on an upstairs level and four windows with shades were looking out. But I didn't catch on to those.

Running in out of the sun, you met what seemed total obscurity inside. There were almost tangible smells—licorice recently sucked in a child's cheek, dill pickle brine that had leaked through a paper sack in a fresh trail across the wooden floor, ammonia-loaded ice that had been hoisted from wet croker sacks and slammed into the icebox with its sweet butter at the door, and perhaps the smell of still untrapped mice.

Then through the motes of cracker dust, cornmeal dust, the Gold Dust of the Gold Dust Twins that the floor had been swept out with, the realities emerged. Shelves climbed to high reach all the way around, set out with not too much of any one thing but a lot of things—lard, molasses, vinegar, starch, matches, kerosene, Octagon soap (about a year's worth of octagon-shaped coupons cut out and saved brought a signet ring addressed to you in the mail). It was up to you to remember what you came for, while your eye traveled from cans of sardines to tin whistles to ice cream salt to harmonicas to flypaper (over your head, batting around on a thread beneath the blades of the ceiling fan, stuck with its testimonial catch).

Its confusion may have been in the eye of its beholder. Enchantment is cast upon you by all those things you weren't sup-

posed to have need for, to lure you close to wooden tops you'd
outgrown, boy's marbles and agates in little net pouches, small
rubber balls that wouldn't bounce straight, frail, frazzly kite
string, clay bubble pipes that would snap off in your teeth, the
stiffest scissors. You could contemplate those long narrow boxes
of sparklers gathering dust while you waited for it to be the
Fourth of July or Christmas, and noisemakers in the shape of tin
frogs for somebody's birthday party you hadn't been invited to
yet, and see that they were all marvelous.

You might not have even looked for Mr. Sessions when he
came around his store cheese (as big as a doll's house) and in
front of the counter looking for you. When you'd finally asked
him for, and received from him in its paper bag, whatever single
thing it was that you had been sent for, the nickel that was left
over was yours to spend.

Down at a child's eye level, inside those glass jars with mouths
in their sides through which the grocer could run his scoop or a
child's hand might be invited to reach for a choice, were
wineballs, all-day suckers, gumdrops, peppermints. Making a
row under the glass of a counter were the Tootsie Rolls, Hershey
bars, Goo Goo Clusters, Baby Ruths. And whatever was the
name of those pastilles that came stacked in a cardboard cylin-
der with a cardboard lid? They were thin and dry, about the size
of tiddledywinks, and in the shape of twisted rosettes. A kind of
chocolate dust came out with them when you shook them out in
your hand. Were they chocolate? I'd say, rather, they were
brown. They didn't taste of anything at all, unless it was wood.
Their attraction was the number you got for a nickel.

Making up your mind, you circled the store around and
around, around the pickle barrel, around the tower of Crackerjack boxes; Mr. Sessions had built it for us himself on top of a
packing case, like a house of cards.

If it seemed too hot for Crackerjacks, I might get a cold drink.
Mr. Sessions might have already stationed himself by the cold-
drinks barrel, like a mind reader. Deep in ice water that looked
black as ink, murky shapes—that would come up as Coca-Colas,
Orange Crushes, and various flavors of pop—were all swimming
around together. When you gave the word, Mr. Sessions
plunged his bare arm in to the elbow and fished out your choice,

first try. I favored a locally bottled concoction called Lake's Celery. (What else could it be called? It was made by a Mr. Lake out of celery. It was a popular drink here for years but was not known universally, as I found out when I arrived in New York and ordered one in the Astor bar.) You drank on the premises, with feet set wide apart to miss the drip, and gave him back his bottle and your nickel.

But he didn't hurry you off. A standing scales was by the door, with a stack of iron weights and a brass slide on the balance arm, that would weigh you up to three hundred pounds. Mr. Sessions, whose hands were gentle and smelled of carbolic, would lift you up and set your feet on the platform, hold your loaf of bread for you, and, taking his time while you stood still for him, he would make certain of what you weighed today. He could even remember what you weighed the last time, so you could subtract and announce how much you'd gained. That was goodbye.

Is there always a hard way to go home? From the Little Store, you could go partway through the sewer. If your brothers had called you a scare-cat, then, across the next street beyond the Little Store, it was possible to enter this sewer by passing through a privet hedge, climbing down into the bed of a creek, and going into its mouth on your knees. The sewer—it might have been no more than a "storm sewer"—came out and emptied here, where Town Creek, a sandy, most often shallow little stream that ambled through Jackson on its way to the Pearl River, ran along the edge of the cemetery. You could go in darkness through this tunnel to where you next saw light (if you ever did) and climb out through the culvert at your own street corner.

I was a scare-cat, all right, but I was a reader with my own refuge in storybooks. Making my way under the sidewalk, under the street and the streetcar track, under the Little Store, down there in the wet dark by myself, I could be Persephone entering into my six-months' sojourn underground—though I didn't suppose Persephone had to crawl, hanging onto a loaf of bread, and come out through the teeth of an iron grating. Mother Demeter would indeed be wondering where she could find me and mad when she knew. "Now am I going to have to start marching to the Little Store for *myself?*"

I couldn't picture it. Indeed I'm unable today to picture the Little Store with a grown person in it, except for Mr. Sessions and the lady who helped him, who belonged there. We children thought it was ours. The happiness of errands was in part that of running for the moment away from home, a free spirit. I believed the Little Store to be a center of the outside world and hence of happiness—as I believed what I found in the Crackerjack box to be a genuine prize, which was as simply as I believed in the Golden Fleece.

But a day came when I ran to the store to discover, sitting on the front, a grown person after all—more than a grown person. It was the Monkey Man, together with his monkey. His grinding-organ was lowered to the step beside him. In my whole life so far, I must have laid eyes on the Monkey Man no more than five or six times. An itinerant of rare and wayward appearances, he was not punctual like the gypsies, who every year with the first cool days of fall showed up in the aisles of Woolworth's. You never knew when the Monkey Man might decide to favor Jackson, or which way he'd go. Sometimes you heard him as close as the next street, and then he didn't come up yours.

But now I saw the Monkey Man at the Little Store, where I'd never seen him before. I'd never seen him sitting down. Low on that familiar doorstep, he was not the same any longer, and neither was his monkey. They looked just like an old man and an old friend of his that wore a fez, meeting quietly together, tired, and resting, with their eyes fixed on some place far away, and not the same place. Yet their romance for me didn't have it in its power to waver. I simply didn't know how to step around them, to proceed on into the Little Store for my mother's emergency as if nothing had happened. If I could have gone in there after it, whatever it was I would have given it to them—putting it into the monkey's cool little fingers. I would have given them the Little Store itself.

In my memory they are still attached to the store—so are all the others. Everyone I saw on my way seemed to me then part of my errand, and in a way they were. As I myself, the free spirit, was part of it, too.

All the years we lived in that house where we children were born, the same people lived in the other houses on our street, too. People changed through the arithmetic of birth, marriage, and death, but not by going away. So families just accrued stories, which through the fullness of time, in those times, their own lives made. And I grew up in those.

But I didn't know there'd ever been a story at the Little Store, one that was going on while I was there. Of course, all the time, the Sessions had been living right overhead there, in the upstairs rooms behind the little railed porch and the shaded windows; but I think we children never thought of that. Did I fail to see them as a family because they weren't living in an ordinary house? Because I so seldom saw them close together, or having anything to say to each other? She sat in the back of the store, her pencil over a ledger, while he stood and waited on children to make up their minds. They worked in twin black eyeshades, held on their gray heads by elastic bands. It may be harder to recognize kindness—or unkindness, either—in a face whose eyes are in shadow. His face underneath his shade was as round as the little wooden wheels in the Tinkertoy box. So was her face. I didn't know, perhaps didn't even wonder: were they husband and wife or brother and sister? Were they father and mother? There were a few other persons, of various ages, wandering singly in by the back door and out. But none of their relationships could I imagine, when I'd never seen them sitting down together around their own table.

The possibility that they had any other life at all, anything beyond what we could see within the four walls of the Little Store, occurred to me only when tragedy struck their family. There was some act of violence. The shock to the neighborhood traveled to the children, of course; but I couldn't find out from my parents what had happened. My parents held it back from me, as they had already held back many things, "until the time comes for you to know."

You could find out some of these things by looking in the unabridged dictionary and the encyclopedia—kept to hand in our dining room—but you couldn't find out there what had happened to the family who for all the years of your life had lived upstairs over the Little Store, who had never been anything but patient and kind to children, who never once had sent us away.

All I ever knew was its aftermath: they were the only people ever known to me who simply vanished. At the point where their life overlapped into ours, the story broke off.

We weren't being sent to the neighborhood grocery for facts of life, or death. But of course those are what we were on the track of anyway. With the loaf of bread and the Crackerjack prize, I was bringing home the intimations of pride and disgrace, and rumors and early news of people coming to hurt one another, while others practiced for joy—storing up a portion for myself of the human mystery.

The Psychiatrist

BY ALEXANDER THEROUX

The notorious Marquis de Sade, ruminating on the subject of man's greatest torment, perversely concluded that it was the impossibility of offending nature. For the sake of dialectic (auditor implied), I would answer him—disallowing, cheerfully, the topics of incest, eco-disasters, and the mysterious "sins against the Holy Ghost"—by pointing to the new Sosostrises of the twentieth century, replete with their wicked packs of cards: the little oracular thumbfumblers and professional witch doctors of unfathomable obscurity who, with an eye on a patient's insurance portfolio and a big appetite for symbols, perch like kites at the heads of their couches and, in some kind of official jingbang, arrogantly sniff, prod, and poke about the human brain.

Alchemyville, all out!

Hello, Dr. Pangloss.

I'm talking about the psychiatrist!

The psychiatrist—you begin with a sigh and end with a *triste* —what exactly does he do? He studies monkeys, examines criminals, administers drugs, testifies in legal proceedings, signs commitment papers, occasionally fools around with biochemical research, but best of all loves just to sit around on his buns.

The archetypical picture you have of him—don't be diffident, he loves that—is quite accurate, if you want the truth of it. Inside the psychiatrist's waiting room on the Formica table sit a few glossy mags, a glass ball filled with hard candy, and a library copy of *Fun with Amphetamines*. The one tight little plant is a mother-in-law's tongue. But come into the procrastinarium. The couch, a kind of modified Gatch bed, is over there, and on that far wall is a portrait of either Babinski or a monkey wearing a necktie, whereas the psychiatrist wears a suit the color of creepmice, went to Yale, and is a New Yorker—and, of course, like all New Yorkers, he wrote the book. He owns racks of bitten pipes, a wall of shiny textbooks, a big bumbershoot, an abstract of Josef Albers, and a secretary named Miss Scheingold, who appears and disappears on tiptoe with a cruelly sharpened pencil and perfect custody of the eyes.

Okay, you are troubled. So you decide to visit a psychiatrist. The secret conviction you have that what you are about to go through will perhaps, like Dr. Johnson's marriage, be a triumph of hope over experience is well-founded. He has slow and easy hummocks, this cineast who slumps down passively to watch the X-rated movies in your head. But he's a great figure of fun, sitting there in his big chocolate chair, muttering words to himself that have the most unviolaceous combinations since the cave age, and tapping a wise index finger on his cuff, while, always, in his face waits a knowing smile, backlit, not visible, informed by more years of exploration than had Magellan, Vasco da Gama, and the Cabots, father and son, combined. But don't be fooled. Skrimshandering the brain is not just cutting pie. The psychiatrist is working with matters often more delicate than the underside of an onion thrip. He's a great little guy, though you should understand that so burdensome is his work, so effortful, so exclusively *profound,* he can get testy. Snappish.

All right, the son of a bitch can be a real quince.

Let's to your inculpation. It's natural enough: your onetime grimwig of a girl friend left you and ran off on her fat legs with a Dutch swabbie, you got depressed, you worried, you started sighing—"whuffs"—and you needed to talk to someone. And so The Man is now listening to you—and, if you're lucky, avoiding during your session the cryprint on the intercom ("Mrs. Beedie is here, Doctor")—and owling you with that satrapic countenance of his through malicious black spectacles while chewing like a camel, side to side, to the twitches of his fashioned goatee. You dislike his air of superiority: it appears in the nostrils, the eyebrows. The klaft of hair swept down to hide his baldness is in itself reason enough to send you into immediate convulsions of loathing. You go through customs—name, address, age, general complaint—and start to talk. He grunts. You keep talking. He shifts in his seat. And you talk some more. He's circling his foot, meditatively. No, he'd rather you not go for a pee just yet.

The monologue begins to bore you, so just for the hell of it you decide to ask a ridiculous question. Naturally, you know the answer (a Dutch *custom?* fewtering ducks *aboardships?*), but it's your money, so why not put the ball in his court? But still the good doctor says nothing, only lights a cigarette, recrosses his legs, and taps off a fez of red ash. And you? Don't rush him, for godsake, and stop whining! You're "ventilating," you insignificant little underbutler, can't you understand? Show some patience, for while you're lying there and nattering on like a damfool in the lay terms psychiatrists despise, who can tell what terrible maniopsychomotorchondrodystopical chimeras this brave chap might suddenly stare upon? His subject, you stupid bisoignon, is nothing less than the human mind! He's a *psychiatrist:* a doctor of the *soul!*

"What's in the brain," asks the poet, "that ink may character?" Who will step forward to answer? A phylactery in which is written the queerest, most inexplicable hieroglyphics, each brain is unique, and simply to try to hypostatize it into one entity or to see it under the guise of one name is to play a joke on yourself.

"That subtle knot," as Donne called it, is surely the single most complex apparat that was, is, or ever will be: a twin-halved casserole of thalamus, cerebrum, and midpiece covered with a wrinkled layer of gray matter and seamed up in a labyrinth of ways. Fifty ounces, five less for woman, something along the lines of a small bag of topsoil, this ball of ropes, juices, and fatty folds is so soft that only the slightest pressure is needed to push one's finger deeply into it, and when so insulted its frail lights flicker out. But don't be taken in by the photoplates you once saw that show it, uncased from its bony cranial brainbox, the gubbins of sheep-belly, clay squelch, a pile of doo-doo. It seems, in fact, a blasphemy indeed not to pay it constant and revered attention. How explain that man has apotheosized the sun, trees, emperors, and not the human brain? It is the enchanted loom. It alone equips us with sapience. It sits in perpetual vigilance, a miraculous Triassic ooze through which pound ideas big as brontosaurs and into which pass smells as delicate as motes. It is a filigree of radial bundles, dendrites, and fifteen thousand million (say that out loud) intercommunicating nerve cells which allow for an infinite permutation of thoughts and outreach all possibilities of all conceivable human mental requirements. It is guessed that the number of its behavior patterns reaches to the order of $10^{300,000}$, a figure so monstrous that, written out, it alone would fill a book. What we can legitimately say of the brain could be bounded in a nutshell, and where nothing can be said, no one would . . .

Good God, I was going to write *no one would try!*

How could I have forgotten all those fulgences, degreed psychofantasts, and wonderful priestcats of wit and curiosity who, each with the enthusiasm of a Jebusite and the eyes of a croupier, would dare anything dareable and disbelieve all dares that weren't? For to the psychiatrist the brain presents no baffle whatsoever. But you say one of its watch lights blinked? Dimmed? Browned out? Quick, find them a pattern, give it a name, identify it with a Greek myth, but in any case let them into that thinkball, a massive Gulliver these little nairns will circumscribe with packthread—and soon conquer! You smell of your grief. The odor is there, isn't it? And they've not noses? Now get back on that couch, take a breath, resume. Dose of salts. World of good. And don't think. Talk. Ventilate. *Ventilate, you bastard!*

"*Just then.* Where did you go?" the doctor quickly asks. He vaults to the edge of his chair.

Go? you exclaim: *you're right in the same room!*

But the session has dynamized. And then you see what he's getting at: in a little epiphany born of the methodological idolatry he loves, the psychiatrist is convinced you just "traveled" somewhere. In your mind, see? So, naturally he wants to follow, and preferably—at least if the $35 to $50 you're paying him per half hour is any indication—first-class. You grab your armpits, make a groan, and roll over. It only whets his appetite. Psychiatrists are always anxious to deal with a person who appears to want to have nothing to do with them.

Ploys: his shucks-it-can't-be-all-that-bad-you-should-see-my-mother-in-law trapfall fails. He'd like to pry a dream or two out of you. Dreams are to a psychiatrist what valerian is to a cat;

merely mention one in passing and they zoom forward as if they were going to hear the thousand and second tale of Scheherazade, Mrs. Eddy's posthumous telephone call, the sound of one hand clapping. Daniels. Veritable Daniels. But your dream proves useless: you can only remember about dreaming being awake when falling asleep you always wake up and forget to remember your dream. So the psychiatrist takes up a few quiddative darts and randomly pitches some at you. Do you keep an ant farm? Do you have tarry bowel movements? Do you call lines "wrinkles"? Do you have an unnatural urinating posture? Do you remember if your mother ever referred to your penis as a "bow-wow"? He asks you, point-blank, why you keep looking at the doorknob.

A fart? That's your answer?

So you're going to be uncooperative. The psychiatrist walks to the window, peers through the blinds, and swiftly turns for a Parthian shot.

"Your girl friend, you want to kill her."

"*No.*"

He smiles at you with his eyes closed. "Bite her? Punch her in the umbo? Raft off her head?"

Your silence has implications.

The psychiatrist bends his head forward and left, a radar to pick up the slightest of clues. Not a toehold: you're a tough little towser. Ah, but fear not, he'll get you to budge, and to that end maintains a battery of psychodynamic cattle prods which, employed, could keep you in that office until tomorrow come never, squinting at Rorschach inkblots; commenting on thematic apperceptions; copying out the nine Bender Gestalt patterns; doing the draw-a-person game; completing sentences; associating words; or filling out the five hundred fifty questions of the multiphasic personality inventories. Solutions, each one gayer and more beribboned than the next, far exceed problems. The psychiatrist is a conjurer with more rabbits than you've hats. Your pea is nothing to his thimbles.

"Tell me. Has your mother ever bumboated to Holland? I ask that for a reason. I notice you're itching."

Here the psychiatrist swings off his glasses, and, so incredibly beyond common understanding is the thought about to be uttered, so unbearably weighty, he lowers his head to pinch his zygomatic arch and sighs dolefully. The genii of Charcot, Janet, and Bernheim oracularly inspirit the air over his head as he coughs professionally and delivers: "The family constellation in cases of the dry type of neurodermatitis—itch freaks, why hedge?—is often that of a hostile dependent maternal relationship in which itching and scratching symbolize anger at the mother figure handled masochistically due to guilt. Now, you see, your girl friend. . . ."

You make a gesture with your finger.

The psychiatrist taps a paradiddle on his thigh with his pencil and nuncupates, profoundly, *Nmmnmmmmnn.*

Be warned of this: everything you do (or don't do) *means* something, if to no one else then at least to the great group of chemotherapeuts and omniscients who so willingly take you in hand—a latching maneuver, as we've seen, invariably on the back right trouser pocket. You present enthymemes, you are to believe, to which they alone can supply the correct premises. Theirs is a proud and elitist secrecy—like the "Illuminati," the order of Templars, Freemasons—with an undivulged motto called a fee and a private handshake, which is in fact a fierce grip on your poor brainstem. The idea, you see, is that you are hopelessly out of it. They know everything; you know squat. And all the status-bestowing formulae, abstrusions, classificatory schemes, insane coinages, and neo-Germanic jargon-mongering in the psychiatrist's therapeutic armamentarium is sent out in a speculative philosophical fog to shore up that position. Thesis: it can't be right if it's not complicated enough.

O Psychosophs! Opifexes! Artists!

Subplots beget subplots, spawn like flies. But as they're poised and tense like frogs waiting for slips of the tongue, maladroit self-disclosures, mistakes and errors, and dream pictures, as they attempt to break through one's "character armor" with that shameless, anti-populist, crumb-grabbing way of theirs, they frequently expect nothing of the psychotic patient short of a lifetime rehearsal of his agonies and a bankroll thick as a tumor to underscore his sincerity. The patient, too often, is there not to seek answers but rather to give evidence. Original sin is wondering what it is. Hello, Joseph K. Sit down.

A good question in analysis can save months of wasted time.

Dr. Freud, allow him this, constantly talked with his patients. A satchelmouth. A real bailer. And while that rara avis, the dedicated psychiatrist, *can* perhaps lead his patient out by suggestion, persuasion, abreaction, even hypnosis and the wise employment of pharmaceuticals, what of the quack? Who can ever say? For, more often than not, these mind-snatching hoodoos are either mute as Violenta or as impersonal as umpires, with personalities like the insipid snails of Burgundy, which, in their natural state, are less succulent than a rubber eraser. It's so swimmingly scientific. They sit by, yawping and yawning, as powerful and ungetatable as Nobodaddy. The psychiatrist contemplates the life around him as in a mirror—the glass of the Lady of Shalott—scarcely counting himself among anyone. A good many of them, I hear, actually take pride in their non-personalities—and, of course, cunningly—for while they sit back, professionally refined out of existence like the abstract God of the Anglican Prayer Book, "without passion or parts," the charlatanry of these crypto-geniuses successfully works two ways: (1) it cannot be legitimately assessed, and (2) it can keep you effectively suppressed.

Deep magicians. *Deep* magicians.

Psychiatrists are the new monks, their offices the secular monasteries against whose walls come to wail, while seeking to be shriven, the guilt-ridden, the sinner, the troubled-in-mind. Officially, there are about 25,000 registered psychiatrists in this country. It may disturb you to know that only about one fourth of the people practicing the craft in the United States have been certified; the rest of them, shingling out, for all I know, under such titles as mediums, mesmerizers, head counselors, kludds, or Wizards of Oz, are nothing more than a lot of horoscopical busybodies, clinical psychologists, and social adjusters with a passion for tampering and who, just for kicks, decide to have a passing shy at the brain to test their own oblique theories as to why people honk out, are a bit voom-voomed, have guests in their attic.

But there's nothing funny about it. There are more mental patients occupying hospital beds in this country than all other sick people *combined*. You're surprised? The world, shrinking, can bring one every bit of international bad news in five minutes. Ours is a standardized, bureaucratized, cyberneticized society.

Women, becoming mannish, wear pantsuits and bark; men grow
into fops. The family unit has been ideologically discredited, and
there is, in general, an almost total loss of a sense of place. There
are thirty million people living below the official poverty line.
We suffer from overpopulation, joblessness, crass exploitation on
a thousand fronts. And perhaps the darkest fact of all, there has
been effected—in terms civic, political, economic, moral, and
religious—an almost total lack of faith.

Which of us, then, can have the immodesty to be shocked to
see so many pour in off the street for succor? It's a Boschian
nightmare: enuretics, dyssocials, mirror-gazers, compulsive fin-
gersuckers, intracranial star-trekkers, cataplects and schizo-
phrenes, fire-setters, malingerers, fecal impactees, metopon-users,
tic-sufferers, hebephrenics, chronic squinters, feebs, smeckers
and bindle stiffs, pogues and kid-simples, yen-shee-munchers and
CKX'ers and all the countless others getting the wrong orders
from headquarters.

Of course you're worried. The mere quantification of it all! But
your sorcerer, your cerebratonic, your quacksalver is smacking
his lips with the damnedest satisfaction, for is not the brain of
man no more complex than your garden-variety melon?

You disagree? Be careful. That alone could serve as your mit-
timus to bedlam.

You're pressing your eyes, reflecting, and finding the phos-
phenes you see angelic, nonconnotative, and, thank God, all
your own, but then—by dint of a cough for attention—you look
up to meet once again the hydropic face, the chin of which is
being stroked, gravely, studiously, by the festinating pull of a
thin, goatish hand. The psychiatrist extends you a tin box of
sweets.

"All right. Now draw another octahedron, but this time . . ."

"I'm tired," you grizzle.

You devour a bonbon. The doctor follows your movements.

"Excuse me, I notice you're swallowing." The psychiatrist's
mind is trip-hammer fast.

You snort.

"After each bite, I mean."

You look sarcastically at the ceiling, then, coming frontal, snap
at him in frank disgust.

"I'm eating a candy!"

The psychiatrist, interlacing his fingers neatly, smiles and corrects you. "A chocolate."

"So?"

"A Dutch chocolate."

"Sour."

"Semisweet."

"Randomly selected."

"*Taken*," the psychiatrist stands up and, pacing the room with his hands locked deliberatingly behind him, continues, "with unnatural relish from a tin with a fat white-capped *frokin*, notice, painted on its side and who, if you weren't lying to me, bears a more than passing resemblance to the fickle bimbo, she of the blubberful legs, whom you can't deny you not twenty minutes ago described as having broken your heart." The psychiatrist bends over you with his nose in your face and, smiling triumphantly, asks, "Coincidence?"

You're speechless with angry amazement.

You decide to give the smug doctor measure for measure, and so snatch up another bonbon—and swallow *vividly*. Your throatball bounces.

With a patronizing smile of pity, the kind that tries to indict, the psychomach turns and proceeds to speak to you in that lessoning, grammar-school tone which affects itself with those over-pronounced declarative sentences one usually reserves for out-and-out simpletons, nonagenarians, and myna birds. "Swallowing," he deblaterates, "is a funny thing. Everyone swallows. I swallow. You swallow. He, she, or it swallows. But it is my educated judgment that *your* swallowing corresponds, as it often will—oh, yes, as it often will, indeed—less to a nutritional need than to a compulsive necessity for an effective sexual and moral order, notwithstanding girl friends and girl befrienders. You have a tropism. Buy it." He checks his watch.

"Mrs. Beedie is still here, Doctor," the intercom sputters.

Time is nearly up.

"Let's to some basics, shall we?" The psychiatrist takes up a clipboard, into which he inserts a questionnaire and then, prepared with a raised pencil, states in a bored, businesslike tone, "Comment yes or no."

You pipe up, "Yes or no."

"Facetiousness," snarls the psychiatrist, his face a nagnail, "is no extenuation. Now, comment. Do you ever hear sirens? Do you have modest stools? Did you ever wish to become a forest ranger? Do you ever open doors and think you're going out when you're coming in? Do you enjoy the taste of pigloaf? Do blue blebs ever appear on your face? Have you ever inserted a finger into your podex? Are your flatulencies sour? Do you dribble?"

Dribble? Dribble, for chrissake?

What, you begin to fear, can this penny-almanacking son of a bitch be getting at? Swiftly it occurs to you that with the simple press of a button he could summon to his aid a company of goons ravenous to pounce on you, truss you into a daft jacket, and fling you headlong into a rubber room to rot away the rest of your life under the wardenship of six sadistic dykes! This is a joke? Scenarios scribble themselves out in your brain. The "drastics," for example. What about the insulin shock treatment, say, where, plunked down, one is gavaged like a silly poppet with coma doses five or six times a week only to awaken with a bone-chilling kikiriki and zombie away your laters in aftershock, twitching and hiccuping? Or how about that brainchild of Dr. Egas Moniz, *Nobel Prize-winner,* who, in 1935, by severing the thalamus from the frontal lobe, created in the miracle of prefrontal lobotomy the possibility of spending the rest of your days with a perpetual grin and the I.Q. of a toaster? And then there was that marvelous little bit of recreation invented in 1938 by those two psychosurgical *menaechmi* Cerletti and Bini, where you skip breakfast, void, pluck out your dentures, and then, rubbed over the temples with electrode paste and mouth-gagged, are strapped down onto a table to be electroconvulsed by 130 volts into a profane and violent unconsciousness. It's too much. By now you're perspiring into your eyes. You ask the psychiatrist to give you a glass of water; he does.

But not before making a quick Sherlockian entry in his notebook under your bio: "Xerostome? Chronic?"

Ah, he is tracing down clues.

There is of course something to be said for the experience of repeatedly seeing patients, the results candling up, as can perhaps happen, into a bright empirical wisdom. But to my mind the psychiatrist's is basically a tradesman's knowledge, not a scientific one, and during the long three years—the mean requirement for analysis—psychiatrists, to say nothing of their hapless patients, rather resemble the wind-eaters of Ruach who subsist on mill drafts, puffs, and unbitable gusts. Indeed, one can't but begin to realize that the psychiatrist and his patient are a *contiguum,* two bodies exactly next to each other which do not, however, compose a unity—certainly not fundwise, in any case. Not that any of these matters has called into question even the most half-witted psychiatrist's credibility with the public. Really, it's a phenomenon as to why not. Juries are impressed with them. Guidance counselors seek their guidance. Graduate students in education courses quote them. Psychiatrists worm their way onto federal committees, school boards, and into every last goddamn congress, conference, survey, and seminar. The social sciences are gaga for them. Psychiatry *itself* is in fashion, the blind hodipecks who work it in style, and the wretched excesses on this score finally giving us every third college girl wearing granny glasses and jeans with mushrooms sewn on, holding an unread copy of Heidegger, introducing herself with the proud moue, "I'm in analysis."

Famous for their chronic mutism, psychiatrists, especially when visited by one of their infrequent ideas, can show a real *loquentia praecox,* and at such times they could talk a vulture off a rubbish tip. You hear them on the radio—being interviewed, being fussy—usually on Sunday night, late. And every time you turn on your television set there's always some big-titted, overbejeweled lady psychiatrist from Beverly Hills constantly interrupting someone, smoking herself into fidgets, and ready to pontificate at the drop of a doubt on any subject from sex to slaver, always with a know-it-all smirk and three face-lifts to prop it up. "I think the wonderful young people today, my goodness," she says in that punishing, grainy voice that's always too loud, "are trying to tell us something. Their 'new morality' is an inverse psychodramatic contraindication which . . ."

In matters of the printed word? Ye gods, what a nauseating spate of nature mysticism has been unleashed in the name of psychiatry and sincerity! Monographs written by Latvian doctors, magazine articles indited by boffo man 'n' wife clinicians, manuals pounded out by *actual Ph.D.s,* and books on and often entitled—dangerous games, awareness, self-defeat and self-worth, inventive divorce, hidden anger, how to free your creativity, open marriage, and antiphon after antiphon of those frank, clarifying John-and-Mary dialogues, and always this drivel comes at you in the same gray narcosynthetic trappings: insane Greco-modernized nouns, a mess of disturbable verbs, the exotic illnesses and fetishes italicized, and, along with the sixty over-simplifications you find on every page, unending supply of those gripping life-bright case histories you love ("A twenty-two-year-old Chinese girl named W— came into my office and complained of jaundice . . ." or, "Vernon, fifty-one, who lived in Farmville, Virginia, began to claim that he was the papal nuncio, and then one day . . .").

They hide behind methodology. They evade in the guise of objectivity. They use stats as camouflage and the nomenclature of Albanian boiler engineers. They try to shove their guess-timates down our craw in the name of medical fact, when, in fact, ninety percent of it all is nothing more than nebulous, untestable, pseudotheoretical hogshit where self-reliance be-comes "need autonomy" and near electrocution is termed "main-tenance treatment." Their subject, mind you? The human mind. Their aim? To enhance it. But in the process how many of these intercranial spelunkers, ask yourself, while claiming to do the op-posite, actually diminish it? "Shrink" applies: the label fits the psychiatrist as perfectly as a stretch sock. The difference be-tween the rapist and the therapist—Nabokov's correct—is a mat-ter of spacing.

A psychiatrist from the gallery is on his feet, waving, pan-furious with an objection. Yes? I'm sorry, could you please lower your voice? Okay, agreed, few patients *are* left still locked in at-tics, chained up, leered at, baited, whipped by the "cat," or fed foo-foo from tin plates shoved under a sealed door. Yet, granting that, I wonder just how much of a consolation that can be to all the disappointed analysands who, weekly, sometimes daily, are forced not only to buy you for a friend but have to sit by with a fistful of sweaty placebos while you all circle and recircle about in games of psychotherapeutical pin-the-tail-on-the- . . .

"Say no more."

"What?"

The psychiatrist claps his hands. "The session's up."

You sit up—dammit!—interrupted in the middle of what you felt, finally, a profitable-to-pursue monologue on your box-ankled former girl friend's infidelity and the hint you only just remembered but somehow failed to put into context way back on the very night of your engagement to her, when, having dragged you off to a tattoo parlor, she went and had commemoratively needled on her ample right thigh a violet tulip within the bulbed turban of which, you also now wistfully recall, was ordered this inscription:

> *Pieter*
> *S.S. Slaapkamer*
> *1973*

And now, just when you're beginning to dig in, he blows the goddamn whistle?

"You mean it's *over?*"

The psychiatrist looks at you, emotionless, unconcerned, his face as cold and depthless as stamped tin. You don't tug Superman's cape.

"Miss Scheingold will make your next appointment. Good afternoon."

"And then another one, and another one, and another one, and. . . ."

To your diagnosis the psychiatrist will later add "whining."

"As long," he says, shrugging, "as it takes to get you well. Rome—well, you know. Frankly, I suspect the problem here rests more with your mother than with your girl friend, though no less with your girl friend than your mother, which allows for the distinct possibility, of course, that it could be your *girl friend's mother*."

It's the madness of rush hour now. Driving home, you're fishtailing in and out of the heavy traffic and, to dispel the gloom you feel, you click on the radio. Light classical. Ballroom. You then cock a detective ear to the speaker, realizing it's more than a familiarity with the piece of music you suddenly hear that causes the slow, then knowing, now rueful smile which, as you goose the car onto the freeway, flowers into that loud quacking laughter alone reserved for the recognition of and homage to the kind of coincidence that announces itself—you're *certain* of this —only once in a lifetime.

It's a Viennese waltz.

The Drive-in Movie

BY WILLIAM PRICE FOX

Back in the fifties, I worked out at the Starlite. I took the tickets and popped the corn. I hung the speakers, cleaned off the graffiti and tapped my flashlight on the fenders of the lovers whose heads had dropped below the window level. "Okay, back row for that! Back row!" On the men's rooms walls it usually ran, "Gertrude does it, Edith won't. Mabel can't."

In the women's it was more explicit. We used to say, "Lord, that's nasty."

Dewey Corbin is now running my old Starlite. Dewey, a religious man who helps out in church work and Little League, doesn't show X-rated films and is careful with the Rs. He charges three dollars a car for *Gentle Ben* and no one has to hide in the trunk or down on the floorboards. In front of his panoramic screen, children play on the swing set and the slides, in the sandbox and the pool. In the wintertime the pool is filled with hay. Years ago, Dewey decided that rather than have the kids sneak in over the fence, or under it, he'd let them in free to sit up front and help with the baby-sitting. These kids are now teen-agers and loyal to Dewey; they make sure nothing gets too wild or out of hand out at the Starlite.

Dewey walked me through the concession stand. My old phone-booth-size popcorn stand had been stretched out sixty feet and now handles Pronto Pups, hamburgers, French fries, cold drinks and ice cream. The counter help are uniformed, trimmed and polished and look as if they've done time down at Disney World. Outside, the old ramps and speaker stations and guide lights looked the same. Dewey said, "I guess it hasn't changed too much. Same old rules. No lights on the screen. And if you want to make out, go to the back row. . . . If I see the heads going down, I kick them out. We keep it a family operation."

At the new Starlite, it seemed, the only change since I worked there was the hardware and price of popcorn. But then as the *Billy Jack* sound track came crackling in over the speakers I wondered if the crowd had changed, and if so, who would know.

In Charlotte, there's Bob McClure, who, as they say in the trade, "knows it from its inception." He produced *Preacherman* and *Hot Summer in Barefoot County.* McClure, a soft-spoken snappy dresser, has his walls covered with eight by tens of Tarzan and Jane, Clark Gable and James Cagney, and featured in the center is a big one-sheet of Tom Mix riding through 1935 with the Texas Rangers. On his desk is a bottle of Scotch, a bottle of vodka, a king-size Gatorade and a poster of his newest release. The red, yellow and blue flyer had it all: bedroom eyes, thighs, cleavage, moonlight and across the bottom, picking up where Mel Brooks had left off, forked lightning backing up *Blazing Stewardesses.*

We talked about the early drive-in days. "Hell, it started right around here. All of it. I got a buddy who booked them." He telephoned Hugh Sykes, who said he would be right over, and I eased in front of the Gatorade and headed for the Scotch.

Hugh Sykes drinks his vodka straight, wears French slacks and flies his own airplane. He jiggled his Gucci loafers like expensive daggers as he and McClure went back over the forties trying to pin down where the first feature flickered out over the first cow pasture. The story goes that an enterprising farmer set up two telephone poles and a screen in a flat field and with a movie and a projector went into business and launched an era. Much conversation passed as to whether it was a cow pasture in South Carolina or a bean field in North Carolina. The consensus seemed to be toward the beans. What the movie was is lost back there in the Carolina dust, but Sykes remembered that the farmer had charged twenty-five cents a carload and had set up a "foghorn-blast speaker" at the side of the screen.

McClure remembered the crowd. "See, this was way before TV came along and those old farm boys would watch anything moving. Anything. They'd come right in the middle of the story and it wouldn't matter a bit. And then a lot of kids came out on the field and got in behind the cars and lay out there on blankets and watched it. See, it was a novelty and, of course, everyone wanted to see who all was out there. I guess at first it was probably more like a social occasion than anything else."

Sykes talked about the commerce. "You could rent a movie for twelve dollars a week. So after your first fifty cars or so, you were into straight profit. Those monkeys made money. Big money."

They talked on, about how the first owners sunk decoy poles to let everyone think they were planning to open up a second place to keep the competition down, about the first angled ramps and the early speakers and how boiled peanuts were the first item at the concession stands because no one had a popcorn machine. And then sliding along through the forties they talked about some long-forgotten night when Tex Ritter, with no stage to work from, hunched down over his guitar and played *Rye Whiskey and Boll Weevil* up on top of the concession stand. As they talked on I couldn't help thinking about what a fine night it must have been back there lying out under the stars in that first field eating peanuts and watching all this and wondering where it was all going.

"Starlite, starbrite . . . Lord, don't let it rain tonight." At the drive-ins across the country, they all agree on one thing: if you're going to show an Ingmar Bergman Festival, do it in the rain. Out under the stars you will find no retrospectives of Eisenstein or salutes to Fellini. *Citizen Kane,* with a personal appearance of Mister Welles himself, would languish, but anything that Elvis touches will run forever. There are all kinds of promotions to bring the cars in; an Easter Eve Show will run *The Robe, The Sign of the Cross* and end at dawn with *The Ten Commandments* and a forty-foot-high cross against the screen and the local minister asking for flashing lights and horns for those who love the Lord. A Halloween Show might go all out and give away a free coffin, a cemetery plot and a free funeral. A triple-feature

Laugh-O-Rama lucky-number holder might take home a year's supscription of Kentucky Fried Chicken and a trunk load of name-brand chick-peas. They have tried, and are trying still, train rides and pony rides, beauty shops and barbershops, bingo, laundrymats, car washes, merry-go-rounds and swimming pools.

Promoter Terry Holman is locally famous for his giveaway of a dead body during a five-feature Horrorthon. It was a frozen turkey. He runs a four-hundred-fifty-car-capacity setup eight miles out from Columbia. It has air-conditioning units equipped with window gaskets that keep the mosquitoes out and a transmitter system where you can dial the sound track on your car radio; if you have stereo so much the better. Holman's location is perfect, with tall trees for a road screen on one side and a truck stop on the other. The drivers park their trailers and drive over in the tractors. With their diesel stacks the rigs are over twelve feet high and Holman makes them park at the back.

"My biggest problem isn't good movies, it's vandalism," he says. "I lost three air-conditioning units last month. Those things weigh damn near a hundred pounds. Hell, they'll steal anything, steal the speakers and take them over to Georgia and sell them to another drive-in."

Holman, an enterprising promoter, not only sells beer cheaper than the bars in town, but he also supplies the country with most of its X-rated soft porns. Down here where the Jesus Saves signs are thicker than red-necks at a white-sock sale the fundamentalists and the pornographers have arm wrestled to a draw. In the men's rooms, Bible-college students still scotch-tape pictures of Jesus over the vending machines for PROLONG and DELAY and the devil's latest, hottest novelty, a red, white and blue Bicentennial contraceptive. But for Holman there is no problem. "The Pentecostals will line up for Pat Boone's *The Cross and the Switchblade* and anything with an Art Linkletter voice-over. But then there're a lot of folks down here who would just as soon see what Linda Lovelace is doing, too. You want to know the best drive-in movie ever made? *Thunder Road.* Don't ask me why. Maybe it's the chases, maybe it's Robert Mitchum. But it's a door-buster. I could bring it in tomorrow and I'd be packed." The last time he booked *Thunder Road* he set up a moonshine still with dry ice boiling up to look like it was cooking and a local deputy standing by to tell the people about lead poisoning and the bacteriology of what happens when small creatures of the night drop into the mash vats.

"It's all a matter of shekels. A good movie will bring in the shekels, a bad one won't." He waved his hand disgustedly at the *Great Gatsby* poster on his wall. "A real turkey. Now what I want to know is why in the hell a nice guy like that who can make *Jeremiah Johnson* can get talked into doing a loser like that. That really gets me."

Down here where the cottonmouth and the possum roam and up to the soybean prairies around Des Moines, if a fan wants to sweat out the Pronto Pup line at the concession stand or move in on his girl friend, he wants to be able to resurface into the simple plot he left behind. An angry drive-in crowd leaning on horns and flashing lights quickly gets the message back to the owner and the producers. Some say that this is the kind of feedback that brought Rome to its knees. But Terry Holman would argue that he is merely bringing the people what they want to see.

Across the border and up where the red clay gets redder, I asked a Georgia owner if he really bought the stolen speakers from the Carolina drive-ins.

"Hell, yeah. They buy ours. Friend, this is a very competitive business. Listen, you printing this?"

"I'd like to."

"Well, take my name and place off. I'm in the divorce courts right now and we're getting ready to divide things up. I got to keep me a low profile."

"I'll call you Max and we'll move it close to Augusta."

"Fair enough."

Max under-belts his stomach low and on his forearm is his wife's name tattooed in blue with a recently etched red line running through it. Popping open two beers, he slid me one and then for absolutely no reason launched into a monologue on the Great Depression—"I was in Savannah, Georgia, and I saw a wharf rat sitting on a garbage can eating an onion. Now a wharf rat is probably the smartest animal that travels on four feet. Friend, I want you to know that rat was sitting there eating that onion and that rat was crying real tears. That's how hard times were down here."

Max's office is built in behind his concession stand and, like Holman's and Mc'Clure's, his walls are lined with one-sheets and glossies. A small refrigerator was loaded down with six-packs of Miller High Life and on the wall above it was a mica-flecked sign: BOWLING—A DRINKING MAN'S SPORT.

Max has been in the drive-in business since the early forties and I asked him if the crowd had changed since then.

"Damn right. Sex is different now. Back in the forties and fifties it was all rassling and steaming up the windows. Now they come out here with pillows and plug in eight-track stereos. Can't you see some old leather-backed greaser with a set of pillows?"

He popped a beer and watched the foam run. "I can look out some nights on my back row and I won't see a single head. Not one. Everybody's going at it. I could be running black leader. But I'll tell you something, we don't have any trouble out here. I mean none. Kids are more sophisticated."

I asked him if the older crowd was getting smarter, too.

He belched and headed for the refrigerator. "TV's changing them. It'll probably wind up burying them though. They're all beginning to sound the same. Biggest week we had was the week right after Kennedy was assassinated. They lined up out here for two and three hours. Face it, they were cut off from their crap on the tube. The next big surge was during the moonshots. The moonshots were the best thing that's happened to drive-ins since Elvis. Another thing you can bet on is that everything comes in waves. They build up, they top out and then they drop. Beach-blanket stuff was hot for a while. Then it was Steve Reeves and the weight lifters. Now it looks like it's horror stuff and the oc-cult. You got to keep stirring it up and trying something else, be-cause nothing lasts. Nothing."

He smiled and polished up a line behind his eyes that he'd been saving. "If the price of gasoline hits a buck a gallon we're going to be sucking wind out here in the turpentine. You know what I told an old boy one night? I said dollar gas is going to do for the drive-in what panty hose has done for finger fucking." He leaned over to make sure I'd got it down right. Then he opened two more beers. "I been shoveling this crap to them for thirty years now. Sometimes, when I get drunk enough, I get a little sad about it all." I checked his eyes to see if he was joking.

"I mean it. Friend, that crowd out there is the crowd that

skinned through high school on C-minuses and D's. They're still wearing their football sweaters. And I mean they don't read one book a year, any year. But all I got to do is remind myself of that rat eating that onion and I get over it. People went hungry back then and kids didn't have any shoes. Those people have come a long ways. Now days some old boy who's worked his ass off all week humping a pulpwood truck can look back in his station wagon and see his kids safe and sleeping and he can open a cool one and maybe reach over and grab the old lady. When you stop and figure it out, we're giving them a helluva bargain. I don't give a damn what's up there on the screen. The kids are sharper, too. Fast. Fast as lightning. You know when they screw out there when we got a good show on? During the cartoon."

He got up and hitched his stomach around the edge of the desk and hollered out, "Alice!"

A voice came back. "She ain't here."

"How about Fern?"

"She's gone too."

Finally he called a girl in. "Jessica, come in here, honey."

She stood in the doorway with her hip sprung out looking like one of the blazing stewardesses. Her blouse was cut off at the second rib.

Max said, "Honey, you ain't wearing no bra under that thing."

"It's hot out there."

He introduced me and when it was clear that the only Esquire she'd ever heard of was the shoe polish, he told her to tell us about an incident from the year before.

She started in about riding around one night and he stopped her. "No that ain't it. The Camaro."

"Oh, that."

She spoke flat as if giving directions to downtown Augusta. "We were doing it in this '73 Camaro."

She looked at me. "You know, screwing?"

I said I knew and asked, "Front seat?"

"Naw, you can't do it there. Anyhow, this acne case comes up and asks us if we wanted to buy some Girl Scout Cookies. Now talk about embarrassing. My boyfriend told the kid to come back later. And you know what that little shit did? He just hung there in the doorjamb and said he'd wait and see if he could learn something new—I mean he wasn't even eleven years old."

As Jessica left, Max winked. "What'd I tell you. Want another beer?"

"Don't mind if I do."

The last show was over and the cars were leaving the lot when Max stripped the plastic from another six-pack. Max said, "They're smarter out there, more direct." And I agreed. In an indoor movie house a bored customer will groan and twist in his seat and maybe bitch out in the lobby after the show is over. But out in the cars, out under the stars, drinking beer and eating chicken and making love, it's still a buyer's market and it's different. Out here, they've been secure enough long enough to flash their lights and blow their horns and pound on the doors and hoods until the producers have finally had to give them exactly what they want.

Max said, "They ain't so shy any more; now they're a pain in the ass." Then sitting back he watched a beetle circling the ceiling light and had the last word. "But you know, when you get old and fat and maybe have to go the aluminum walker route, this is the way to do it. I'll tell you the God's own truth. I got two passes to *Jaws* in my pocket right this minute, and I'm passing. I'd rather see it in my Buick. Friend, I got me a little refrigerator in there and you talk about something that's convenient . . ."

The Schoolmarm

BY MERLE MILLER

I never knew her first name, and neither did my mother, who at eighty-seven still has an insatiable curiosity about everything about everybody. She always makes use of such information, too. Some people call it gossiping; she calls it analyzing people.

But Miss Brhel was simply Miss Brhel. Her given name must have appeared on the records of Abbott School someplace. Being a true and the only son of my mother I once looked carefully everyplace I could think of while wasting my time and the taxpayers' money for fifteen dollars a month snooping around the principal's office in the pay of a boondoggle that may have saved the republic, called the National Youth Administration. I never found Miss Brhel's first name, though.

All the other teachers in Marshalltown, Iowa, in those days, the late twenties and thirties, had first names. Miss Cholly's was Lola. The boys called her that within her hearing and whistled slightly as she passed; Lola heard them and smiled. She wore *red* crepe de chine, a sheer material with, as my mother so often put it, "nothing decent underneath." Lola Cholly slapped me twice, allegedly for pushing in line, which was a felony, but she never proved it; punishment always came before trial.

Lola Cholly also gave me Cs and a 3 in Conduct, which was the worst; everybody else, even Mr. Haug in manual training in high school, gave me almost all As and a 1 in Conduct, although, of course, I didn't conduct myself; I conformed as much as I could, not too.

After the Lola Cholly shame, my mother led a reluctant battalion of one, me, to Abbott School to find out why. Lola said, "People like him make me nervous." People like *me*. Who else was there, for heaven's sake?

Some thirty years after I escaped to New York and other fashionable spas, my mother, a great believer in direct cause and effect and still possessed of total recall, reported, with some satisfaction, "Lola Cholly died last winter, *riddled* with cancer. And I guess you know why." Thirty-some years later, mind you.

Except for Lola Cholly and Miss Brhel, all the other teachers wore sensible below-the-knee dresses of subdued colors, mauve being the most daring; brown was the most common. Miss Brhel wore white shirtwaists that were not at all masculine, although each had a collar that buttoned high on her neck and French cuffs in which she wore black cloth links. Her black wool skirts reached the third button of her shoes. The other teachers wore pumps. It seems to me that everybody of every sex wore long underwear most of the time.

What Miss Brhel wore, outside anyway, never changed, and her hair, always white, was gathered into a tight, almost angry bun on top of her head. She never wore any makeup, but then neither did the others, except, sometimes, a hint of powder. Lola Cholly was accused of rouge, but they never proved it on her, any more than she had a court case for my line-pushing.

I thought Miss Brhel was fifty, to say the least, but then I thought that of Ruth Outland, the only other schoolmarm I ever had. It turns out she was thirty-nine. Ruth Outland officially taught journalism, but her curiosity and information were as wide and as deep as Plato's. So were Miss Brhel's.

At the end of the year Ruth Outland asked each of us to put down on paper the reason we had taken her class. I said, "I wanted to learn how to write, and now I do know how." I was almost sixteen.

Both Ruth Outland and Miss Brhel were, as I said, schoolmarms. Don't look in the dictionary; it will tell you nothing. The other day I asked my friend and classmate, Neil Naiden, who has become a very good and very successful Washington attorney—

almost all the best and the smartest of us left town at the earliest opportunity—to define the difference between a schoolteacher and a schoolmarm. He said, "A schoolmarm made going to school seem worthwhile." I go along with that.

In those days merely attending school was quite an undertaking. In Iowa, at least, there was no such thing as a split session. Iowans are and always have been great believers in the powers of education, or so they say. Even then the people were ninety-nine-percent literate. They could read but didn't, don't now. In Marshalltown it's mostly the *Times-Republican* and who spent the day shopping in Cedar Rapids or has a great granddaughter visiting from Dubuque.

The first school bell in the morning was at 8:40, and you had to be in your seat at 8:45 when the tardy bell rang. I forget what happened when you were tardy; I never was.

We marched into class; it wasn't exactly a goose step, but if they'd thought they could get away with it, they would have. Not that Germans were popular. The German language was removed from the entire curriculum during the First World War and was never returned.

Recess was at ten and lasted fifteen minutes; it was preceded by the order, "Turn and stand." Turn in your seat, then stand. How did we manage it? Why?

I can never remember anybody complaining, though, including me; as I say, as best I could, I conformed.

It's a wonder we didn't all turn Ku Klux Klanners. There were a number of those around, wearing their over-priced sheets, including two uncles who shall remain nameless; as a friend once said, they might as well; they had all the other attributes of bastards.

Twice I saw crosses burning on somone's lawn. I forget whose. There were maybe five black families in town, as invisible to me as to everyone else, and I called them what the others did, too. There weren't enough Catholics in town for Al Smith to carry a single ward when he ran for President in 1928, but the Catholic kids—the "mackerel snappers"—were tougher than the Protestants. I know because I fairly regularly got beat up by both, and the Catholics didn't stop with just one black eye and a single kick in the nuts.

But the cowards in bed sheets didn't have the guts to monkey around with the Catholics. Maybe it was the Jews, three, maybe four families of them.

All the Jews, parents and children, were my best friends, and none of them ever laid a finger on me, which is one reason I almost forgave a Jewish girl for being valedictorian of our high-school class; I was salutatorian, a mark of shame I'll bear to my grave, and so will my mother, who will outlive me; she may outlive all of us.

Recess. It lasted fifteen minutes in the morning and again in the afternoon, after each of which we all marched into class again. At ten or twelve we were marched out of class, raced home, gulped dinner (supper was at five-thirty at the latest), rushed back to school, and lined up.

I remember once asking Miss Brhel, "Why do we have to *march* into class? We're not exactly soldiers, are we?"

She sighed, took off the pince-nez (have I mentioned them, that?), wiped it thoughtfully with a white handkerchief edged with lace, and said, "That is a question that probes so deeply into the idiocy of the human race that I fear I cannot answer it. If you ever can, you will have become a valued philosopher."

Alas.

But can you imagine one person keeping thirty to forty preadolescents quiet let alone interested in anything for almost seven hours a day? We weren't paroled until ten of four.

Miss Brhel did. I wish I could tell you more about her, but I don't know where she came from, where she was educated (The Normal School at Cedar Falls?). I don't even know where she lived. At some boardinghouse, no doubt. Not the Larsons'. At the Larsons' the teachers were said to be wild; they lived it up in the evenings by gossiping, smoking cigarettes (first being sure that no matter what the season all windows in whatever room were open), and Lola Cholly was said to drink an entire glass (size unknown) of sherry before supper, right out in front of everybody.

I do not know what Miss Brhel did in the evenings; she probably read. I know one thing: during all the years I worked at the Casino, she never showed up, not even for the Joan Crawford or Errol Flynn movies.

It was never spoken of, except by my mother, disapprovingly, of course, but Miss Brhel never went to church on Sundays, although she did once tell me, "Several men of dubious intellect have tried to convince me of what they refer to as their faith. Faith is what cannot be proven and, thus, is likely to be a lot of nonsense."

I don't even know what finally happened to Miss Brhel. The first year I was in New York she simply didn't allow her contract to be renewed; she left town, and, as my mother said, "Nobody's seen hide nor hair of her since. I'm glad you were fortunate enough to have had the advantage of her tutelage, however."

Tutelage. What an inadequate word to describe what went on in Miss Brhel's classroom. In the first place, on the very first day she said, "Good morning, ladies and gentlemen, and welcome to sixth grade." *Ladies and gentlemen.* Those eleven-year-old hoodlums, us?

Nobody laughed, though, not even Tony Genero, who was fourteen and had beat me up more than all the Catholic and Protestant kids put together. I did his math, and he stopped. Miss Brhel only said, "Your efforts for him haven't improved Master Genero's arithmetic, though they may have had some beneficial effect on you." That year Tony did try, with no help from me, to memorize *The Children's Hour.* He almost succeeded, too, and Miss Brhel praised him so much that you'd have thought he had dashed off *Inferno* in a spare moment.

We did a lot of memorization in those days, and I remember asking Miss Brhel if *The Children's Hour* was any good. She said, "Well, it's not quite as bad as *Hiawatha,* but perhaps you would find it more rewarding to concern yourself with some of the work of Emily Dickinson." I did, and I did.

Miss Brhel made spelling a game, and it was nice to win, which I almost always did and Tony Genero almost always didn't, but it was no sin to lose. Miss Brhel was a praiser, not a blamer.

I think, too, that there was a schoolboard rule that all hands or fingernails or both were to be inspected by every grade-school teacher every morning. Miss Brhel never put up with such nonsense. The first day she said, "I have never been sure that cleanliness is next to godliness, whatever that means. Clean people do smell better, of course, but on the other hand, it's easier for some people to keep clean than it is for others. And it must never be forgotten that, in his entire life, so far as is known, Frederick the

Great never took a bath. That did not, however, prevent him from becoming a great ruler, although he went to war a good deal; soldiers seldom bathe."

I don't know how or why Miss Brhel's heresies were tolerated. I do remember that each morning after the first she said, "Good morning, ladies and gentlemen. Despite the weather I anticipate that we will have a pleasant and productive day." The weather was always the worst. As I recall, it started snowing around Labor Day, got down to below zero shortly thereafter and stayed there until about Easter when it started being 97° in the shade. There were no springs or autumns, never.

But despite the weather, in sixth grade at Abbot School days were pleasant and, for a surprising number of us, productive. Miss Brhel's was the only class in school in which when the teacher left the room all hell didn't break loose.

I couldn't explain it then and can't now, except to say that she respected us all, every one, and we respected her back, all, every one. And that all by itself was and is a miracle. Ladies and gentlemen we were, if only briefly.

I haven't mentioned that she read aloud to us. Mark Twain was her favorite, and we got a lot of Dickens. *Twelfth Night* is the only Shakespeare I remember but what a lovely beginning.

Some other time I'll tell you about Alice Storey who, incredible, was the chief librarian at the Carnegie and who let me read everything and anything in the library from the time I was eleven on—perhaps Miss Brhel's influence. They were friends. The last time I saw Miss Storey I was in my mid-twenties and had just published a widely acclaimed best-selling novel. Miss Storey said, "I won't say Miss Brhel would have been proud of you. She always was, all of you."

By that time Tony Genero, who had been the best-looking boy in town, had lost his looks, owned a big trucking company, weighed three hundred pounds, and thought that the John Birch Society was "a little too pinko for my taste." Dull. The only time he smiled was when I asked if he remembered Miss Brhel.

He said, "She was the only goddamn teacher I ever paid any attention to; she was really something, *really* something."

Then, I regret to report, he recited the entire first stanza of *The Children's Hour,* worse yet, accurately.

Jazz and the Duke

BY GORDON PARKS

Jazz. (according to The
Oxford Universal Dictionary
          on
Historical Principles)
Is a kind of music
In syncopated time
        as played
By Negro bands in the U.S.
        and
Music. Is a fine art concerned
With the beauty of form
And the expression of thought
        and feeling.
Negro. (also nigger, esp. a male)
Is one distinguished by
Black skin
Woolly hair
Flat nose
        and
Thick protruding lips.
     [Thus defined in
This same eminent tome
Edited by C. T. Onions C.B.E., F.B.A.
        and

Other corresponding fellows
Of the Mediaeval Academy
                of America.]
Well,
Question not these lettered
Fellows of Oxford.
                Jazz,
The meaning of it,
Is as evasive as silence.
Name one who could
Accurately define this
Passional art that slices
And churns one's senses
Into so many delicate
                barbarous
And uncountable patterns.
But alas for me
One definition would suffice.
Jazz (n). EDWARD KENNEDY ELLINGTON
Also known as Duke, Big Red, Monster,
                duc, duk, ducem.

Edward Kennedy Ellington counted on going to heaven, have
no doubt. But the inevitability of death, especially his own, was
not his favorite subject. Yet one suspects that he gave deep
thought to it in the last few years—what with all the sacred
music he began composing. I once warned him that St. Peter
couldn't be jived by all that heavenly jazz he was putting down.
He just laughed.

I don't know if Edward made it through the exalted gates—I
hope he did. In any case there is an inordinate amount of interest in his ultimate abode among the surviving Ellington alumni.
They're passing the rumor that Edward is scheming to have the
rest of the band join him as quickly as possible. No one loved
Ellington's music more than Edward. He would want those
around him who played it best. Was it a coincidence that four
giants in the saxophone section, Ben Webster, Paul Gonsalves,
Johnny Hodges and Harry Carney, recently departed on their
final trip? So have Tyree Glenn, trombone, and Joe Benjamin,
bass. There is a suspicion that Billy Strayhorn, Edward's friend

and arranger, went ahead in 1967 to make arrangements of a different kind for the rest of the band.

And what a band! I traveled with it on assignment for several months in the mid-fifties, a hard time when high salaries and costly transportation had killed off most of the big jazz bands. As one famous group after another foundered, Edward's distinguished career made an even steeper ascent. He wanted to hear his music. In order to hear it, he had to keep the band together. So instead of relaxing with his vast royalties he lived as he had to, on the brutal road of one-nighters and exhausting recording dates, "bearing beautiful fruit," and paying for it with an aging body and his life's savings.

Edward called himself the piano player in the band. But his best instrument was the band itself. He put every fiber of himself into it from the day of its inception over fifty years before. And that instrument could unfold softly like a flower or explode like a bomb. Traveling with it was a journey of sweet madness—standing there offstage in the magic wings each night, showered with its overpowering stomping sound, the curtain going up to ringing applause, and elegant Edward bouncing onstage smiling waving shouting we love you we love you madly then sliding under the keyboard thumping out his staccato beat as the band rose rocking and ablowing and ascreaming all around everything and everybody with Sammy Woodyard drumming hard sweating driving the wailing brass into frenzied madness and Johnny Hodges stepping out front alto sax dead center legs akimbo zombie cool eyes unfocused to infuriate the whole band with that arrogant kiss-my-ass tone of his as the brass screamed back as Edward impishly whipped up more tension Edward having fun Edward pounding Hodges higher and higher to his sharpest bossiest sound a withering onslaught blowing the phalanx of angry trumpets and trombones to gentle wailing until Cootie Williams' lone horn growled a final growl and died as Hodges contemptuously booted out his final arrogant note to applause applause and more applause with Edward smiling rising shouting Johnny Hodges Johnny Hodges Johnny Hodges. Thank you ladies and gentlemen. That was *Things Ain't What They Used To Be,* written especially for me by my forty-year-old son, Mercer, on my sixteenth birthday—about sixteen years ago. The applause showers Edward and he smiles and blows kisses to the ecstatic gallery. We love you! We love you madly! It was like that every night.

Edward wrote to the limits of his instrument and his performers. He grooved their individual styles into the distinctive Ellington sound. Each man was at his very best within that sound. Now and then one of them left to try it on his own, only to return disillusioned to the nest. Johnny Hodges was with Edward for forty years. Harry Carney joined up in 1927 and never left. Edward the magus, the wizard, the villain, the lover, the enchanter, the necromancer. He was the great conjurer of passion, emotion and soul. And what magicians to help stir the sorcerer's caldron! Hodges with *Passion Flower,* Cootie Williams, "a bitch on anything," Ben Webster with *Cotton Tail,* Ray Nance with *Take the A Train,* Lawrence Brown with *Do Nothin' Till You Hear From Me,* Juan Tizol with *Caravan* and Cat Anderson with his stratospheric trumpeting. And who could forget Paul Gonsalves, sweating through twenty-seven choruses of Edward's *Diminuendo and Crescendo in Blue* at the 1956 Newport festival, where acres of Ellington fans went into a hypnotic frenzy for several hours? But praise is for all the sidemen who held Ellington chairs. It's blasphemous to mention one without mentioning all of them.

I was seventeen when I first saw Duke Ellington in an alley back of the Orpheum Theater in Minneapolis, Minnesota. He arrived for his performance that summer afternoon in a cream-colored LaSalle convertible driven by Big Nate, a noted racketeer off the Northside. Elegantly attired in Eton-stripe trousers and afternoon coat, Edward alighted and started through a line of admirers who hung around the stage door. I pushed forward and shoved a piece of paper into his face for an autograph. Big Nate shoved me back.

"Git the hell outa here, kid!"

Duke turned and softly reprimanded Big Nate. "We don't treat our public like that, Nate." He motioned me forward, asked my name, and signed my paper. I was astonished to read that I had been dubbed *Sir* Gordon by the famous Duke of Ellington and went around calling myself *Sir* for weeks.

For me, and many other black young people then, his importance as a human being transcended his importance as a musician. We had been assaulted by Hollywood's grinning darky

types all of our young lives. It was refreshing to be a part of
Duke Ellington's audience. Ellington never grinned. He smiled.
Ellington never shuffled. He strode. It was "Good afternoon ladies and gentlemen," never "How y'all doin'?" At his performances we sat up high in our seats. We wanted to be seen by the
whites in the audience. We wanted them to know that this elegant, handsome and awe-inspiring man playing that ever-so-fine
music on that golden stage dressed in those fine clothes before
that big beautiful black band was black—like us.

A few years later, when I was still a hungry young dude visiting a Kansas City whorehouse, Ellington, without knowing it at
the time, favored me again. His recording of *Sophisticated Lady*
laid more heavily upon the lady than I did; the music drove her
to remorseful thoughts and melancholy tears. The lady gave me
back my money, which she knew I needed badly, then treated
me to a midnight supper of pig knuckles, collard greens and corn
bread. Many years later I told Edward the story and thanked
him for the warm body and the soulful repast he had granted me
that long-past night. He laughed. "That, my good friend, was
Ellington generosity touching you. You can now add splendor to
this night by repaying me with a big New York steak."

"And the warm body?" I asked.

"Mention it not. I am submerged in them. Come on, let's find a
good steak house."

Lurking inconspicuously inside Edward's genius was Billy
Strayhorn. Small, chubby and bespectacled, Billy looked like a
young college professor. He called Edward "Monster." Edward
called him "Swee' Pea." Others dubbed Billy Ellington's alter
ego. But Edward corrected this. "Let's not go overboard. Pea is
only my right arm, left foot, eyes, stomach, ears and soul, not my
ego." Strayhorn's compositions were some of the most beautiful
and exciting the band ever played: *Take the A Train,* the band's
theme, *Lush Life, Chelsea Bridge, Passion Flower.* His classical
and modern background served Edward well, as arranger, com-
poser and critic.

"Ellington without Swee' Pea would be like apple pie without
apples," Edward once quipped. During the whole of one night in
San Francisco, I watched the two of them write and arrange a
number to be recorded the next morning. An unbelievably
bad horror movie preceded the ordeal. At about one-thirty Ed-

ward switched off the television set. "That flick," he said with a yawn, "was the worst. No other has aroused my imperial displeasure so thoroughly." He picked up some manuscript paper and handed it to Strayhorn. "Gather up the genius, Swee' Pea. The maestro is limp at the heels." He then flopped down on the couch. Turning to me he mumbled wearily, "You are about to witness a remote and covetous collaboration between flower and beast." Five minutes later he was snoring deeply. Strayhorn worked.

It was well past three when Strayhorn shook Edward's shoulder. "Wake up, Monster. I stopped on C minor. Take it from there." Edward rose slowly, yawned and stumbled over to the manuscript. Strayhorn took the couch.

"C minor. C minor. How indelicate of you, Pea. C minor." Edward was mumbling himself back to consciousness. "Working with you is like tearing one's heart in half. C minor. How dull. How unimaginative to awaken one and assign him to such an ordinary chord. C minor. You *are* a slaughterer of the innocent." Strayhorn snored peacefully now. Edward worked. In a couple of hours he roused Strayhorn and they worked together. And so it went until the piece was finished at dawn. Four hours later the big band was rocking the studio with their arrangement. And no one knew where the Monster started or Swee' Pea left off. Only one big fine sound, one grand, remote and covetous collaboration.

A young reporter had an appointment with Edward the same evening after the recording date. Edward, exhausted from the night's work, tried to put him off until the following afternoon. The young reporter was insistent. Then Patricia Willard, Duke's press assistant, tried. But the reporter, using the deadline ploy, still insisted. Edward, kindhearted man, gave in. At least the reporter thought he did.

REPORTER: Would you mind if I used a tape recorder?
EDWARD: You won't need one.
R: Oh, well, I know you're tired and . . .
E: Very.
R: . . . and I appreciate your granting me this interview.
E: Inner-view. Call it an inner-view.

R: Fine. Inner-view. That's fine. Now, Mr. Ellington, where is home for you?

E: Digsville, jazzville, jumpsville, wherever we are making good sounds.

R: Well, let me put it like this. Where do you go back to after all these other places?

E: Soulsville, another place for good sounds.

R: Speaking of sounds. What makes yours so different?

E: Some very different and unusual cats.

R: Is there much of a turnover in your band?

E: Turnover?

R: Yes. You know, men leaving, new ones coming in.

E: No one leaves the Ellington Institution. Some drift away now and then. And they drift right back—now and then.

R: How old were you when you realized you were going to be famous?

E: (yawning) Famous?

R: Yes. When you finally knew you were going to make it.

E: Make it? We're still making it. We're almost virginal.

R: Would you say it was about 1927 when you opened up at the Cotton Club in New York?

E: We started making lots of noise about then.

R: (eagerly) Could you tell me what it was like, Duke, the Cotton Club? It must have been great, it . . .

E: I was only sixteen at the time. I don't remember much about it.

R: (smiling nervously) Oh, come on, Duke. Who were some of the famous names and faces who came to see you?

E: (squinting) Well, I'm sorry. I don't remember names. But I always forget faces.

R: (rubbing brow) Er, yes, I see. Well, were your parents very talented? Did one or both of them pass somethng on to you?

E: (yawning, stretching) Indeed so. Mamma was very pretty and Papa was very intelligent. They both gave very generously of themselves to me.

R: You seem very sleepy, Mr. Ellington. Perhaps we
should put this interview off until tomorrow.

E: Inner-view.

R: Yes. Inner-view. How stupid of me.

E: Yes. You are a very perceptive young man. I accept
your suggestion [rising, extending his hand]. Until
tomorrow afternoon then.

R: One last question until tomorrow. If you had it all to
do over again, would you do anything differently?

E: Of course not—but I doubt it.

R: Well, well . . . Okay, tomorrow afternoon, Mr.
Ellington.

E: Tomorrow afternoon.

I read somewhere that Edward was influenced by Debussy,
Respighi and Stravinsky. If that is so, their protégé served them
well. But Edward's music was what Edward lived. Truly a night
creature, he wrote about night people and places where good
times and bad times hung out together. He wrote about smoke-
filled bars, dance halls, pubs, after-hours spots, cabarets, night-
clubs, brothels, bedrooms, barbecue joints, even chicken shacks
—from Kansas City all the way to Addis Ababa. He loved the
exotic, and he wrote about royalty, the desert, the jungle, the
rivers. He wrote about God. He had a streak of melancholy, and
his soul was marinated in the blues, *Pauline's Blues, C-Jam
Blues, Paris Blues, Blues In Orbit*. The blues was a gray day
hanging around, a purple dress shimmying by on Beale Street,
bourbon dripping from a dark sky. Blues was a last kiss. Blues
was those nighttime ladies he so passionately celebrated in song,
the satin dolls, the sophisticated ladies, the black beauties,
Madam Zajj. Even his most urbane music had a touch of the
blues.

He loved those ladies. Those ladies loved him. They
"smothered him with divine adoration from Sugar Hill to Java
Pachacha," wherever that happens to be. On ladies, he ex-
pounded, "I do not wish to disenchant you, my friend, but fair
lady's power lies not in her soft beautiful arms. It's discreetly
concealed midway between her upper left thigh and her lower
right hip. Love her madly, Friday through Friday if necessary,

respect her. But watch her. She has more ways to destroy you than the Soviet Army."

According to Edward, he wrote his first copyrighted tune back in 1923. It was called *Blind Man's Buff*. He was only three years old at the time, it seems, just four years before he took his band into Harlem's Cotton Club. His last copyrighted composition, *Amour, Amour*, was written in 1973. But of course this was quite some time after he matured into manhood—after he had learned what a "rikiti" could do to an unwise "rokito." By then he had composed well over a thousand other things, including *Sonnet for Caesar, Tutti for Cootie* and a sacred concert that included *The Majesty of God*. Other titles: *Malletoba Spank, Girdle Hurdle, Honchi Chonch, La De Doody Doo, Dooji Wooji, Fugeaditti, Rhapsoditti, Purple Gazelle,* and *You're Just an Old Antidisestablishmentarianismist.* "The last one wasn't played much on radio. The announcers had a bad time with it."

There were those who found fault with Edward. Some accused him of playing the egos of his men against one another. There were others who thought he played the ladies too much. Well, he never drew any of my personal sweat. The only thing I faulted him for was eating too much ice cream every night. He downed several quarts in one sitting. We talked about this. He had a weird notion that this indulgence increased his sexual powers. But I halfway persuaded him that the chill factor might just have the opposite effect. Soon after, large lumps of hot fudge were added to the ritual.

Edward did seem somewhat of a mystery sometimes, even to himself. And that's probably the way he wanted it. It wasn't his thing to be thoroughly understood. Those who knew him didn't try—they just sat back and enjoyed him. And there was plenty to enjoy; he was generous, kind, intelligent and entertaining. But his inner life and feelings were as personal to him as his music. He guarded them with passion. Anyone who pried too deeply was cleverly rebuffed. How did he get that scar on his cheek? "At my sixth bullfight in lower Spanishotozfol. No, in all seriousness, I got it umpiring a duel between a pink baboon and a three-legged giraffe in back of a Japanese supermarket in eastern Turkey." Ask him why he didn't indulge in outdoor sports and you would be informed that he feared fresh-air poisoning. Press him to evaluate jazz and he would lament having stopped using the term at his last Bar Mitzvah. He would admit, under duress, that jazz spelled backward was zzaj, or Zajj as in *Madam Zajj*. And who did he admire most as a child? "My mother of course. Only my sister had a mother as fine as mine."

If a telephone rang within ten yards of him he went for it. "I'm a telephone freak, the greatest invention since peanut brittle. The only way to keep me from answering one is to padlock my lips. Even then I'll try sign language." Knowing this I called him in distress early one morning. My daughter was threatening to quit college and marry a Frenchman. I had to find some way to stop her. "Stop her? Come, come, my friend. Why should you expect a lovely lass like that to be practical and grammatic—when she is so rightfully inclined to be romantic? Forget it. Order the Champagne and flowers, then call your favorite preacher." It was questionable advice, I thought at the time. But I took it.

Now there were some white people who confused Edward's looks with mine. (We both had bags under our eyes.) On a plane between Rio de Janeiro I sat across from the senator from Minnesota, Hubert Humphrey. I strongly sensed some concern in his party as to my identity. After some whispering a man leaned over. "Pardon me, sir. The senator wants to know if you're Duke Ellington?"

"No, I'm not," I answered politely.

There was another whispered conference. Then, after about ten minutes, the gentleman leaned over again. "Sorry, but are you by any chance Cab Calloway?"

"No," I replied politely. Then, as the gentleman turned away dejected, I suggested, "How about Martin Luther King?"

The last, and final time I hope, this confusion came about was when I hailed a taxi to go pay my final respects to Edward in New York. The taxi driver did a double take, "Ah, ah, gee, for a second I thought . . ."

"Yes, I know," I interjected, "I'm going to see who you thought I was. Take me up to Cooke's funeral parlor." Elegant Edward to the last, he lay in state in evening dress and patent-leather slippers. He appeared to have lost his fear of the inevitable; he seemed fulfilled. But with the energy and the mischief gone, he was a smaller man than I remembered.

Edward avoided flying whenever he could. "I don't like pushing my luck. If God intended me to fly he would have leased me

some wings." The others would go on by bus or plane. Harry
Carney, who had been with Edward longer than anyone else in
the band, became his driving companion or better his private
chauffeur. The three of us were approaching San Francisco early
one morning after an overnight drive from Los Angeles. In the
distance the Golden Gate Bridge floated eerily in the dawn mist
rising above the bay. Harry called Edward, who was asleep in
the back seat. "Hey, Big Red, wake up and look over yonder.
Looks like something you might want to write about." Duke
stirred awake, wiped his eyes and looked at the bridge. "Majestic. Majestic. Goddamn those white people are smart," he mumbled and fell back to sleep.

When we reached our hotel, Paul Gonsalves was stumbling
out, stoned out of his mind. Edward sleepily looked him over.

"Where you headed so early, my man?"

"Fishing," Paul answered without stopping.

"Fishing? You're not dressed for fishing, man."

"Shit, Duke, I ain't trying to impress no fish. I just wanna
catch some of the bastards. See you later."

"Somebody's going to have to double on tenor tonight," Edward said. Carney agreed. Inside the lobby, we ran into Ray
Nance. He was disheveled and seemed to have been awake all
night. He approached Edward quietly, very quietly. "Hey, Big
Red, let me hold fifty bills till payday. I just lost my damn wallet."

"Where'd you lose you wallet?"

"Hell, if I knew I'd go find it, Red."

"You guys got a crap shoot going?"

"Yeah, a little one up in Cootie's room. Why?"

"Why that's where you lost your wallet, sweetheart." He dug
into his pockets and handed Ray the money. Ray took it without
any fuss. That same afternoon Ray bought me a drink at the bar.
He had found his wallet, and about a hundred bucks besides.
Someone else had probably lost his wallet by now.

For Edward, Duke, Monster, Big Red, or whatever one chose
to call him, there were problems like this every day. All kinds of
problems, little ones, mediocre ones, big ones. But more important there was the band each day. For with it came the solitude
that only Edward's true mistress could bring, this mistress of
desire, of wonder as old as the sun, this mistress as beautiful as

a full moon above sea mists. Her name was music, and he loved her with impassioned madness. He is gone now from this place he used to call "the forest." But here he was more than just a leaf. A big lush green part of this place is thick with his foliage.

Corn

BY JULIA CHILD

Despite its mighty historical significance, I must confess I never paid corn much mind, except to gorge upon it fresh from the cob and to enjoy an occasional corn muffin or wedge of spider bread when my avoirdupois would permit. Then I read Evan Jones's book, *American Food: The Gastronomic Story*, which goes at length into colonial ways with fresh corn: puddings, corn oysters, succotash, hominy and the Virginia penchant for grits and pork, and, of course, the use of cornmeal, the only grain the early ancestral cooks had at first. In fact, it was this book that set me off on a corn spree.

Thinking delicious thoughts of fresh corn pudding one February morning as I slushed through the snowy sidewalks to our local supermarket, I noticed fresh ears of corn in the refrigerated vegetable case. Of course it had been there all along; I had scorned it, however, as being out of season. But now, with that fresh corn pudding rather than corn on the cob in mind, I gathered six of the finest, fattest ears and bore them home.

Fresh corn pudding calls for grating the corn, which means the kernels are slit open so that the soft milky pulp can be squeezed out. Fortunately, at Christmas my California brother-in-law had sent me a corn grater, a beautiful piece of nicely finished natural wood about ten inches long and two and a half inches wide that stands on sturdy stubby legs. It has a hole in its center, across the middle of which is an upended metal plate; near the hole is a row of small steel spikes spaced at quarter-inch intervals. You lay the husked ear of corn on the wood and push it against the spikes; these open the hulls as the kernels scrape over them, and the metal plate squeezes out the pulp, which, in turn, falls through the hole into a waiting bowl. Zip, zip, zip, and six ears of corn are done in a flash.

Even that out-of-season out-of-state February fresh corn was delicious grated, mixed with eggs and cream and a bit of cheese, and baked in the oven as though it were a quiche without a shell. A few days later I made fresh corn crepes, using my marvelous grater again. Then I stewed fresh corn kernels with minced scallions and cream, and I tried frozen corn kernels the same way, finding them surprisingly good. I made corn chowder, following Sandra Oddo's clever suggestion in her big book, *Home Made*, of first simmering the stripped fresh corncobs for twenty minutes in the soup liquid, to gather all possible flavor before proceeding to the rest of the cooking. I would have stayed happily on my fresh corn kick had I not been switched to cornmeal by being asked to appear with James Beard in a speculative television pilot show for a putative series on American cooking from the Pilgrims to the present day. That meant Revolutionary Bicentennial cooking, and a dish made from dried corn rather than fresh corn kernels, because it was largely cornmeal that nourished those early settlers during the long winter months.

Jim charged himself with a New England fish chowder, and I did Indian pudding. I chose the pudding because my husband, Paul, a New Englander, adores Indian pudding and during all the years of our marriage I had never made it for him. Frankly, I, a Californian, had never even heard of Indian pudding until we settled in the Boston area, and besides, a dessert mush of cornmeal and molasses topped by ice cream did not fire me with an uncontrollable urge toward the kitchen.

I had my first Indian pudding, finally, in a small restaurant in Lexington, Massachusetts, run by an Armenian chef. It was a deep molasses brown, with a deliciously long-cooked, spice-baked-in, almost caramelized taste. Its rather stern and earthy quality held character through the accompaniment of rich vanilla ice cream and this, said Paul, should be my touchstone if I ever got around to making Indian pudding for him.

The taste and texture of that experience lingered when I went into my I.P. experimental phase some fifteen years later. First was the research into old sources. Recipes for Indian pudding abound, as Craig Claiborne found when he ran one in the New York *Times* some months ago and received a spate of angry letters from those presuming to hold their own secret of the one, the only, the true and historic Indian pudding—which did not happen to be his version. Some recipes are very plain—cornmeal, molasses, salt, and whole milk. Others use skimmed milk or water, or brown or white sugar along with molasses. Some include eggs; some, raisins; and some, sliced or grated raw apple, like my recipe here. You can boil it all up in a cloth bag, which sounds a very British way with a pudding, or you can bake it slowly all day. When you are in a hurry, you can make a hasty pudding by stirring and stirring your mixture on top of the stove for a good half hour and, as one old recipe puts it, "letting it boil between whiles, and when it is so thick that you stir it with great difficulty, it is about right." Remembering my long-cooked touchstone, I based the following on a recipe from Mrs. Child's *American Frugal Housewife*, first published in Boston in 1829, and now reissued in facsimile by the Ohio State University Libraries. Mrs. Child (no relation to me) was Lydia Maria Child, writer, editor, poet, friend of Whittier, Lowell, and Bryant, and the author of "Over the river and through the wood, to grandfather's house we'll go . . ." In addition, she was a leader in almost every area of reform, according to the foreword of the new edition, being active in women's rights, religious freedom, the fight against capital punishment, and the antislavery movement. How she found time to make Indian pudding during her unusually busy life, we shall never know, but perhaps she readied it for the oven after lunch and let it slowly bake its allotted time all afternoon while she tended to higher affairs. Here is my version, then, of Mrs. Child's pudding, tasted and approved by my husband, Paul:

INDIAN PUDDING

For about 6 cups, serving 6 to 8 people. (Cooking time, 5 to 6 hours)

¼ cup finely ground yellow cornmeal, preferably hand- or stone-ground (not degerminated), from the health-food section of your market

2 cups cold milk, either regular or low-fat
2 to 3 Tb butter; or fresh beef suet, chopped
1 tsp salt
2 tsp fragrant ginger powder (you may also add cinnamon, nut-
    meg, cloves, or other spices; I happen to like ginger alone)
A scant ½ cup excellent non-sulfurated dark molasses
A small apple, peeled, cored, and coarsely grated (a scant cup)
1 cup additional milk
To serve with the pudding: vanilla ice cream; or lightly whipped
    and sweetened cream; or custard sauce; or heavy cream and
    sugar.

Place the cornmeal in a heavy-bottomed two-quart saucepan
and gradually beat in the milk with a wire whip. Set over moderately high heat, add the butter or suet, salt, ginger, and molasses.
Bring to the boil, stirring and beating with a wire whip to be sure
all is smooth, then grate in the apple. Boil 10 to 15 minutes, stirring frequently with a wooden spoon until you have a thick por-
ridge-like mixture. (Meanwhile, heat oven to 350 degrees.) This
preliminary cooking may be done ahead; set aside or refrigerate,
and bring to the boil again before proceeding.

Turn the hot pudding mixture into a buttered two-quart baking dish and set uncovered in middle level of 350-degree oven
for 20 minutes, or until bubbling. Stir up the pudding, blend in
½ cup of the additional milk, clean sides of dish with a rubber
spatula, and turn oven down to 250 degrees. Bake 1½ to 2 hours
longer.

Stir up again as before and pour over the surface of the pudding the remaining ½ cup milk, letting it float on top. Continue
baking uncovered another 3 to 4 hours; the top will glaze over. If
you are not ready to serve by that time, cover the pudding and
keep it warm but not too hot or it will dry out.

Serve the pudding warm, with the ice cream, whipped cream,
custard sauce, or cream and sugar passed separately.

Just as American as Indian pudding is Pennsylvania Dutch
scrapple, which, when homemade, can be delicious indeed—
sage-flavored sausage slices, fragrant and meaty yet not heavily
so. When you eat it for the first time, you wonder what this
breakfast accompaniment to your fried or poached eggs could
be, this savory something with its crisp toasty outside and its ten-

der, almost melting, interior. It's scrapple, and what it's made of sounds just as unpromising as the mush and molasses of Indian pudding: scrapple is mush and pork. But there is scrapple and scrapple.

Originally and traditionally, scrapple, like all sausage products, was an appetizing way to make use of pork scraps on the farm after the annual pig slaughtering, butchering, salting, and smoking. The Dutch settlers boiled up all edible leftovers—hog's heads, pig's knuckles, liver and lights, and scraps in general— then shredded or chopped the cooked meat; with the broth from that pork cooking, they made a thick cornmeal mush. Finally, they cooked mush and meat together with sage and seasonings, turned it into molds or casings, chilled it, and it was ready for slicing and cooking.

That's the old way of going about scrapple, the scrappy scrapple as I call it; far better to my mind is scrapple made with your own sausage meat and a delicious broth concocted from roasted pork bones and vegetables in which to cook the cornmeal. This is definitely not a fast-food operation, but there is no difficulty to it, making sausage meat being no more of a trick than grinding your own hamburger, and stock being no trick at all. Furthermore, you can ready parts of it whenever you have a spare moment in the kitchen, freeze what you've made, and do the final cooking when it suits you. Your reward will be a tasty dish that you probably won't want to confine to breakfast; you'll be bringing it out for informal meals, serving brown and crusty slices of scrapple as you would pork chops, with fried apple rings and fresh peas or broccoli or steamed cabbage wedges. And you'll be serving a hearty as well as economical meal, since the cornmeal acts as a meat stretcher—a porkburger helper, in other words.

My scrapple experience grew out of my Indian pudding days. I had plenty of cornmeal left on hand and, prompted by Evan Jones's book, I went into a scrapple syndrome. Once again I found you need to use hand- or stone-ground cornmeal, the fine yellow type you see in the health-food section of your market; the degerminated boxed kind just does not have a comparable texture and flavor. Then, as to whether or not to cook the sausage meat before combining it with the cornmeal mixture, I have tried both systems; while cooked sausage meat makes a stiffer final scrapple, easier for later slicing and frying, the uncooked sausage blended into and baked with the cornmeal gives a subtler taste and texture. Finally, the following recipe does not pretend to be either historical or traditional; it is a modern-day personal scrapple designed not for farmers but for us city-living cooks who like to fool around in the kitchen.

YOUR OWN HOMEMADE SCRAPPLE
For 4 to 5 cups of scrapple

Homemade sausage meat (6 cups)
6 cups fresh pork—4 cups lean and 2 cups fat—such as country-style spareribs, shoulder, pork chop tails, or loin or leg meat, plus hard fat-covering from a loin roast
2½ tsp salt
2 tsp finely ground sage
1 tsp ground thyme
½ tsp freshly ground pepper
Cut meat and fat into strips and put through the medium blade of a meat grinder. Vigorously beat in the seasonings, pack into a bowl, cover, and refrigerate. (A day or two of refrigeration before cooking makes for better flavor; you may freeze the sausage meat for a week or so if you are not ready to make your scrapple.)

Homemade meat stock
3 to 4 cups pork bones or a mixture of pork, veal, and/or beef bones (preferably with some meat attached), sawed or chopped into 2- to 3-inch pieces
1 cup each, roughly chopped onions and carrots
About 6 cups liquid, which may include 2 cups or so of other meat stock or of canned beef bouillon
1 tsp (or to taste) salt
The following, tied in washed cheesecloth: 1 tsp thyme, 1 tsp sage, 4 cloves or allspice berries, a small handful of celery leaves and parsley stems, 2 large unpeeled cloves of garlic.
Roast the bones with the chopped onions and carrots in a shallow pan in the upper third of a 450-degree oven, turning and basting them several times with accumulated fat. Cook for about 30 minutes or until nicely browned. Scrape into a large saucepan; discard fat. Deglaze roasting pan by pouring in a cup or so

of hot water and scraping up coagulated juices with a wooden spoon; pour this liquid into the pan with the bones and add remaining liquid. Bring to the boil, skim off scum for a few minutes, add salt and herb packet, cover partially, and simmer slowly for 3 to 4 hours, adding more water if liquid evaporates below the top of the ingredients. Strain, degrease, and correct seasoning. (Refrigerate or freeze until ready for use.)

The cornmeal base
4 cups pork stock (preceding recipe)
1 cup hand- or stone-ground fine yellow cornmeal
½ cup water
1 tsp finely ground sage; more to taste
Salt to taste

Bring the pork stock to the boil in a heavy-bottomed saucepan. Meanwhile, place the cornmeal in a bowl and blend in the cold water; gradually stir in about 1 cup of the hot stock, then beat the cornmeal mixture into the saucepan of stock. Boil, stirring with a wooden spoon and reaching all over bottom of pan, for 5 minutes or more, until mixture is quite thick and heavy. Then cover the saucepan and set it in another and larger pan of simmering water; cook 30 minutes. Uncover and set saucepan over moderately high heat; boil and stir 10 minutes or so—or as long as you have the patience—until mixture is very thick and a mound lifted in the spoon holds its shape. (The thicker the better, or the final scrapple will be too loose for easy sautéing.) Taste and correct seasoning; it should be delicious just as it is. (Refrigerate or freeze if you are not ready to continue; reheat over simmering water, stirring and beating.)

The scrapple
Preheat oven to 300 degrees. Stir the sausage meat into the hot cornmeal mixture and bring to the boil, beating vigorously to break up the sausage and mix it with the cornmeal. Boil, beating and stirring, for 5 minutes, then taste and carefully correct seasoning, adding more salt, pepper, and sage as necessary— scrapple usually has quite a strong sage taste, but the decision is up to you. Turn the scrapple into a flameproof baking dish, bring to the simmer on top of the stove, lay a round of wax paper over the scrapple, and cover the dish. Bake for about 1¼ hours and

remove from the oven. Immediately degrease the surface—skim off floating fat with a large kitchen spoon, then press the spoon into the surface, squeezing out residual fat. (Reserve fat for sautéing scrapple later.)

Line the bottom of a bread pan or pans with wax paper (for easy unmolding), and smooth in the scrapple. Cover surface with wax paper and chill for 24 hours, then cover airtight. (Scrapple will keep in the refrigerator for 2 weeks or more; it will freeze, but lose its character if kept too long—a month or so is about the limit, I think.)

To serve scrapple

Either unmold the scrapple (run a thin-bladed knife between it and the bread pan, then invert the pan and give a hefty shake) and cut crosswise slices—I like them ½ inch thick—or cut slices from the bread pan—in which case the first slice is the most difficult. Dredge each slice in flour and sauté rather slowly in hot skimmed-off cooking fat or in rendered pork fat or butter; when bottom is brown and crusty, turn and brown the other side. (If your original cornmeal mixture was soft, your scrapple slices will be hard to turn: instead of trying with a spatula, then, place a cookie sheet over the frying pan and reverse scrapple onto cookie sheet; slide the slices, browned side up, from cookie sheet into frying pan.) Serve on hot plates and accompany with fried or poached eggs and, if you wish, with broiled tomatoes or sautéed tomato or apple slices.

Gas Stations

BY MAX APPLE

Chances are you've been here, too. World's largest, eighty-three pumps, forty-one urinals, advertised on road signs as far east as Iowa. Oasis, Wyoming, U.S. 40, hard to miss as you whiz on by. Even Jack Kerouac on an overnight cross-country spin used to stop here for soft ice cream. In the golden days, they had their own tables, all those fifties beats, way in the back by the truckers' shower room. They lumbered in with the long-haulers, left their motors running just like the diesel men, wore leather, too, drank half cups of coffee. The truckers said shit more. Busboys, in retrospect, could tell them apart by the poems on the napkins.

The counter is fifteen yards long and there must be two hundred tables. The waitresses wear roller skates except when carrying expensive meals. Everyone chews gum. The girls are all named Ellie. At their waists, just above the apron, they make change like bus drivers out of metal slots. Quarters fly onto tables, dimes trickle down their legs.

I order hashbrowns and eggs, whole-wheat toast and coffee. My Chevy is being gassed out front, pump number forty-eight. The place mat tells the incredible story of the man who made all this possible. He dreamed a dream fifty years ago on a cold hillside. He was a Wyoming shepherd boy nuzzled against members of his flock in the biting wind. He dreamed that all his bleating herds became Cashmere goats at five times the price, that Wyoming shriveled up and dove into Texas. He awoke with frostbitten ears, fingers iced into the wool he clutched. While that man awaited the slow rising sun to warm his limbs and awaken his herds, he vowed a vow.

"This won't be a barren wasteland," he vowed. "Men will know that here I froze one night so that after this men shall freeze here no more." He slapped his herd with a long crook. His collies awoke as if it were spring and stretched on their forepaws. The man spit into the icy wind. He named the spot Oasis.

I look up from this saga on the place mat to recall, in the midst of travel, the tiny oasis of my youth, Ted Johnson's Standard. On our own block flew the Texaco star and the Mobil horse, but you couldn't pay us not to fill our Pontiac at Ted Johnson's Standard. He was the magician of the fan belt. With an old rag and one tough weathered hand, he took on radiators foaming and in flame. Where other men displayed girly calendars, Ted Johnson hung the green cross of safety.

Although he looked like Smokey the Bear, it was engine neglect and rowdy driving that he cautioned against. Whenever a kid short-cut onto Bridge Street across his pumps, old Ted raised the finger of warning. "Stay to the right, sonny," he would yell, shaking his gray head over the lapse in safety. He had spotless pumps, his rest rooms glowed in the dark, he bleached the windshield sponges, but it was safety that drew us all to Ted. He wouldn't take your money until he had checked your spare. And it must have worked. He never lost a regular customer to a traffic fatality. He kept the number of deathless days posted above his cash register. At night, after he counted his receipts, Ted read the obituaries and added another safety day. I remember at least 7,300. Twenty years of Ted's customers rolling down the road with their spare tires at the ready. They didn't need their suction-cup saints. Ted passed out his own stick-on mottoes for the dashboard.

> DON'T SWITCH LANES
> ALWAYS SIGNAL FIRST
> USE THE REARVIEW MIRROR

Yes, Ted Johnson's Standard, here in the middle of the world's biggest rest area, I long for you. They don't clean my windshield, and my hood is tinkered with less than a fat girl's skirt. At night, Ted, they don't even make change and in the best of times you have to beg for the rest-room key.

You treated our cars, Ted, like princes from afar. The way Abraham must have washed the feet of angels, so you sponged windshields fore and aft. And those glass-headed pumps of yours looked like the Statue of Liberty lowering her torch to us, cozying up to our rear end.

My waitress rolls up. Her name is Ellie. "We're out of eggs," she says, "how about oatmeal. Twice the protein and none of that troublesome cholesterol. A man your age can't be too careful."

"I'm only thirty," I tell her.

"Not so young. In Korea, in the middle of veins, they found cholesterol at nineteen. The oatmeal's on special today. Think about it." I think about oatmeal while I continue the place-mat saga of Oasis, Wyoming. In 1930, there wasn't a road within a hundred miles. The shepherd boy was twenty-eight then and rode the freight to Grand Forks, North Dakota. With his stick and his collie and his dream, he rode east and almost succumbed, once in Kansas City and again in Chicago, to a fortune in the stockyards. By 1940, he had made a million in suet and owned a mansion on Lake Shore Drive. Big stockmen from all over came by to sample his roast beef and pork chops and talk business. Swift and Armour sent him Christmas gifts. The dog was his only memento of Wyoming.

Still, the millionaire was restless. His vow came back to trouble him. The autumn of 1941 was the worst freeze Chicago ever knew. By October the leaves in all their splendor froze upon the limbs. Thanksgiving was twenty-two below zero, the average for November. People coughed chilled blood into the streets. The stockyards closed. On December 7, the Japanese attacked Pearl Harbor and the millionaire suet man knew the Jonah. "I hustled ass back to Wyoming," he said, "before the enemy could make it his own."

First he leveled the land and built towers of fluorescent lamps. There was still no road within fifty miles, but now the man thought of nothing but his vow. "The road will come," he said, and he invested his million in a pinball arcade, a small wax museum, and the earliest version of the restaurant. The gas pumps were an afterthought.

Ellie brings me oatmeal.

"No charge if you don't like it," she says. "They've got twenty pounds of it in the kitchen. It'll be lumpy by noon anyway." She looks over my shoulder while I taste. Her long hair touches the milk in the spoon, the steam rises to both our nostrils.

"It's good," I say.

"It has to be," Ellie answers, "the big boss eats it himself." She nods toward a bald man about twelve tables east of me. He wears a baggy thin-lapelled suit and is daydreaming through his smoky windows. When I finish breakfast, I walk over to shake the hand of the man whose history has filled my place mat. He attempts to smile for me but can't quite do it.

"Troubles," I ask, "when you have eighty-three pumps and are a place-mat legend?" He collapses over the table. He buries his head in his hands.

"Personal problems?" I ask. "Health? Marital? Emotional?"

He picks up his head. "Psychiatrist?" he inquires.

"Only a traveler," I respond, "heading west." He sits up and looks around to make sure that nobody is listening to us. He pulls me close to his shrunken lips. "Arabs," he moans into my ear. "When they couldn't buy the Alamo they started putting the pressure on Oasis. They want Coney Island, too, and Disneyland. Our government is worrying about U.S. Steel and Armour beef, they don't know the desires of desert folk. I do. My people come from Lebanon, also a land of milk and honey."

To cheer the man, I tell him about Ted Johnson's Standard, the example that has strengthened me through breakfast. "A white tile building," I tell him, "round as a mosque. Inside, it was like a solarium. Cut flowers bloomed from the carcasses of dried-out batteries. The Lions Club glass and the March of Dimes cup twinkled in their fullness. Only one grade of motor oil there, the very best, and six-ply treads, mufflers with welded reinforcements, belts and hoses of the finest India rubber. . . ."

"Enough," says the Oasis man, "you're just a pisscall romantic mooning over the good old days of Rockefeller. Wake up. Ted's Standard belongs to O.P.E.C. now. It flies the sign of the Crescent. Turbaned attendants laugh at the idea of a comfort station. They mix foreign coinage in your change."

"What about your help?" I motion toward my Chevy where a swarthy man peeks beneath the hood. He wipes the oil stick clean with his lips and spits into the radiator.

"Just Mormons in makeup," the Oasis man says. "You can't find a real Arab out here, but I do my best. I want to get the country ready for what's coming. I give out free headdresses all through the holy month of Ramadan. For a nickel, I'll sell you an ALLAH LIVES bumper sticker. We closed down on the day Faisal was assassinated. You can't buck the future."

"And what about the Ted Johnsons?" I ask. "The men in uniform who made our stations great?"

"Underground," he says, "with the hat blockers and egg candlers, praying for the resurrection of the downtown."

"I don't believe it's so bleak," I say.

"Bleak for you and me," the Oasis man answers, "not so bleak along the Nile and the Euphrates. Every thousand years or so Mesopotamia gets a shot in the arm. It's just history. You can't buck it. You go along."

"I don't see it that way, Mr. Big, no sir, I don't."

Ellie rolls up with another ladle of oatmeal for the boss. "Beware," he says, "watch out for price-fixing in radial tires and don't believe what the company tells you about STP." He rouses himself for a moment from his melancholy. "We serve three thousand meals a day here. Where are you headed, California?"

"Righto," I say, not even surprised that he has guessed it.

"Your own station or a dealer owned?"

"Franchise direct from J. Paul Getty, option to buy in five years." The Oasis man can tell that I'm proud of myself.

"Dummy," he says, "in five years you'll be a slave in Tunis." Ellie pulls up a chair and joins us.

"No," I say, "in five years I'll be like Ted Johnson. I'll be fixing flats and tuning engines in the happy hills outside San Francisco. I'll have an '81 Chevy, loaded, and watch the Golden Gate Bridge hanging in the fog."

"More oatmeal for you two?" Ellie asks. "It'll all be lumps by noon." Her perfect legs in their black hose roll toward the kitchen. Sparks fly from her wheels.

"Young man," he tells me, looking away now, through the window at what is visible from this angle of his eighty-three pumps, "take it from the King of Octane, there's not a fart's chance for you out there. Go back to school. Learn dentistry. The third world will need attention to its teeth."

Ellie is back with oatmeal and hot coffee. She sits with us, makes a thin bridge out of her fingers, rests her chin on it as she stares at my oatmeal.

"You've had your day, Mr. Oasis," I tell him: "If the place mat is to be trusted, you've been hot and cold, rich and poor. Now you can sit at your window and watch the cash roll in. Ted Johnson never looked up except when he had a car on the rack. He called his place a service station. Your name was your credit over there."

The millionaire's mouth finally makes it into a huge smile. "How many pumps will you have?" he asks.

"Three," I tell him loudly. "One each, regular, premium, and no lead and no locks on the rest room." He breaks into giggles. People at other tables are looking but I don't care.

"That's right," I continue, "and rubber machines and ten-cent Cokes if I can get them." He is almost rolling in the aisle now. Tears of happiness leak from the corners of his eyes. "Firecrackers and recaps," I continue, "wheels balanced by hand, and even mufflers and pipes."

"Stop," he yelps amid his giggles. "I can't take any more." But I want to go on. "I'll lend out tools, too, and give a dollar's worth to anyone who's broke."

Ellie looks into my heart. "Take me with you," she says. "I'll check crankcase oil and clean windshields. I don't want to be a harem girl." Her look is as grim as mine. We leave him howling at the table. I pay my bill and buy her a pair of magnetic dogs. Beside my Chevy, Ellie removes her roller skates. Her black hose hooked around my antenna rise in the wind. Through the rearview mirror, I see in pursuit the disguised Mormons. Awkwardly they mount their camels and raise curved swards to the east. My electric starter drowns their desert shrieks. Three hundred and forty cubic inches rumble. I buckle up, Ellie moves close. Careful on the curves, amid kisses and hopes, I give her the gas.

The Mink Coat

BY NORA EPHRON

I think it was about 1954 when my mother got her mink. A
Beverly Hills furrier had run into some difficulty with the
Internal Revenue Service and he was selling off his coats. My
mother would never have bought anything wholesale—she dis-
approved of it on grounds that I never understood but later
came to suspect had something to do with being the daughter of a garment salesman—but there was a distinction between
buying wholesale and getting a good price. She got a good price.
It was an enormous mink. A tent. It came to her ankles, and at
least two people could have fitted under it. The skins were
worked vertically. I did not know this at the time. I did not know
much of anything at the time, much less anything about the way
mink skins were worked. A few years later, when I knew, all the
furriers in America decided to work the skins horizontally; when
I heard about it, I instantly understood that it would not make
her happy to be wearing an Old Mink. But she always pretended
that things like that meant nothing to her. She was a career
woman who was defiant about not being like the other mothers,
the other mothers who played canasta all day and went to P.T.A.
meetings and wore perfume and talked of hemlines; she hated to
shop, hated buying clothes. Once a year, after my father had
nagged her into it, she would go off to a fashionable ladies'
clothing store on Wilshire Boulevard and submit to having a
year's supply of clothing brought to her in a dressing room larger

than my current apartment. She grumbled throughout. I thought she was mad. Now I understand.

My guess is that my father paid for the mink, wrote the check for it—but he did not *buy* it for her. My parents worked together, wrote together, and there was no separation between his money and hers. That was important. Beverly Hills was a place where the other mothers wore minks their husbands had bought them. They would come to dinner. The maid would take the coats upstairs and lay them on my mother's bed. Dozens of them, silver, brown, black, all of them lined with what seemed like satin and monogrammed by hand with initials, three initials. I would creep into the bedroom and lie on the bed and roll over them and smell the odd and indescribable smell of the fur. Other children grow up loving the smell of fresh-cut grass and raked leaves; I grew up in Beverly Hills loving the smell of mink, the smell of the pavement after it rained, and the smell of dollar bills. A few years ago, I went back to Beverly Hills and all I could smell was jasmine, and I realized that that smell had always been there and I had never known it.

My mother wore the mink for years. She wore it through the horizontal period and into another vertical period, but it never became fashionable again; by the time vertical skins were back, furriers were cutting minks close and fitted. Eventually, she stopped wearing it and went back to cloth coats. She and my father had moved back to New York and she had less patience than ever for shopping. And then she was sick and went to bed. One Thanksgiving she was too sick to come to the table. My mother loved Thanksgiving almost as much as she loved making a show of normal family life. I knew she was dying.

The months went by, and she hung on. In the hospital, then out, then back in. She was drugged, and wretchedly thin, and her throat was so dry, or so clogged with mucus, that I could not understand anything she tried to say to me. If I nodded at her as if I understood, she would become furious because she knew I hadn't; if I said, "What?" or, "I don't understand," she would become furious at the effort it would take to say it again. And I was furious, too, because I was there for some kind of answer— what kind of answer? what was the question? I don't know, but I wanted one, a big one, and there was no chance of getting it. The Thorazine kept her quiet and groggy and hallucinating.

When the nurse would bring in lunch, soft food, no salt allowed, she would look around almost brightly and say, "I think I'll take it in the living room." I would become so angry at her at moments like that, so impatient. I wanted to say, damn you, there is no living room, you're in a hospital, you're dying, you're going off without having explained any of it. And she would look up and open her mouth just slightly, and I would put another spoonful into it.

Then it was September. Fall. The room had a nice view of Gracie Mansion and the leaves were turning. It was a corner room on the sixth floor, which is, for those who care, a little like being seated at the right table. She did care. She managed, almost until the end, to keep up appearances. If the nurse was new, she would raise herself a bit, lift her arm in a dear and pathetic waft, and introduce us formally. "Miss Browning," she would say, "my daughter, Mrs. Greenburg." (My mother and the fish market were the only people who ever thought of me as Mrs. Greenburg.) Then she would collapse back onto the pillow and manage a bare flicker of a smile. I found it unbearable to be there and unbearable not to be there. I was conscious that I was going through an experience that writers write about, that I should be acutely aware of what was happening, but I hated that consciousness. And I could not look at her. She would moan with pain, and the nurse would reach under her, move her slightly, and the sheet would fall away and I would catch a glimpse of her legs, her beautiful legs now drained of muscle tone, gone to bones. The hallucinations went on. Then, one day, suddenly, she came into focus, knew exactly who I was, and like a witch, what I was thinking. "You're a reporter," she said to me. "Take notes."

Two days after she died, my sisters and I spent an afternoon— how to put this?—disposing of her possessions. It was an extremely odd day. People kept dropping in, somber people, to pay their respects to my father; in the bedroom were the four of us, not at all somber, relieved, really, that it was finally over, and finding a small and genuine pleasure in the trivial problem of what to do with her things. In the midst of it, my mother's friend Sylvia came into the room. Sylvia, who snitched on me when I told her my first dirty joke, Sylvia, who my mother always said wore her girdle to bed—Sylvia came in and saw us trying on our mother's clothes.

"I have to talk to you," she said to me. "Alone."

We went into the dining room.

"There's something I have to tell you," she said.

"Of course," I said.

"Don't tell your sisters," she said.

"What is it?" I said.

"Lamston's has paper underpants in stock," she said. "I bought you a pair."

Most of my mother's clothes were sent to charity. And the evening dresses, the beautiful chiffon Galanos dresses my father had bought her, were too big for any of us. But there was the mink. And there I was. The eldest. The most grown-up. It occurred to me I could cut it down to size or line another coat with it. Something. I took it.

A few weeks later, one of my sisters called. Did I take the mink? she asked. Yes. It's not fair, she said. She didn't even have a winter coat and I had hundreds and a big apartment and a rich husband and now I had the mink, too. You can have half of it, I said. She didn't want half of it. She didn't have the money for a winter coat much less the money to turn half a mink into something. What do you want? I said. She didn't know. There were three more phone calls, each uglier and more vituperative, thirty years of sibling rivalry come to a head over an eighteen-year-old mink. I have to make it clear that I was as awful as she was. I wanted the mink.

Finally, one day, we met in front of the Ritz Thrift Shop on Fifty-seventh Street. I was carrying the mink. She was barely speaking to me. We went inside, and a lady came over. We said we wanted to sell the mink. The lady took the fur in her hands and turned it over, peeling away the coat lining to look at the underside of the skins. She spent a good half second with it. "I won't give you a nickel for it," she said. The skins were worthless. Shot. Something like that. We walked out onto Fifty-seventh Street carrying the mink. It was suddenly a burden, a useless assemblage of old worn-out pelts. I didn't want it. She didn't want it. A year later, my maid asked for it and I gave it to her. Shortly thereafter, my maid's apartment was robbed and the burglar got the mink.

I will never have one. I know that now. And like a lot of things I will never have, I have mixed feelings about it. I mean, I could have one if I wanted one. I could squirrel away every extra nickel and buy myself, maybe not a perfect mink, but something made of mink noses or mink eyes or whatever spare parts make up that category of coats they call fun furs. But I don't really want one: a mink coat is serious, and I would have to change my life to go with it.

But I love her for having bought one. She had the only kind of mink worth having, the kind you pay for yourself. That is not the answer I was looking for, but it will have to do.